HOW POSTMODERNISM SERVES (MY) FAITH

Questioning Truth in Language, Philosophy and Art

Crystal L. Downing

IVP Academic

An imprint of InterVarsity Press
Downers Grove, Illinois

InterVarsity Press
P.O. Box 1400, Downers Grove, IL 60515-1426
World Wide Web: www.ivpress.com
E-mail: mail@ivpress.com

InterVarsity Press® is the book-publishing division of InterVarsity Christian Fellowship/USA®, a student movement active on campus at hundreds of universities, colleges and schools of nursing in the United States of America, and a member movement of the International Fellowship of Evangelical Students. For information about local and regional activities, write Public Relations Dept., InterVarsity Christian Fellowship/USA, 6400 Schroeder Rd., P.O. Box 7895, Madison, WI 53707-7895, or visit the IVCF website at <www.intervarsity.org>.

Scripture quotations, unless otherwise noted, are from the New Revised Standard Version of the Bible, copyright 1989 by the Division of Christian Education of the National Council of the Churches of Christ in the USA. Used by permission. All rights reserved.

Design: Cindy Kiple
Images: Carlo Maria Mariani/Licensed by VAGA, New York, NY

ISBN-10: 0-8308-2758-7
ISBN-13: 978-0-8308-2758-9

Printed in the United States of America ∞

Library of Congress Cataloging-in-Publication Data

Downing, Crystal.
  How postmodernism serves (my) faith: questioning truth in language,
  philosophy, and art/Crystal Downing.
     p. cm.
  Includes bibliographical references and indexes.
  ISBN-13: 978-0-8308-2758-9 (pbk.: alk. paper)
  ISBN-10: 0-8308-2758-7 (pbk.: alk. paper)
  1. Postmodernism—Religious aspects—Christianity. I. Title.
  BR115.P74D69 2006
  261.5—dc22

                                                                          2006003974

P	19	18	17	16	15	14	13	12	11	10	9	8	7	6	5	4	3	2	1
Y	21	20	19	18	17	16	15	14	13	12	11	10	09	08	07	06				

For my mother, father, sister and brother

and the house we called home

Contents

List of Illustrations

Acknowledgments

This book reached its present form thanks to the encouragement of Julianna Gustafson, the enthusiasm of Giles Anderson, the consultation of Maria Frawley and the commentary of Donald Richmond. But its content had been brewing for decades, malted by substantive conversations with dozens of brilliant and supportive friends, five of whom stand out for the way they helped me understand postmodernism and its relation to Christianity: Kathleen Lundeen, Sandra Stanley, Rebecca Adams, Samuel Smith and especially Julia Kasdorf, who effectively models the transmission of theory through personal narrative. Would that I could write as well as she.

I am also indebted to my colleagues at Messiah College, especially the members of the English Department, including our wonderful secretary, Gina Hale, who have provided a loving environment that has nurtured my scholarship. Outside the department, two colleagues have been especially supportive of my work: the mathematician Gene Chase, who repeatedly showers me with reading material and encouragement, and the biblical scholar John Yeatts. The latter not only solicited my first national address on postmodernism and faith but continues to have me speak on the subject to his honors class every semester.

I also want to thank those colleagues at Messiah College who graciously shared their disciplinary knowledge for this project, taking time to answer questions I encountered during the writing process: John Beaney, Lois Beck, Ron Burwell, Robin Collins, Dean Curry, Ted Davis, John Eby, John Fea, Milton Gaither, Doug Jacobsen, Liz Kielley, Lawrie Merz, Caleb Miller, Dee Porterfield, Ted Prescott, Morris Sider, Brian Smith and David Weaver-Zercher. Responding beyond the call of duty were several generous members of the faculty who either read part of the manuscript or gifted me with helpful publications: Susanna Bede Caroselli, Mike Cosby, Julian Gutierrez-Albilla, Joseph Huffman, Christine Perrin, Tim Schoettle, Samuel Smith, Susi Stanley, Pauline Stevick and Kim Yunez.

In addition to supportive colleagues, I am blessed with intellectually energized students. Many of the ideas found in these pages developed during discussions both inside the classroom and out, especially with Aaron Dahlstrom, Sharon Hewitt, Lucas Sheaffer, Rebecca Buckham, Rachel Petersen, Janel Atlas and Emily Rainville. The latter three, the wonderful Rachel, Janel and Emily, read drafts of this book, providing insightful responses to both form and content. Also informing these pages are ideas generated during a seven-week-long chapel series during fall 2004, when I joined sixteen students and my insightful colleague Chad Frey to discuss Brian McLaren's *A New Kind of Christian*.

I would be remiss not to mention the staff at InterVarsity Press, who have contributed to this book with insight and grace. Gary Deddo, my editor, is both brilliant and judicious, and this is a better book because of him. All deficiencies within the book I claim as my own.

My last but unending thanks go to my best reader and better friend, David C. Downing, of whom I can say much, but perhaps *il miglior fabbro* is enough.

PART ONE

Situating This Book

Introduction

LINING UP THE DUCKS: CHRISTIANITY AND POSTMODERNISM

With tears streaking their dirty faces, two little girls raced from window to window, madly closing curtains, and then took refuge under the dining-room table, carefully pulling the chairs in close around them. Sobs shaking their small frames, the sisters clung to each other as they crouched in their makeshift fortress. No imaginary monster or neighborhood bully generated their fear. This time a bomb threatened their very lives, as the older sister well knew. In her first-grade class, she had been trained to recognize and react immediately to multiple air-raid warnings. One kind of siren indicated that the class must line up at the door and then file out to the playground. Another, the most fun to practice, directed students to quickly walk home. The third sent everyone scurrying to the classroom's windowless wall, pressing fearful faces against cinderblock. The last, and scariest of all, was the "Duck and Cover" siren, and every child knew what it meant: "Get under your desks with arms over your heads! The communists are dropping an atom bomb!" No child thought to ask why the communists would think to send an atom bomb toward their sleepy suburb of San Francisco. All they knew is what adults taught them: communists wanted to destroy their country.

It was a Duck-and-Cover siren that shattered the sisters' complacent world that sunny summer day. The first-grader thought of conversations she had heard while eating dinner at the table above her. Her father, an engineer (but not the kind that drives trains, she often had to explain), sometimes discussed his special training in air-raid shelter design, and he would speculate where best to dig one on his own property. So this little girl was very much aware of the communist threat.

She was I: a child born into and nurtured by the Cold War, too young to have heard of Joe McCarthy but old enough to know "Better dead than red." Under the dining-room table, however, I was not yet ready to die.

The Postmodern Threat

I recount my childhood trauma in order to set up an analogy for how many individuals have responded to "postmodernism": as a threat to what Americans, especially people of faith, hold dear. Communism was to many in the middle of the twentieth century what postmodernism was, and still is, to many after its turn: an ideology that dismisses God and undermines cultural values; a worldview that calls truth as we know it into question; a force that subverts the fundamental assumptions on which the United States was established, destabilizing institutions that made it great.

The analogy, of course, is not exact. Communism was a political ideology, while postmodernism questions any political commitment, analyzing how and why people fiercely stand for and by the truth claims of their political, as well as all other, ideals. From the perspective of those who initiated it, postmodernism is not an "ideology" or "worldview" at all. *Exposé* might be a better word for it: postmodernism exposes the shaky foundations on which ideologies and worldviews rest. (Not coincidentally, Marxist intellectuals were among the first to attack postmodernism, for it questioned their ideology.)[1]

Despite this and other differences, the analogy between communism and postmodernism may be helpful for several reasons. First, my duck-and-cover under the dining-room table was based on legitimate fears. Communists did indeed see themselves as adversaries of U.S. capitalism, maintain-

---

[1] I disagree with Myron Penner when he calls postmodernism a "worldview." I think he is more accurate when he refers to it as an "ethos," an "intellectual attitude or frame of mind that shapes the style and substance of thought and provides one with a starting point for reflection." See his introduction to *Christianity and the Postmodern Turn: Six Views*, ed. Myron B. Penner (Grand Rapids: Brazos, 2005), p. 17.

ing that military force was a necessary means to establish their power. Joseph Stalin, though long dead by the time of my dining-room drama, believed that it was expedient for millions to die so that one ideology might live—an ironic reversal of Caiaphas's statement about Christ, that it was "expedient" for one man to die so that many people might live (John 18:14). To complete the analogy, then, just as communism is inherently antagonistic toward free-market economics, postmodernism is inherently antagonistic toward evangelism, seeming to undermine the call to world mission.

Second, the real shortsightedness of 1960s duck-and-cover drills lay in the assumption that hiding under a desk or table would provide protection from an atomic blast. So also a duck-and-cover attitude toward postmodernism provides no protection. It must be studied and understood. Perhaps if more people in the 1950s and 1960s had probed and prodded, rather than feared, Soviet communism, they might have discovered something that became clear during the 1990s: the Russians did not have the economic resources to overthrow the United States and elevate communism to the reigning ideology. Similarly, if Christians probed and prodded postmodernism, they would discover that it does not have the power to destroy the truths that they cherish.

Ironically, both communism and postmodernism were generated by impulses consonant with Christianity. *The Communist Manifesto* of 1848 was partially based on Friedrich Engels's 1844 sojourn in Manchester, England, where laissez-faire economics had led to deplorable conditions for the working class. With no government controls over factory conditions, workers had no recourse when machinery put out their eyes or severed their fingers. Their wounds would fester in the only dwellings they could afford: overcrowded tenements where Engels saw them forced to "wade through puddles of stale urine and excrement."[2] It is no wonder that he and Karl Marx chose a model for government harmonious with Christ's directive to the rich young man—"sell your possessions, and give the money to the poor" (Matthew 19:21)—as well as with Acts 2:43-47 and 4:32-35, which recount how resources were shared commonly in the early church. Of course, the coerced collectivism of Soviet communism was no solution, and today only the most die-hard ideologue thinks that communism can work on a na-

---

[2]Friedrich Engels, *The Condition of the Working Class,* in *The Norton Anthology of English Literature: The Victorian Age,* ed. M. H. Abrams and Stephen Greenblatt, 7th ed. (New York: W. W. Norton, 2000), 2B:1707.

tional level. But its original impulse—to remedy the flaws in capitalism—should be valued by Christians. So also the early impulse of postmodernism—to remedy the flaws in modernism—should be valued by Christians.

Unfortunately, remedies often create their own excesses as one extreme elicits an equal and opposite reaction. Marxism became an excuse, if not impetus, for purges and genocide. And even though postmodernists will never exile people to gulags or invade Eastern Europe with tanks, many Christians worry that the invasion of North America by postmodern theory has sent Christianity into exile, that postmodernism is slowly conquering society with its weapons of mass destruction: atheism, nihilism, relativism, skepticism and immorality.

That's why I'm writing this book: to explore when such worries are warranted and when they are not.

Judging Postmodernism

The first thing I want to emphasize is that perspectives on life should not be judged by the people who misuse them. After all, thousands have been killed in the name of Christ. When I told a non-Christian English professor that I believe in the resurrected Christ, she snapped back, "What about the Crusades? What about the Inquisition?" I could only respond that an earnest seeker after the truths of existence does not reject an answer because of the fanatical excesses of its followers.

In this book I want to say the same thing about postmodernism: it should not be judged by problematic practices carried out in its name. This is not to suggest that Christianity and postmodernism are comparable answers to the meaning of life. The first is based on a certain person—the incarnation of God on earth—while the second is based upon a certain attitude: a suspicion of ready answers, an emphasis on the limitations of language, an awareness of the artifices of tradition. This book will bring the postmodern attitude to bear on following Christ, using my own experience for the argument's core. In the language of evangelical Christianity, my personal testimony will serve as a witness to my understanding of a life in Christ. In the language of postmodernism, I will acknowledge the *positionality* of my beliefs.

After hearing me speak at secular conferences, some non-Christian scholars have described me as a "postmodern Christian." Because earnest defenders as well as energetic critics of Christianity would equally consider the phrase "postmodern Christian" an oxymoron (like "jumbo shrimp"), I am willing, if hesitant, to accept the label, enjoying a position between opposing camps. This does not mean I am lukewarm about my faith. It is the heat of my commitment to Christ that has warmed me to postmodernism. This book will argue, in fact, that postmodernism serves faith. It certainly has served mine.

Escaping from the Duck-and-Cover

What about the little girls whimpering under the dining-room table? What saved them from their tearful turmoil? Their halo-encircled mother, back-lit from the midday sun, entered from a door to the outside. I still remember peeking out from under the table as I heard the click of the latch and the squeak of the door hinges. A confused look wrinkled Mother's brow as her eyes, adjusting to the darkened room, beheld two chairs moving mysteriously away from the table, followed by two sobbing girls who clutched at her for comfort.

Though the halo vanished when she shut the door, Mother did indeed bring comfort, explaining that the siren was simply a scheduled test of the city's civil defense system; there was no imminent peril. Similarly, I would like to suggest that sirens about postmodernism might best be seen as helpful tests of our faith defense systems rather than signs of imminent demise. In fact, I want to change the siren image altogether by considering the origin of the word *siren*—a strategy that, in my experience, both postmodernists and pastors love to employ.

According to the *Oxford English Dictionary (OED)*, the word *siren* first appears in Homer's famous epic *The Odyssey*, referring to sea nymphs whose beautiful singing lured sailors toward dangerous rocks, where their ships crashed and foundered.[3] Odysseus, the hero of Homer's tale, desires to hear the sirens' song as he sails home from the Trojan War. He therefore has his men tie him to the crosslike mast of his ship where he can listen while they, with plugged ears, safely sail around the rocks. And though the seductive music nearly overpowers him, Odysseus makes it through without submitting to its tempting lure.

I assume that anyone picking up a book with a title like *How Postmodernism Serves (My) Faith* wants neither to crash their ship of faith nor to im-

---

[3]The *Oxford English Dictionary*, considered the definitive scholarly source for word origins, is employed throughout this book, cited as *OED*.

itate sailors who, with ears plugged to isolate them from their surroundings, merely followed the dictates of a human (and hence flawed) authority. This book is meant to encourage Christians in their own odyssey: ones who can revel in the siren song of postmodernism exactly because they are tied to the mastlike cross of faith.

Defining Postmodernism

By now you are probably asking, "What exactly *is* postmodernism?" This is like asking, "What exactly *is* Christianity?" On one level the answers are easy, indicated by the names themselves: *Christ*ianity follows the teachings of Christ; *post*modernism follows the teachings of modernism. The word *follows,* of course, has different—almost opposite—meanings in my two definitions: the Christian accedes to (follows) the words of Christ in order to affirm their truth, while the postmodernist supersedes (follows) the words of modernists in order to question their truth.

What I have done here, as I will do throughout this book, is to illustrate one component of postmodernism, knowing that illustration is often the best way to clarify complex ideas. In this case, I have shown that even a simple word like *follows* is not one-dimensional; it changes meaning depending on its context. Ironically, Marxist theorists, believing postmodernism to be merely an extension and intensification of modernist consumerism, would prefer the first meaning of *follows.* To them postmodernism accedes to "the logic of late capitalism," as Fredric Jameson famously put it.[4] As we can see, the word *follows* is influenced not only by its context but also by assumptions the reader brings to it. Language is slippery.

Even the statement "Christianity follows the teachings of Christ" is a bit slippery. Many people use it merely to endorse an ethical system based on Christ's Sermon on the Mount. Others regard following Jesus to be an issue of belief more than practice, pointing out that Christ's most important teaching is "For God so loved the world that he gave his only Son, so that everyone who believes in him may not perish but may have eternal life" (John 3:16). Indeed, if we were to ask Christians around America to state the top ten essentials for following Christ, we would get different lists depending on whether the respondents were Lutheran, Pentecostal, Mennonite or Eastern Orthodox. In fact, the essentials for Christian practice would differ even

---

[4]Fredric Jameson, "Postmodernism, or the Cultural Logic of Late Capitalism," *New Left Review* 146 (1984): 53-93.

within each of these denominations depending on the location and ethnicity of individual congregations. And I won't even mention the difference between U.S. Episcopalians or Catholics and those in Africa or Ireland (but, of course, I just did: another way that language doesn't always do what it claims).

Definitions of postmodernism differ as dramatically. Some theorists proclaim that it is passé, while others continue to publish books and articles reveling in its relevance.[5] One specialist, Eleanor Heartney, comments in 2001 that "even the most ardent advocates of postmodernism have been forced to admit that the term has become discredited by its very popularity." However, she goes on to assert that "postmodernism has remade the world in ways that can never be retracted."[6] In other words, whether or not one regards our times as "postpostmodern," as some do, postmodernism has been a culture-changing movement that must be taken seriously and studied.

Dismissing Postmodernism

In my experience, scholars who dismiss postmodernism by denying its lasting relevance are often those who never liked it in the first place: people who were molded by modernist assumptions—like Marxist critics, scientists religiously devoted to evolutionary theory, emphatic adherents to secular humanism.[7] Ironically, their forebears said the same thing about Christianity in the 1920s and 1930s: that it was passé, defunct—at least for the well educated. Postmodernism and Christianity make odd bedfellows, both having been disdained by the same kind of people.

This is why I want to address, and possibly redress, the duck-and-cover repudiation of postmodernism by Christians. For example, Gene Edward Veith Jr., in his book *Postmodern Times: A Christian Guide to Contemporary Thought and Culture,* seems to regard everything he doesn't like about the 1990s as "postmodern": the animal rights movement, "collaborative learning," television remote controls, just to name a few.[8] On one level he is right: con-

---

[5]Brian McHale argued in 2004 that the term *postmodernism* is still useful. See *The Obligation Toward the Difficult Whole: Postmodernist Long Poems* (Tuscaloosa: University of Alabama Press, 2004).

[6]Eleanor Heartney, *Postmodernism* (Cambridge: Cambridge University Press, 2001), p. 77.

[7]I will make the case in chapter four that Christians who revile postmodernism are often thinking like modernists.

[8]Gene Edward Veith Jr., *Postmodern Times: A Christian Guide to Contemporary Thought and Culture* (Wheaton, Ill.: Crossway, 1994), pp. 74, 183, 81. This book was employed as a textbook for Focus on the Family college courses as late as 2004.

temporary culture is indeed "postmodern." We have been in the midst of "postmodernity" for at least a quarter of a century now—the same way nineteenth-century English citizens had been in the midst of "Victorian" culture even before Victoria came to the throne in 1837. (Traditionally, the Victorian era starts with the passage of the First Reform Bill in 1832.) With the benefit of hindsight, historians and sociologists identify cultural trends as beginning before the people living in that culture are ever aware of them. Veith, however, does not always honor the intelligent distinction he makes between postmodernity, the era, and postmodernism the attitude.[9] Though Queen Victoria's attitudes affected the era during which she reigned (1837-1901)—some for good, some for ill—she didn't *cause* the "Victorian" conditions that Engels witnessed in 1844 Manchester. Similarly, the attitude we call "postmodernism" didn't cause all the ills (which are legion) of postmodernity. Besides, I know earnest Christians who endorse animal rights (C. S. Lewis actually argued that our pets would be in heaven), collaborative learning (a model very close to my Sunday school experience) and even remote controls.

Those willing to enter the theater of postmodernism obviously see it in a radically different light from those who stand outside protesting that its performances are evil. This point, itself, is an assumption of postmodernism: that the way we see reality depends on our perspective and that our perspective is molded by our *situatedness*.

Postmodern Situatedness

I did not fully understand "situatedness" until I moved to Pennsylvania after having grown up and earned my Ph.D. in California. My first May in Pennsylvania, I was home alone one night when a window-rattling thunderclap extinguished the lights. Trying to remember where I had stored the candles, I suddenly noticed a camera flash coming from the deck outside the living-room window—then another. My hands protectively crossed my chest as I ran behind the kitchen wall, assuming that some peeping Tom was taking photographs. Slowly peeking around the wall, I witnessed multiple flashes, as though a whole crew of paparazzi were in my yard. But as I stared, I noticed that some of the flashbulbs were coming from the tops of trees, a good thirty feet above the ground.

Only then did I feel appropriately stupid: these were no peeping pa-

---

[9]Ibid., pp. 19, 24.

parazzi with invasive cameras. I was seeing fireflies. My confusion turned to delight as I ran out onto the deck to watch more closely. Even then, however, I perceived with California eyes. For as I watched the bugs flashing against the distant trees, it looked exactly to me like a television commercial for Mr. Clean, as though the trees were sparkling from a fresh washing up. What really were being washed up were my watching eyes; by moving cross-country, I was finally experiencing what postmodernists had told me: the perceptions one takes for granted often turn out to be flies in the night.

Let me give an example related to faith. During the U.S. Civil War, earnest Christians from both the North and the South believed that God was on their side, and both appealed to the truth of Scripture in their rhetoric. Christian slave owners quoted Ephesians 6:5, "Slaves, obey your earthly masters with fear and trembling," to legitimize their practice. And they justified their fugitive slave laws by citing Genesis 16, where an angel tells a runaway slave, Hagar, to return to her masters, Abram and Sarai. Many regarded the subordination of blacks to whites as a fundamental principle of God's creation, established in Genesis 1:4: "God separated the light from the darkness."[10]

In contrast, some Christians in the North led the abolitionist movement and participated in the Underground Railroad, illegally smuggling runaway slaves all the way to Canada. They broke the law believing that the truth of verses they read in their King James Bibles—"Render therefore unto Caesar the things which are Caesar's" (Matthew 22:21) or "Obey them that have the rule over you, and submit yourselves" (Hebrews 13:17)—was superseded by the truth of Galatians 3:28: "There is neither Jew nor Greek, there is neither bond nor free, there is neither male nor female: for ye are all one in Christ Jesus."

Both sets of Christians equally believed the Bible to be universally true, but each interpreted it from their own context.[11] Postmodernism, in recognition of realities like this, encourages attempts to understand the conflicting "truths" of each group and to acknowledge their "situatedness." This is not the same as accepting all "truths" as equally valid, which is how many peo-

---

[10]For a rigorous discussion of how Southern slaveholders used the Bible to justify their practices, see Elizabeth Fox-Genovese and Eugene Genovese, *The Mind of the Master Class: History and Faith in the Southern Slaveholders' Worldview* (Cambridge: Cambridge University Press, 2005). The interpretation of Genesis 1:4 was recounted to me by a pastor in South Carolina, who heard it used to justify segregation as late as the 1980s.

[11]Rex Koivisto, an evangelical theologian at Multnomah Bible College, rightly notes that all Christians "interpret out of a cultural, historical context, through an ecclesiastical context, looking for the Bible's relevance to cultural problems." See *One Lord, One Faith: A Theology for Cross-Denominational Renewal* (Wheaton, Ill.: Bridgepoint/Victor, 1993), p. 136.

ple interpret postmodernism, leading them to accuse it of nihilistic relativism. This accusation, though completely understandable, unfortunately generates a duck-and-cover attitude toward postmodernism.

From Duck-and-Cover to Duck-and-Rabbit

Instead of the "duck and cover!" response, which dismisses postmodernism with accusations of radical relativism, it is more helpful to see postmodernism as presenting the famous "duck or rabbit?" conundrum—see figure 1.1.

Figure 1.1. Duck or rabbit?

Since the 1930s, scholars have been analyzing why some people when they look at this figure first see a duck, and why others see a rabbit. Today they might analyze why some people, when they look at affirmative action, see reverse discrimination, while others see a necessary counterbalance to racist practices. The postmodernist, however, would concentrate on the ability to change one's initial perception through an intentional switch in focus: seeing the duck's beak as a rabbit's long ears. This does not mean that the form can be whatever one wants it to be—an accusation often leveled at postmodernism. The shape of the image delimits how one can interpret it.

Christian Ducks (or Rabbits)

While critics have accused postmodernists of dismissing historical facts by reducing them to the artificial constructions of culture or the manipulations of the power elite, this is the case for only the most radical. As Linda Hutcheon notes, for most postmodernists "past events existed empirically, but in epistemological terms we can only know them today through texts. Past events are given meaning, not existence, by their representation in history."[12]

---

[12]Linda Hutcheon, *The Politics of Postmodernism* (New York: Routledge, 1989), p. 82.

Christians should be familiar with this approach. Faced with the exact same facts in Scripture, some readers see ducks, others see rabbits. For example, I grew up in an evangelical church that was extremely suspicious about the practice of *glossolalia,* the Greek term for "speaking in tongues." I was taught that this style of worship ceased to be appropriate after the first century of the church's existence, primarily because the loss of control represented by glossolalia could be manipulated by Satan. Pentecostal Christians, however, regard the *fact* of Pentecost, when the apostles "began to speak in other languages, as the Spirit gave them ability" (Acts 2:4), as still applicable to current followers of Christ. After all, they point out, Paul gives explicit instructions about employing the gift of tongues (1 Corinthians 12:7-11) only fourteen verses after he gives guidelines for the Lord's Supper (1 Corinthians 11:23-26), one of the prescriptions most universally followed by Christians.

Yet in the very same chapter in which he exhorts us about the Lord's Supper, Paul also speaks about the veiling of women, giving prescriptions that most Christians today ignore. Thus, when conservative Anabaptists—certain Amish and Mennonite believers—still take seriously the prayer veil, women wearing head coverings over hair that they do not cut (1 Corinthians 11:15), we need to take note: why do they interpret as relevant biblical practices that others believe no longer applicable? It's like the duck/rabbit conundrum: people who see a duck perceive it as facing to the left, while those recognizing a rabbit see it facing right. So also Christians dismissing the veiling of women perceive the passage about it in 1 Corinthians 11 as looking back to outmoded cultural contexts, usually symbolized to the left on a timeline; those honoring the head covering look to the right on the timeline, seeing its relevance now and into the future.

Significantly, once one sees both duck and rabbit, she can flip back and forth in perspective, recognizing both as present in the drawing. I hope to do the same in this book, flipping back and forth between the strengths and weaknesses of postmodern discourse, as well as of Christian rhetoric. In this introduction I have primarily focused on postmodernism as facing a positive direction, largely because many Christians regard it with a duck-and-cover attitude. But I am very aware of its problems, and in the final chapters of the book I will mount my most rigorous critiques.

An Overview of the Book

Because postmodernism is more sophisticated than many people realize, I start by setting up a simple scaffolding on which to build toward more and more complex ideas. I therefore advise that you read the chapters in the order I give them. The analysis found in later chapters will make much more sense in light of earlier discussions.

In chapter one I tell my own story, explaining how a fascination with language contributed not only to my Christian journey but also to my interest in postmodernism. As I outline my own history, I demonstrate why we should take seriously postmodern views of history.

Because postmodernism developed in response to modernism, chapter two presents key thinkers who contributed to the construction of modernism in philosophy, science and the arts. At the end of the chapter, I highlight several postmodern thinkers who challenged modernist assumptions in philosophy and science.

I devote chapter three entirely to the arts, since technically this is where postmodernism began. Though numerous other Christians have written helpful works on postmodernism, they have tended to focus on the differences between modernism and postmodernism in philosophy and theology. In contrast, my book gives more attention to the modernist mystification of art in order to explain how postmodernism has undermined assumptions of secular humanism.

Chapter four addresses a key concern of Christians: postmodern antifoundationalism. In this chapter I adopt ideas from postmodern neopragmatists and Christians in the Radical Orthodoxy movement (as well as from my Sunday school experience) in order to challenge readers in their assessment of foundations. Ultimately, I suggest that Christian foundationalism reflects modernist values more than it does Christian orthodoxy.

The next two chapters grapple with poststructuralism, a fundamental ingredient of contemporary theory often overlooked by theological engagements with postmodernism. After explaining "structuralism" and the "poststructuralist" response, chapter five outlines one aspect of poststructuralism, the "deconstruction" made famous by Jacques Derrida, and suggests ways that it resonates with biblical teaching. Chapter six discusses how postmodern theorists developed Ludwig von Wittgenstein's idea of "language games," explaining how these games contributed to what is commonly called "the cultural construction of knowledge." To make my analysis more accessible, I use my childhood fascination with construction paper as a metaphor, relating the construction of knowledge to ways that we see Christ.

Chapter seven discusses the complex philosophical issue of relativism. After providing a historical overview of relativism, I illustrate several different kinds that are manifest in postmodern thought. I argue that some forms of relativism are more philosophically viable than others and suggest how Christians might respond to the intellectually irresponsible yet often-heard phrase "Everything is relative."

In chapter eight I continue my critique by suggesting that many of those Christians who denounce postmodernism often demonstrate its most pervasive attribute: what critics call the "commodification of identity." I encourage Christians to demonstrate instead the biblical injunctions to be in the world but not of it, to be wise as serpents but gentle as doves, and I show how postmodernism might help in the process. After discussing pluralism within the Bible itself, I close the book with the issue of evangelism, suggesting how Christians might use postmodern paradigms to help share the truth of Christ.

Navigating This Book

Throughout the book I have tried to make the complicated discourse of postmodernism as understandable as possible. Accessibility, however, inevitably simplifies, eliminating the nuances of complex issues and arguments. It reminds me of the first time I went skiing. A friend took me up the slope (after I had fallen off the T-bar at least eleven times) and then instructed me to keep my skis straight as I went off the hill and to "go pigeon-toed" if I wanted to slow down. Next she dug in her poles and pushed off the mountain, leaving me to fend for myself. I soon discovered that her explanation was simpler in the hearing than the doing. Racing faster and faster down the snowy slope in terror, I was unable to get my skis into a pigeon-toed position. Hence, as the ski lodge loomed closer and closer, threatening to halt my progress all too dramatically, I stopped the only way I knew how: by ducking into a snowbank, covering my ineptitude with icy crystals. As I hurled my body into the wall of snow, I realized that I had entirely missed the nuances of skiing.

Having learned from my skiing "duck and cover," I want to take my readers down the slippery slope of postmodernism with care. I have an advantage over some of the ski-instructor Christians who have written books attacking postmodernism. While Christian critics too often play telephone, relying on summaries from other people attacking postmodernism, I have read many (certainly not all) of the famous theorists whose writings helped shape postmodern discourse: Friedrich Nietzsche, Martin Heidegger, Michael Polanyi, Mikhail Bakhtin, Thomas Kuhn, Jacques Derrida, Paul de Man, Michel Foucault, Roland Barthes, Jean Baudrillard, Jean-François Lyotard, Jacques Lacan, Julia Kristeva, Luce Irigaray, Terry Eagleton, Fredric Jameson, Edward Said, Richard Rorty, Stanley Fish, Linda Hutcheon, Jonathan Culler, Jane Gallup, Judith Butler and so on. Were I to outline the thought of each, I'm sure many of my readers would soon be hurling themselves into intellectual snowbanks. Instead, having grappled firsthand with the writings of these theorists, I hope to present their accumulated wisdom (or perversity—duck or rabbit?) as simply as possible.

Rather than expecting readers to go down the hill by themselves, I employ analogies from my own experience as well as examples from contemporary culture to tangibly illustrate not only the theory but also its application to Christianity. Periodically I will refer to more scholarly works, just in case readers want to dig their ski poles into more difficult runs. However, I tend to avoid the moguls of postmodern theology, not only because they are beyond my expertise but also because other Christians have negotiated them so well.[13] Instead, I focus my attention on the postmodern view of language, discussing its influence not only on philosophy and art but also on contemporary social

---

[13]Most accessible of all is Brian McLaren's *A New Kind of Christian: A Tale of Two Friends on a Spiritual Journey* (San Francisco: Jossey-Bass, 2001). Also accessible is J. Richard Middleton and Brian J. Walsh, *Truth Is Stranger Than It Used to Be* (Downers Grove, Ill.: InterVarsity Press, 1995), which brings postmodern views of the self into conversation with biblical views of identity. For the historical development of postmodern ideas in philosophy, see Stanley J. Grenz, *A Primer on Postmodernism* (Grand Rapids: Eerdmans, 1996). For more scholarly engagement between postmodernism and Christian theology, I recommend Merold Westphal, *Overcoming Onto-theology* (New York: Fordham University Press, 2001); Stanley J. Grenz and John R. Franke, *Beyond Foundationalism: Shaping Theology in a Postmodern Context* (Louisville, Ky.: Westminster John Knox, 2001); and Robert C. Greer, *Mapping Postmodernism: A Survey of Christian Options* (Downers Grove, Ill.: InterVarsity Press, 2003). There are also several essays I have found especially helpful: Philip D. Kenneson, "There's No Such Thing as Objective Truth, and It's a Good Thing, Too," in *Christian Apologetics in the Postmodern World*, ed. Timothy R. Phillips and Dennis L. Okholm (Downers Grove, Ill.: InterVarsity Press, 1995); Mark R. Schwehn, "Christianity and Postmodernism: Uneasy Allies," in *Christianity and Culture in the Crossfire*, ed. David A. Hoekema and Bobby Fong (Grand Rapids: Eerdmans, 1997); and James K. A. Smith, "A Little Story About Metanarratives: Lyotard, Religion and Postmodernism Revisited," in *Christianity and the Postmodern Turn: Six Views*, ed. Myron B. Penner (Grand Rapids: Brazos, 2005). For the best overview of differences between modernist and postmodern theologies, see Nancey Murphy and James William McClendon Jr., "Distinguishing Modern and Postmodern Theologies," *Modern Theology* 5, no. 3 (April 1989): 191-214.

values. I sometimes play with language, as do many postmodernists, creating puns and inserting parentheses into words or phrases to expose how language can, with barely noticeable traces, quickly change meaning. In another postmodern move, I often juxtapose homey illustrations to serious theoretical issues. This may bother readers who feel jarred by sudden transitions from powdery whimsy to crusty scholarship. But those who make it to the end of this book without abandoning their skis should be able to explain why my style reflects the influence of postmodernism.

I do not claim to be an expert instructor. Because postmodernism is as multifarious as the culture in which it is embedded, I cannot discuss its every aspect. Furthermore, what is a "duck" to me will be a "rabbit" to someone else. Instead, think of me as someone who has learned that to duck and cover is not the best response to the sirens of our culture.

1   Posting (My) Life

BIOGRAPHICAL BACKGROUNDS

Ayear after crawling out from under the dining-room table, I experienced another dramatic moment, again on my knees with my sister. We were saying our evening prayers in matching pink flannel pajamas, the attached feet cushioning our toes against the cold wooden floor. As Daddy knelt at the side of the bed with us, I prayed aloud, "Dear Jesus, I want to be born again."

I still recall that moment in vivid detail, not because I immediately felt saved but because I looked up to see my father in tears. I suddenly discovered that words wield enough power to make grown men cry.

This power, in fact, is what got me down on my knees in the first place. Earlier that same day, in the Blue Room at church, a Sunday school teacher had illustrated Christ's admonition to Nicodemus, "Ye must be born again" (John 3:7 KJV), in flannelgraph. For those readers who missed Sunday school in the 1960s, a description may be in order. Flannelgraph was the PowerPoint of midcentury Christian education. Television-sized pieces of flannel were layered over each other and stapled to the top of an easel board, each piece printed with a different background scene: a river to illustrate Jesus' baptism, a rock tomb to explain his resurrection, a hill with three crosses to illustrate—well, you know. A Sunday school teacher would flip to the appropriate flannel scene and then attach to it colorful paper figures that had sandpaper glued to their backs. Thus the same material that protected my body in bed also communicated deliverance to my soul.

That Sunday in the Blue Room, stiff petticoats flaring my dress too high to protect my roly-poly legs from the cold metal chair, I could have used some of the flannel being displayed at the front of the room. However, my shivery discomfort was entirely displaced by fascination with the idea of being "born again." My interest had nothing to do with worry over the state of my soul. After all, I had asked Jesus "into my heart" years before (and probably once again under the dining-room table). Rather, my attention was captured by a new way of seeing, by the discovery that something down to earth like the birth of a baby could represent the means to escape earthly things.

"Down to earth" was indeed the way I had interpreted my sister's birth four years earlier. When Mother answered my question "Where do babies came from?" with "God sent your sister to us," I imagined a fully formed infant, conveniently wrapped in diapers, floating down from the sky and negotiating its way around our gargantuan palm tree into Mother's waiting arms. Being "born again," then, guaranteed the process in reverse; it was the means by which I would one day float up to heaven to be received by the waiting arms of Jesus. I did already have that guarantee; I knew that I was saved. But the flannelgraph lesson instilled a desire to appropriate a fascinating new metaphor, to make it my own. Even though I would not have the word *metaphor* in my vocabulary until a decade later, in the Blue Room I had my first glimmer that language can shape perception the way scissors can shape flannel, generating images that explain reality in new ways. The glimmer became a dawning light as I witnessed how my appropriation of the "born again" metaphor affected my father—even though he knew that I had already asked Jesus into my heart.

Pioneering New Paths

Several years later, I was in Pioneer Girls, a Christian alternative to the Girl Scouts that met in the same Blue Room. The Pioneer Girl motto, recited at every club meeting, came from Psalm 119: "Thy word is a lamp unto my feet, and a light unto my path" (Psalm 119:105 KJV). Physical gestures accompanied each recitation: we began "Thy word is a lamp" with elbows down at our side while the right hand made a letter *L* with the thumb and index figure next to the shoulder. Then as we said "unto my feet," the *L* dropped down to our side as we pointed to our feet. Finally, "and a light unto my path" was accompanied by the hand opening up and making an arc to the right, as though pointing out a path beside us. This ritual indicated to me that words were not the only kind of signifiers, that the performance of the body is a type of language. Of course, this was a key message that I was getting in both Sunday school and Pioneer Girls: that human performance testifies to life commitments, that "faith by itself, if it has no works, is dead" (James 2:17). But I was also assimilating a sense that the word by itself, if it has no works, is dead. Like the hand movements accompanying my Pioneer Girl recitation, words were merely signs, constructed by humans, and could only gesture toward significant realities.

Thus in the very same room at my church, though at different moments, I was impressed with both the power and the poverty of language. This dual nature of discourse, especially in relationship to Christianity, eventually led to my fascination with postmodernism, which regards discourse as shaping behavior as well as being shaped by it. Because it molds the humans who shape it, language faces two directions, simultaneously duck and rabbit.

In this chapter, then, I will describe my spiritual and intellectual growth as I moved from Pioneer Girl to Postmodern Woman. For, as my Blue Room experiences imply, spiritual growth for me has usually been tied to reflections about the mediation of language, both of the word and in the Word, which still operates as a lamp unto my feet. I trace my progress down a path lit by the Word (and the word) for two reasons. First, some readers may need convincing that an advocate of postmodernism can also regard herself an orthodox Christian. Second, postmodernism, with its emphasis on the particularity of experience rather than its universality, encourages personal testimony as a way to explain oneself.

Adolescent Anxieties

My self was molded by the language of evangelical Protestantism. And for most evangelicals, human words, in response to and expounding upon the Word of God, are the living stones built into the spiritual house of faith. It is no coincidence that in many Protestant churches the Eucharist "altar" seen at the front of Catholic churches has been replaced by a table on which lies an open Bible, as though acknowledging Martin Luther's famous phrase *sola Scriptura*: "only the Bible" should be our source of Christian truth.

It should not be surprising, then, that watershed moments in my spiritual growth have been tied to the complexities of language. In high school, for example, I became increasingly disturbed by a statement reiterated numerous times in the early chapters of Exodus: "the LORD hardened the heart of Pharaoh" (Exodus 7—14). It didn't seem fair to me that God caused the hardening and then punished the Egyptians for it. The way the language is constructed, it sounds as though God either enjoys human suffering or delights in the creation of evil; if not, why harden a heart and then punish it for being hard?

A balm for this intellectual Gilead came from my pastor, who during a sermon about Pharaoh's heart stated, "The same sun melts butter and hardens clay." With that metaphor I could reconceptualize what appeared to be the arbitrariness of God and believe that, like the sun, God, the light of life, is entirely consistent. It is the nature of the human heart—its consistency affected by external causes—that generates its own demise. This reassurance was accompanied, however, with another unsettling insight: The Bible is not self-interpreting. Humans must infer meaning even as they seek to extract God's truth. And the meaning some humans infer can be as disturbing as the idea of an arbitrary God—such as when Christians justify segregation with "God separated the light from the dark."

A different metaphor helped ease my worry over this issue. A speaker at the Christian college I attended began a talk on Francis Schaeffer's *How Should We Then Live?* by quoting from Psalm 119: "Thy word is a lamp unto my feet, and a light unto my path." Restraining the impulse to sign the letter *L* at my shoulder, I listened as he described two kinds of Christians: those who use the Bible as a lamppost, leaning against it in order to prop up what they want to believe, and those who use the Bible as a light to illuminate their mind. This satisfied my sense that there was a right way to read Scripture and a wrong way.

Later, however, I wondered how one recognized which way was "right." For example, a friend of mine at another Christian college told me that she was going to participate in a debate about pacifism versus just-war theory on her campus. When I asked her which side she was on, she said, "Pacifism! Even though I'm not a pacifist, it's an easier position to support from the New Testament." I was disturbed by more than her flippancy. If, for Christians, the New Testament completes the Old, with Christ's words often challenging ancient paradigms, how can Christians ignore those pacifists who ground their position in the New Testament? Yet most of the Christians I knew were just-war advocates, including those who did not think Vietnam was a just war. Which side was using the Bible as a lamppost, which as an illuminating light? I worried over the fact that the Bible, the inspired Word of God, did not make the "right" interpretation clearer. I was now beginning to feel that the words of Scripture, which had so much power over human behavior, also demonstrated the poverty of language.

The word that nearly broke the camel's back—hindering it, at least, from getting through the eye of a needle—came from a sermon I heard while working on the summer staff of an evangelical conference center. The director was one of the heroes of my adolescence, and I took every opportunity to hear him speak. One morning he gave a powerful sermon, taking as his text a passage from Paul: "Since we have such a hope, we are very bold. We are not like Moses, who would put a veil over his face to keep the Israelites from gazing at it while the radiance was fading away" (2 Corinthians 3:12-13 NIV). He talked from his own experience as the leader of a Christian organization, explaining how he was often tempted to put a veil over his weaknesses so that people would continue to admire the splendor of his Christian maturity. I was profoundly moved by his vulnerability, and even though he did not elaborate on his flaws, I was amazed that this admirable man admitted to any weakness at all.

To make his point, my hero drew our attention to Exodus 34:29-35. The passage recounts how Moses, after being exposed to God's glory on Mount Sinai, discovered when he came down from the mountain that "the skin of his face shone." Because this frightened the Israelites, Moses veiled his face whenever he appeared before them. Centuries later, however, Paul reveals in his letter to the Corinthians that the *real* reason Moses veiled his face was to hide the fact that the shining splendor was fading. While this makes a superb illustration relevant to any Christian leader, I was deeply concerned with what it implied about Scripture. Having been taught that the Bible is without error, I wondered how I was to regard Paul's exposé of Moses' inaccurate account. After all, I was told that Moses wrote the creation account in Genesis; did he misreport that one as well?

When I returned to college the next fall, people responded to my questioning one of several ways:

1. My revered Christian leader (whom they did not know) had misinterpreted what Paul was saying.

2. One minor discrepancy cannot topple all of Scripture.

3. Just as Jesus "fulfilled the law" of the Old Testament, interpreting the Messiah in a new way, so the New Testament fulfills and surmounts the Old, providing new interpretations.

The first answer made me aware, once again, that the Bible is not self-interpreting, that human beings bring their assumptions to their readings. What advantage was there in having an inerrant Bible if Christians, all feeling similarly led by the Holy Spirit, interpret the text differently?

The second answer became unsatisfying when it was delivered by people who at other times decried the "domino effect," wherein skepticism about one element from Scripture causes the whole thing to collapse. For example, they would argue, if people do not believe that the story of Job is historically accurate, they will soon doubt the historicity of the resurrection. This provided no comfort to me, for it turned the Bible into a domino-document: too precarious to be the foundation of faith.

The third response, though far more subtle, left me wondering why some of the Christians who employed it conversely argued vociferously for the literalism of the Old Testament, especially the creation account. They seemed to want it both ways, sometimes arguing for the power, other times for the poverty of the Old Testament. I continued to question how words could adequately contain the profound biblical truths to which they pointed.

True Believers and True Unbelievers: My Grad School Years

A different kind of questioning enveloped me in graduate school, where my fascination with the power and poverty of language led me to pursue a Ph.D. in English. Having immersed myself in Young Life and church youth group throughout my high school years and then attended an evangelical college, where I led Bible studies, helped with local Young Life activities, and served as an assistant to a church youth pastor, I had primarily focused my intellectual inquiry on the language that shaped me at the time: that of evangelical Christianity.

In graduate school in the 1980s, however, I started questioning the language that many of my peers and professors took for granted: a language that dismissed Christianity as intellectually untenable. Because I refused to "hide my light[s] under a bushel"—lights of both intellect and of faith—one of my classmates told me, with sincerity as thick as the Shakespeare anthology he held against his hip, "Crystal, you are the only Christian I've ever met who is the least bit intelligent." High praise indeed! When I told a professor in the Religious Studies Department that I believed in God, he sipped his chardonnay for a moment and then commented, "My, aren't *you* an anachronism!"

The defining moment came at a dinner party hosted by one of my grad-school friends. When someone made a contemptuous remark about be-nighted Christians, my friend blurted out, "Crystal is a Christian, and she's smart."

Ten sets of raised eyebrows turned in my direction. And then the attacks began: "How can you as a woman endorse a misogynistic religion?" "What about the Holocaust?" "How can a good God allow suffering in the world?"

By God's grace, I had reasonably helpful replies to each question, and eventually the protests died out. As my inquisitors redirected eyebrows to enchiladas, one finally broke the silence with "Next time we'll bring our friend John. He can argue better than we can."

This moment was an epiphany as strong as the one wearing flannel in the Blue Room: I realized that Christians are not the only ones who hold on to their beliefs so tightly that they can leave bruises. These graduate students were so committed to their anti-Christian assumptions that they refused to reconsider their position when their criticisms were shown to lack sub-stance. Though they would certainly have described themselves as "liber-als," they were amazingly conservative: in order to keep from changing an opinion, they appealed to an "inerrant" source to conserve their "truth": John, who could argue better than any of them could. I, in contrast, wanted to remain open to the liberation of the Word.

The means to that liberation was provided, ironically, by a Marxist: Fred-ric Jameson, a professor of literature and humanities who mounted some of the earliest scholarly attacks against postmodernism. The title of his book *The Prison House of Language* (1972) became a catch-phrase for the idea that language shapes perception and behavior. When I heard Jameson speak in 1989, I was not surprised at the contempt he expressed for postmodern-ism, for I had learned enough in grad school to know that postmodernism undermined absolutist explanations for reality—like Marxism. Indeed, in 1981 Jameson had written that "the *absolute* horizon of all reading and in-terpretation" is political (emphasis mine), the "political" for most Marxists consisting mainly in class struggle.[1]

As a Christian believing in God as an absolute, I also had stayed clear of postmodern discourse—until Jameson suddenly flannelgraphed me. I re-member where I was sitting in that lecture hall as clearly as I remember the

---

[1]Fredric Jameson, *The Political Unconscious: Narrative as a Socially Symbolic Act* (Ithaca, N.Y.: Cornell University Press, 1981), p. 17.

cold chair against my bare legs in the Blue Room. The sharpened point of my pencil broke when Jameson proclaimed, barely suppressing a sneer, that postmodernism was "like Christian fundamentalism." At first I was chagrined, for Jameson's comment elicited a derisive laugh from many of the listeners, who were delighted at his dismissal of Christianity and postmodernism in one fell sneer. Those listeners were like the graduate students at my friend's dinner party: welcoming any language that might reinforce their belief in the foolishness of orthodox Christianity (or "fundamentalism," as they inaccurately called it). I, however, having questioned the *language* of belief in my Christian upbringing, also wanted to question *this* language of belief: Where did anti-Christian sentiments come from? Which cultural powers had constructed a fortress against faith? Was this fortress vulnerable?

Unwittingly, Jameson gave me a key that might unlock *his* prison house of language. He explained his comparison of Christianity and postmodernism by saying both celebrated "the synchronicity of the non-synchronous" or, in other of his words, "the co-existence of distinct moments in history." Indeed, I thought, orthodox Christians believe that Jesus Christ is as alive today as when he lay in a manger two thousand years ago, and that he preexisted his moment of birth as a cocreator with God: Jesus incarnates the synchronicity of the nonsynchronous.

I also recognized the applicability of the synchronicity of the nonsynchronous to postmodern architecture. Because my doctoral dissertation discussed how nineteenth- and early-twentieth-century English writers described architecture in their texts, I often read books on the history of architecture, enjoying the photographs of contemporary styles. Postmodern buildings disregard historical continuity, playfully juxtaposing styles from nonsynchronous modes. For example, part of a building might look like the Roman Coliseum while another part "quotes" (a favorite word of postmodern architects) a Gothic cathedral, both styles embedded in an obviously high-tech building. Such an edifice illustrates a "co-existence of distinct moments in history." Rather than value historical progress, which Marxists hold so dear, the synchronicity of the nonsynchronous makes fun of it (in both senses of "make fun").

Jameson berates this kind of fun in his oft-reprinted essay from *New Left Review:* "Postmodernism, or the Cultural Logic of Late Capitalism" (1984). Here he despairs that modernist "parody" has been displaced by postmodernist "pastiche." While parody usually has a serious message (best employed, we would assume, in exposés of capitalist excess), pastiche merely plays with historical images. The pastiche of postmodern architecture, then, illustrates one of the basic tenets of postmodernism: history itself is an artificial construction, a narrative fabricated from images of the past that are organized and juxtaposed according to the worldview of the historian. This is an appalling idea to Marxists and other secular humanists who have an evolutionary view of history, believing that society will eventually evolve beyond its need for "the opiate of the masses," to use Marx's famous reference to religion.

Therefore, after hearing a Marxist contemptuously dismiss both Christianity and postmodernism, I decided that rather than taking a duck-and-cover position, I needed to study thinkers whose "synchronicity of the nonsynchronous" aligned them with Christians. Perhaps, I considered, two enemies of the same godless political philosophy might become friends, aiding each other in an appreciation for the God who transcends language. Hence I started studying postmodern views of history to help me understand what was behind the architecture I so enjoyed.

Postmodern Versus Christian Views of History

I discovered that the near-religious belief in progress—a fundamental staple of Marxism and the Enlightenment that fed it—was undermined by Michel Foucault (1926-1984), himself a one-time member of the French Communist Party. Trained as a philosopher, Foucault, who also studied psychology and psychopathology, developed a view of history different from that of his Marxist forebears. Rather than maintaining the Enlightenment model, in which civilization advances through time (which usually meant advancing beyond Christianity and its outdated superstitions), Foucault conceptualized history as falling into discontinuous epochs. Those alive during each epoch perceived and explained reality differently, one epoch being neither more nor less "enlightened" than the next. Foucault supported his theory by exploring how different epochs defined and treated aberrant behavior, like insanity, criminality and sexual deviance. In *Discipline and Punish* (1979), for example, Foucault illustrated how actions regarded as visionary in one era—like the trances of a Christian mystic—might be treated as signs of mental instability in the next.

Some critics of Foucault's postmodernism actually accused it of being "conservative"—because it granted the same level of respect to medieval Christian interpretations of reality as to eighteenth-century dismissals of

Christianity.[2] This disturbed disciples of the "Enlightenment," who liked to perceive themselves as progressing beyond the European "Dark Ages," when Christianity was the ground of all knowledge. However, rather than endorse an evolutionary view of history, Foucault visualized epochs as layered on top of each other—much like the different scenes stapled on top of each other on a flannelgraph easel. One scene does not flow into (evolve into) the next; instead the historian, like the Sunday school teacher, must consciously reveal each layer, defining its significance by the way she places figures into the scene.

Ironically, Christians seem to parallel Marxists more than they do postmodernists in this area. Both have a teleological view of history, regarding time as progressing to a desired end (*telos,* in Greek, means "purpose" or "end"). Christians believe that all of history is aimed toward a purposive end: Christ's dominion over the heavens and the earth. Marxists believe that history is developing toward the "purpose" of a different "end": the end of capitalist dominion over the working classes.

Christians would do well to beware. For in order to achieve this "end," Marxist-Leninism sought to control historical *telos* through violent revolution. And far too many Christians seek to control historical *telos* through violence to revelation. From Hal Lindsey's *The Late Great Planet Earth* in the 1970s to twenty-first-century fictional bestsellers, I have read disturbingly self-assured predictions about the "end times"—despite Christ's statement "But about that day and hour no one knows, neither the angels of heaven, nor the Son, but only the Father" (Matthew 24:36).

Nevertheless, the history of Christianity has been filled with unfulfilled prophecies about the future; Christians in the year 1000 were as convinced of an imminent apocalypse as those a millennium later. In 1793 a U.S. evangelist named Elhanan Winchester addressed the British Parliament, which took seriously his theory that the fall of the Bastille prison, which began the French Revolution, was the first stage in the fulfillment of Revelation 11. That same year he published his talk, writing,

I regard the late events in France, therefore, as Signs of the Times, and they

---

[2]Jürgen Habermas, for example, calls Foucault a "Young Conservative" in "Modernity Versus Postmodernity," *New German Critique,* Winter 1981, p. 13. Bruce Ellis Benson notes that Jacques Derrida, the father of postmodern "deconstruction," has been accused of being "too conservative" as well. See "Traces of God: The Faith of Jacques Derrida," *Books and Culture,* September/October 2000, p. 43.

mark the close of the preceding period with great exactness; and in this light
their consequence is very great: they shew us whereabouts we are, and tend
to confirm the authority of the Scriptures, and especially the book of the Revelation of St. John.[3]

A year later, one of the discoverers of oxygen, Joseph Priestly, published
a sermon similarly arguing that the French Revolution presaged the end
times as outlined in the book of Revelation. As a result, just as Marxists had
to reassess their revolution when Soviet communism did not fulfill their predictions, many Bible believers have had to reassess their revelation when
the apocalypse went unfulfilled.

Most of us, of course, recognize the impossibility of seeing into the future
and know that even the best political pundits, economic analysts and
weather forecasters are often wrong. Postmodernism asserts that just as we
cannot see into the future, neither can we look into the past. In both cases,
we only have clues from which we construct scenarios that individuals either believe or discount. The big difference, of course, is that predictions
about the future can be verified, as when snow arrives the way a forecaster
said it would. But it is impossible to retrieve the past for verification. The
past has ineluctably passed.

At first this idea intimidated me. If history is a human construction, how
can I trust the truths that have been passed down through history? After all,
Christianity is a historical religion, predicated on the fact of Christ's birth,
death and resurrection. The resurrected Christ was the cornerstone to my
faith, and I had booked my retirement in "a house not made with hands" (2
Corinthians 5:1). I was not going to give up on my ages-old lease on life,
even though grad-school peers and professors kept waving eviction notices
in front of my face. History *had* to be true.

Then I attended my first high school reunion.

Interacting with former acquaintances in a strange new setting, I discovered that even the way I told my own history was somewhat artificial. Before
the reunion, I had always described my early life to my husband as a story
of progress: the transition from the air-brain of a high school prom queen
to the scholarly mind of a published graduate student. This Bastille of my

---

[3]Elhanan Winchester, "The Three Woe-Trumpets, of which the first and second are already past
and the third is now begun: under which the seven vials of the wrath of God are to be poured
out upon the world," in *The Norton Anthology of English Literature: The Romantic Period,* ed.
M. H. Abrams and Stephen Greenblatt, 7th ed. (New York: W. W. Norton, 2000), 2B:141.

brain—my own construction of history—was battered down by my former classmates, several of whom told my husband, leaving the "air" out entirely, "Crystal was such a brain."

As soon as we got in the car after the festivities, my husband turned to me saying, "Well, Ms. Alleged Air-Brain, what was *that* all about?!"

Frankly, I was as surprised as he. While I got good grades in high school out of sheer conscientiousness, my embarrassingly low SAT scores attest to the poverty of my mental life. And though I spent time thinking about sermons and biblical language (the only topics I considered worth analyzing), my thoughts in high school centered on boys, proms, popularity (did I mention boys?). To my mind (and in my mind) I was an air-brain. Others, however, seem to have considered me smart.

This contradiction between my self-reporting and reports of my acquaintances suggested to me that postmodernism was onto something: even historical eyewitness accounts may not be entirely "true." Indeed, who was telling the truth about my mental capacities in high school? I? My classmates? My SAT scores? My straight-A average? The postmodernist would say all of these are reporting "truth," each one operating from a different perspective. Truth is situated. This does not deny the fact of my existence, the honesty of my classmates, nor the accuracy of my grades or aptitude scores. No thinking postmodernist denies the reality of facts. Instead, postmodernism calls into question the immediacy of our access to facts, suggesting that prejudices, presuppositions and other constructions of culture tint the glasses through which we view facts—even when those facts appear before our very eyes. In my case I viewed my intelligence through the glasses of insecurity. Noticing (or perhaps just believing) that it wasn't "cool" to be smart in my high school, I discounted my good grades because I wanted to be accepted.

There may be another reason that my "truth" differed from the "truth" of my classmates. Like most people, I wanted to make my personal history a success story. To do so, I needed to conceptualize a deficient past in order to narrate a change for the better. In other words, I wanted to give a *telos* to my life story. I finally understood what I had done when I encountered the extraordinary scholarship of Hayden White, both through his books and in conversation with him.

Hayden White and History as Story

The first book I read by Hayden White, *Metahistory,* discusses how historians, in order to make sense of the facts they have gathered, must organize them into some kind of narrative. But the way they piece together their narratives affects the way their readers view history. For example, similar to my Sunday school teacher's arranging images for a flannelgraph scene, the historian must choose the kind of background on which she will position her material—a backdrop that can affect readers' perceptions.

I became aware of what a difference background can make when, at age eighteen, I read my first Jane Austen novel. In *Pride and Prejudice* (1813), the Bennet sisters, especially the youngest ones, gush over the fact that Redcoats have set up camp near their village. They, along with other unmarried women in town (not to mention their mothers), look forward to the next ball, where they will have a chance to dance and flirt with the handsomely dressed marriageable soldiers. To counter Mr. Bennet's disgust at the silly obsessions of his daughters, Mrs. Bennet remarks, "I remember the time when I liked a red coat myself very well—and indeed so I do still at my heart; and if a smart young colonel, with five or six thousand a year, should want one of my girls, I shall not say nay to him" (chap. 7). I remember being shocked by these attractions to the Redcoats, for throughout my American history lessons Redcoats were despicable: the evil enemy that had to be defeated in order to guarantee freedom, justice and the American way. Though Austen's Redcoats and Redcoats in American Revolutionary days both reflected historical conditions in the late eighteenth century, the soldiers appear quite differently depending on their backdrop: rural England or the American colonies. The very same phrase, "The Redcoats are coming! The Redcoats are coming!" has a radically different meaning depending on who utters it: the infatuated Lydia Bennet or the infuriated Paul Revere.

Though White does not use the language of "backdrop," he does allude to other conditions that change the way readers perceive history. For example, the point at which historians choose to begin their narrative makes a big difference. One historian might begin her history of the American Revolution with the gentlemanly flirtations of Redcoats who follow orderly dance-steps at English balls, in order to emphasize their shock when, after a hazardous voyage across the Atlantic, the tidy soldiers encountered colonists who, rather than fight according to the respected conventions of warfare, sometimes used guerrilla tactics. A different historian will start with the Boston Tea Party to emphasize the frustration—"No taxation without representation!"—that led to revolution, while others will point out that American colonists, taxed at lower rates than citizens in England, had already been offered representation in Parliament. One historian may even want to start her account with the colonists' treatment of the American Indians, a beginning that would put the Revolution in an entirely different light altogether.

Lest readers think I am inventing extremist scenarios, as early as 1962 Thomas J. Pressly wrote a book about the multiple ways Americans have interpreted another American war: "The farther the Civil War receded into the past, the greater the disagreement among twentieth century historians over its causes, and the greater the strength of the emotions with which these divergent viewpoints were upheld."[4]

In *Metahistory,* White provides an explanation for such divergences, discussing how the narrative style a historian chooses is affected by the way his era conceptualizes historical processes: as a pendulum swing, via cause and effect, or through the struggle of competing forces. Depending on assumptions embedded in their culture, some historians script a historical event as Tragedy, others as Comedy, both interpreting the same facts quite differently.

Turning Messy Facts into Tidy Fictions

Hayden White's insight is just as true on the smaller canvas of biography as it is on the larger canvas of American history. Take two reputable biographies about the Christian playwright and essayist Dorothy L. Sayers: James Brabazon's *Dorothy L. Sayers: A Biography* (1981) and Barbara Reynolds's *Dorothy L. Sayers: Her Life and Soul* (1993). To narrate an incident from Sayers's life, both quote from the exact same letter, Brabazon discussing how it illustrates Sayers's weakness, Reynolds her strength. As I argue in my book *Writing Performances: The Stages of Dorothy L. Sayers,* Brabazon turns the history of Sayers into Tragedy, Reynolds into Comedy. The *fact* of the letter is the same for both, but the *truth* about Sayers differs radically.

When I read *Metahistory,* I realized that I had "narrativized"—or scripted—my own biography in the literary genre of Romance, which White defines as "transcendence of the world of experience, . . . victory over it, . . . liberation from it."[5] I saw myself transcending a cultural era that defined fe-

---

[4]Thomas J. Pressly, *Americans Interpret Their Civil War* (New York: Free Press, 1962), p. 9.
[5]Hayden White, *Metahistory: The Historical Imagination in Nineteenth-Century Europe* (Baltimore: Johns Hopkins University Press, 1973), p. 8.

males as adorably vapid; my liberation was declared by my first scholarly publication. Of course, I was not aware of the artifice of my script when I recounted the "truth" of it to my husband. But since high school I had immersed myself in novels that celebrated a woman's "victory over" the expectations of her culture, like the works of Charlotte Brontë, Jane Austen and George Eliot. Furthermore, I had discovered that fascination with tales of human progress—the surmounting of hardship, the transformation of sensibilities, the discovery of capabilities—sells Hollywood tabloids as well as Victorian novels. And I wanted to "sell" myself as having successfully transformed from a ditzy flirt to a dutiful scholar. But if truth be told, at least truth from the perspective of friends past and present, I was quite dutiful in high school and to this day can sometimes be a ditz.

Autobiographies, like biographies, carry with them the prejudices and purposes of the historian—perhaps all the more so for the writer who claims to have no prejudices. We all have biases, and to claim that they don't exist is to bind ourselves all the more to their power. The good historian, of course, gathers as much material from as many sources as possible, weighing the accounts of multiple perspectives to look for a trend in order to construct the most responsible history possible. But even then, history is dependent on the data available.

For an example, let's return to my high school reunion. As Crosby, Stills, Nash and Young blared in the background—on vinyl, no less—my husband and I approached a buffet table where the same heating lamps were hardening rolls and melting butter. Adjacent to the mayonnaise I said "Hi, Amaryllis!" to a woman (name changed to protect the insolent) who literally turned up her nose at me and then sashayed by, without returning my greeting. This was the first time that evening my husband felt led to whisper, "What was *that* all about?" I could only conjecture that it had something to do with the fact that I had run against her for a student body office and won.

I share this sadly humorous tale to make the point that Amaryllis, if still bearing a grudge some ten years later, would most likely give a historian a very different account of the "truth" about Crystal than my dear high school friend Barbara (name accurate to praise the worthy), who has supported me through rough times over the years. What if historians had access only to the account of Amaryllis and her friends? And what if I'm wrong about Amaryllis? Perhaps she stuck her nose in the air because she's allergic to mayonnaise.

This anecdote is meant to illustrate, if even simplistically, what postmodernists mean when they say history is a fiction. The word *fiction* comes from a Latin word which means "to fashion" or "to form"; historians "fashion" their stories out of the available "facts," some of which are "formed" by people like Amaryllis (or me!). Postmodernists are merely recognizing that the people who "live" history as well as those who write about it shape facts according to ways that they themselves have been shaped.

Psychologists provide increasing evidence that the mind often constructs fictions from the facts of experience. Daniel Schacter of Harvard University discusses the problem with memory in his book *The Seven Sins of Memory: How the Mind Forgets and Remembers* (2001). Among Schacter's many intriguing examples is a study undertaken in Holland after a cargo plane accidentally crashed into a huge residential building in 1992. Almost a year after the crash, researchers asked noneyewitnesses the question "Did you see the television film of the moment the plane hit the apartment building?" More than half of the people interviewed confirmed that they had seen the television image and gave detailed accounts of the devastating crash to prove the truth of their answer. Ironically, no image of the crash had ever been shown on television because none existed; television crews had arrived at the scene only after the impact. Nevertheless, in their memory these people had "seen" the crash; they were not lying. But the "truth" they told could only have been construed out of what they later read or heard in the media: speculations about the angle of impact, the direction of the explosion, the fall of the plane.[6]

Postmodern theorists similarly discuss how history is construed out of memories that are molded by one's "situatedness." And for those who consider this idea inimical to Christian orthodoxy, let me quote one of the church's greatest theologians, St. Augustine (354-430), who helped shape what Christians in the West consider orthodox Christianity. In his *Confessions,* Augustine wrote, "When we describe the past, it is not the reality of it we are drawing out of our memories, but only words based on impressions of moments that no longer exist."[7] Just as we do not have direct access to the future, neither do we have direct access to the past.

---

[6]Daniel L. Schacter, *The Seven Sins of Memory: How the Mind Forgets and Remembers* (New York: Houghton Mifflin, 2001), p. 112.

[7]Augustine *Confessions* 11.17. The translation is by Thomas C. Greene and appears in "Forum," *PMLA* 110 (1995): 411.

This, of course, applies to my own descriptions of the past: words based on impressions of moments that no longer exist. Readers must believe that my self-history is as accurate as I can remember it, just as I must believe that the historians I read are attempting to be as faithful to the available data as possible. So also Christians must believe that the Bible, despite its apparent inconsistencies, is the inspired Word of God, a reliable guide to faith and practice. Everything that is constructed from language—like Enlightenment and Marxist negations of Christianity as well as institutional Christianity itself—can only gesture toward, but not completely capture, the truth.

Witnessing to Non-Christians

Ironically, then, while my faith was ridiculed by the secular humanists I encountered in grad school, postmodernism, by drawing attention to the fact that *all* knowledge must be taken on faith, has allowed me to speak about my faith in the secular academy. I could tell that a dramatic change had occurred when, in the mid-1990s, I was asked to speak at a secular conference "as a Christian intellectual" who could justify Christian ethics. The session was titled "Postmodern Ethics," and one of my fellow panelists discussed the ethics of Afrocentrism while the other quite "pornographically" (his word) described the ethics of gay bathhouses. Because of postmodernism, it was expected that respect be accorded to all three of us, who discussed our situatedness as, respectively, a Christian scholar, an African American scholar and a homosexual scholar. In the presentation, I used paradigms from postmodern theory in order to argue that one must believe in some kind of universal absolute in order to legitimize ethics. And then I explained how Christian theology offers the best possible way to conceptualize an ethical absolute. Terrified, knowing that people at the secular conference would be most skeptical of my position, I solicited prayers from friends and family across the country. Though I worked harder on this paper than anything in my life thus far, I still marveled when it was selected, over the other two papers, to be published in the conference journal.[8]

I am not the only Christian who has experienced more openness to religion in the academy thanks to postmodernism. As Christian scholar Wilfred McClay recounts in his book *Religion Returns to the Public Square: Faith and Policy in America,* "In the postmodern dispensation, where knowledge

---

[8]Crystal Downing, "Antiseptic Bakhtin: A Dialogic Christian," *Pacific Coast Philology* 34 (1999): 18-31.

is to be understood as something always rooted in, and inseparable from, the discourse of particular communities, religious assertions have as good a claim as anything else, and a better one than most, to the mantle of 'truth.'"[9] Secular academicians are acknowledging, after centuries of repudiation, that religious conviction is a legitimate ground for knowledge.

This, of course, does not mean that professors around the world are welcoming Christians with open arms. Many were trained in modernist, rather than postmodernist, modes of thought and therefore assume that religion, at best, is irrelevant to intellectual endeavors and, at worst, hinders the objectivity necessary for intellectual progress. For an extreme example, take Richard Dawkins, the famous evolutionary psychologist who published *The Selfish Gene* in 1976, arguing that morals and mores are grounded in evolutionary processes. In 1997 he asserted that "faith is one of the world's great evils, comparable to the smallpox virus but harder to eradicate." And in 2004 he called religion "a dangerous collective delusion" and a "malignant infection."[10] Significantly, Dawkins also attacks postmodernism—perhaps because postmodernism serves faith.

This, however, does not mean that all postmodernists welcome faith. Some like to talk postmodern theory but still retain a modernist view of Christianity (which will be explained in the next chapter). Furthermore, according to my friends who teach in secular universities, some professors feel antagonistic toward Christianity due to the behavior of a small number of Christians themselves. Feeling as disdainful of other faiths as Dawkins is of all faiths, some students demonstrate a double standard: while expecting professors to be open to their Christianity, they put little effort into understanding how or why others believe the way they do.

When this kind of student encounters her mirror opposite—a secular humanist who has already made up her mind about the ills of Christianity—both come away more resistant than ever to the position of the other. The Christian ends up mirroring the anti-Christian: different positions, same tactics. Christ, however, calls us to be in the world but not of the world, loving

[9]Wilfred M. McClay, "Two Concepts of Secularism," in *Religion Returns to the Public Square: Faith and Policy in America*, ed. Hugh Heclo and Wilfred M. McClay (Baltimore: Johns Hopkins University Press, 2003), p. 39. I will give more examples of this openness in chapter eight.

[10]Richard Dawkins, quoted in H. Allen Orr, "A Passion for Evolution," review of *A Devil's Chaplain: Reflection on Hope, Lies, Science and Love*, by Richard Dawkins, *New York Review of Books*, February 26, 2004, p. 28.

people in their fallenness rather than mirroring them. Evangelism not based in genuine love for all of God's creatures tends to alienate rather than convince. To love another means trying to understand what they value and how they think.

Fortunately, most Christian students I encounter realize the importance of God's call to love the world. However, many might also ask, "If we try to understand controversial perspectives, might this not weaken the strength of our dedication to Christian truth? After all," they would assert, "Jesus instructed his disciples, 'Truly I tell you, unless you change and become like children, you will never enter the kingdom of heaven'" (Matthew 18:3). Indeed, I have heard this verse quoted as both a warning against thinking too much and an exhortation that childlike faith accepts the truth of Christianity unquestioningly.

However, it strikes me that one of the characteristics of children most pronounced (in both senses of the word) is their relentless questioning. I first discovered this when I was fifteen, having volunteered to help with a Sunday school class for three-year-olds. I gave stories using two puppets—Polly and Peter—created out of brown paper bags with painted paper faces glued to their bases. Slipping my hands into the bags, I would make Peter and Polly "talk" by working the folds creased into the bottom of the bags. One Sunday, as Polly (or was it Peter?) explained that God was the light of life, a restless member of my (surely) rapt audience piped up, "Teacher, why can't I look at the sun?"

"Because it will hurt your eyes."

"Why?"

"Because the sun can burn you even from far away."

"Why?"

"Because it's a huge ball of fire."

"Why?"

"Because we need its light to live."

"Why?"

At this point, having depleted the breadth of my scientific knowledge, I resorted to one of two authoritative replies modeled by some parents: "Because God made it that way" or "Because I said so."

Unfortunately, too many Christians settle for these kinds of answers, thinking that they fulfill Christ's admonition, "Whoever becomes humble like this child is the greatest in the kingdom of heaven" (Matthew 18:4). It seems to me, however, that a true sign of childlike humility is the recognition that one does not have everything figured out and hence must keep on asking questions.

This chapter, then, has related how my questions about the language of the Bible led to questions about the language of secular humanists, questions that postmodernists were asking as well. My willingness to start asking questions about postmodernism led to the discovery that it serves my faith—not in spite of its view of history but because of it. For postmodernism calls into question historical accounts that proclaimed Christianity a superstitious construct of the past.

How these anti-Christian accounts developed is the subject of the next chapter. But before you turn the page, let me assure you I do not claim to have all the answers. To make such a claim, I would have to draw a veil across my face to hide my lack of splendor.

PART TWO

From Modernism to Postmodernism

2

The Fall of the House of Usher

A HISTORY OF MODERNISM

Oの memorable moment during her preschool years, my sniffling mother was unsettled by a huge linen handkerchief held to her nose by Uncle Doc ("Cockey" to her). When Doc commanded "Blow!" she stamped her foot, pushed away his hand and forcefully insisted, "Yeeeeve it in there, Cockey!"

This, one of my grandmother's favorite stories, strikes me as a whimsical analogy for the way many people regard changes in cultural values. They want to hold on to what they have rather than clear out passages to new perceptions. Of course, when new values and perceptions undermine the possibility of a universal absolute, there is legitimate concern over the loss of certitude. I, as well, would want to "yeeve it in there" if postmodernism were accurately captured in the following definition:

> the consciousness of what once was presumed to be present and is now seen as missing. It might be considered as a series of felt absences . . . knowledge without truth, power without authority, society without spirit, self without identity, politics without virtue, existence without purpose, history without meaning.

This summary by distinguished professor of history John Patrick Diggins describes, however, *modernism* rather than postmodernism.[1] Admittedly,

---

[1] John Patrick Diggins, *The Promise of Pragmatism: Modernism and the Crisis of Knowledge and Authority* (Chicago: University of Chicago Press, 1994), p. 8.

just as many children carry bad habits into adolescence (like refusing to blow their nose), most of Diggins's "without" phrases could describe post-modernity. Nevertheless, his congestion of "withouts" is a symptom of modernism, which must be diagnosed before postmodernism can be treated.

The Difficulty with Defining Modernism

As its name implies, postmodernism is usually defined in contradistinction to modernism—except by some of its Marxist and leftist detractors, who see it as the intensification of everything wrong with capitalism. Most scholars, however, regard postmodernism to be as pluralistic as the phenomena it describes: it is "both a strict and logical continuation of modernist thought and its thoroughgoing revision or reversal."[2] Whichever way you see it, you need to understand the story of modernism in order to have a sense for postmodernism.

Unfortunately, like *postmodernism,* the word *modernism* is employed differently by different kinds of scholars. Art historians identify the word with a trend away from photographic realism that started with late-nineteenth-century French painters (Early Modernism), reaching its climax in the era of Pablo Picasso (High Modernism) and entering its maturity with the abstract expressionism of Late Modernism. In contrast, literary critics and cultural historians use the term *Early Modern* to talk about the period in Europe from around 1500 to 1850. Church historians, meanwhile, often think of modernism in conjunction with the "modernist versus fundamentalist debates" about the Bible that occurred in the United States in the 1920s and 1930s. Despite their differences, all these definitions have one thing in common: a focus on cultural phenomena of Caucasian Europe and America. This is significant in that one characteristic of postmodernism is the valuing and celebration of non-Caucasian voices and styles.

Like the word *Christian,* then, *modernism* means different things to different people. But all definitions can be reduced to two basic categories, which I distinguish by writing capital-*M* "Modernism" versus lowercase-*m* "modernism." In this book (and elsewhere), capital-*M Modernism* refers to early-twentieth-century trends in the arts: painting, poetry, sculpture, architecture, music, theater and so on. Lowercase *modernism* usually "implies a cultish or celebratory approach to what is 'modern,'" as Ludmilla Jordanova

---

[2]Stuart Sim, ed., *The Routledge Companion to Postmodernism* (New York: Routledge, 2001), p. 319.

defines it in her book *History in Practice*.[3] Lowercase *modernism,* as I use it in this book, parallels what C. S. Lewis called "chronological snobbery": "the uncritical acceptance of the intellectual climate common to [one's] age, and the arbitrary discrediting of past thought."[4]

A similar distinction can be made with definitions of the word *postmodernism:* it can refer to specific literary, artistic and architectural forms—usually in contrast to Modernist styles—or it can describe theories that question the cult of modernism. Not surprisingly, the two definitions of modernism (and of postmodernism) are interrelated, for the cultish (or anticultish) trends are reinforced by movements in the arts.

I will discuss how the arts inform both modernism and postmodernism in chapter three. For now, it is best to begin with an overview of the "modern" period in order to explain how the "cultish" celebration of everything "modern" developed. This can be a treacherous undertaking, for as Jordanova notes, "descriptions of a time period . . . are rather slippery and contain hidden agendas. There are many different definitions of modern history."[5] Trying to define such an elastic term is somewhat like looking at a house. Though it is all one structure, the front view can differ considerably from views taken from the back or either of the sides. Some houses in suburban developments look quite impressive from the street, with gables rising above stately brick façades. But a walk around each house reveals that the other three sides are covered in aluminum and vinyl and one side sports no architectural features other than tinny garage doors. Similarly, the house of "modern history," containing several rooms that art historians call "Modernism," looks different depending on where you are standing.

This means, of course, that my history of modernism will differ from that of someone situated elsewhere—especially someone who prefers looking only at the best face of the modern era, which, like the façade of a suburban estate, is quite impressive. Just as I love how many houses look from the street, I value how the modern era, in contrast to what is called the "premodern," led to the increasing egalitarianism of democratic societies. However, when I entered the house of modernism in graduate school, I discovered that its longtime residents were trying to flush Christianity—and thus

---

[3]Ludmilla Jordanova, *History in Practice* (London: Arnold, 2000), p. 125 n. 15.
[4]Janine Goffar, ed., *C. S. Lewis Index: Rumours from the Sculptor's Shop* (Riverside, Calif.: La-Sierra University Press, 1995), p. 98.
[5]Jordanova, *History in Practice,* p. 124.

part of myself—down the drain. They considered religion to be the refuse of a decaying past: the waste matter of the premodern. As recounted in chapter one, I therefore welcomed whatever might bring to ruin an intellectual edifice that posted at its door "Christians not allowed." The fall of modernism served my faith.

Constructing a History of Modernism

When we talk about the "fall" of modernism, we must recognize that the transition from one era to another is a construction of historians—a welcome construction that aids in the recognition and analysis of cultural trends. It is like asking, "In what year did your grandmother fall into old age?" Even though her childhood, young adulthood, middle age and old age are distinct eras in which her appearance has differed considerably, the change is barely perceptible when perceived on a monthly, even yearly, basis. You can therefore talk about her life in terms of continuities: personality characteristics that remain the same over the years, or idiosyncrasies that have intensified in old age. This parallels how scholars on the left, especially the Marxists, talk about the continuities between modernism and postmodernism.

In the life of a person, of course, you can also talk in terms of discontinuities, identifying symbolic events that mark the transition from one era to the next: childhood ends with a confirmation service or a move to college, middle age ends with the advent of either grandchildren or arthritis. The same, then, can be said of the transition from the premodern to the modern and from modernism to postmodernism: despite the apparent continuity between them, historians select symbolic names and dates to identify a moment of change. Furthermore, just as you, a grandchild, may select different events as significant in your grandmother's life than her contemporaries would, various scholars will identify different transitional moments in the life of modernism. Even those people who agree with my assessment of postmodernism might construct its antecedents differently in the tiny entryway of this chapter. Some postmodernists might even accuse me of being too "modernist" in my approach, for I am reinforcing a linear ("modernist") view of history, in which one era develops out of another.[6] I, like any scholar, can only give my point

---

[6]For example, Stanley Hauerwas writes, "I am just postmodern enough not to trust 'postmodern' as a description of our times, for it privileges the practices and intellectual formations of modernity." See his "Preaching as Though We Had Enemies," *First Things* 53 (May 1995) (available at www.firstthings.com).

of view and justify it as responsibly as I am able.

The House of Modernism

To open the door on modernism, we need to unlock the word *modern*. First used in the earliest decades of the sixteenth century, *modern* indicated "the present time" in contrast to the past, from the Latin *modo,* meaning "just now." The words *modernist* (1588) and *modernism* (1757), like the word *Christian,* were initially employed to dismiss something new that challenged the status quo. In fact, Jonathan Swift, famous author of *Gulliver's Travels,* coined the term *modernism* in 1757 to disdainfully denote, ironically enough, new coinages of language. He railed, for example, against the word *mob,* for he believed that the phrase from which it came, *mobile vulgus* (Latin for "movable, changeable common people"), was far preferable. For Swift, it was better to "yeeve it in there" than to develop a "modernism." Until the nineteenth century, then, *modernism* and *modernist* referred to a new trend or word—much as people tend to use the word *modern* today—except that the connotations were usually negative.

By 1887, however, "the spirit of modernism" had developed positive connotations, often distinguishing the modern era from the "medieval" or "Christian" past—so much so that by 1907 *modernist* referred to "one who inclines to, supports, or advocates 'modernism'; a holder of advanced or liberal religious views" *(OED)*. More and more, *modernist* became associated with innovative individuals who, through exercise of innate reasoning abilities and/or artistic talents, become elevated above contemporary institutions and social conventions.

The Elevation of Early Modern Thought

I try to avoid elevators as much as possible, ever since a traumatic experience at the university where I taught immediately after grad school. Late for class, I was the first of about twenty tardy persons to rush into a metal-lined cubicle before its doors closed. Overcrowded, the cubicle groaned as it rose and finally stopped halfway between two floors, prohibiting the doors from opening. Crushed against the back wall, with a mood of restrained panic permeating the space, I started to feel as though I couldn't breathe. In between shoulders, I could just make out a huge pair of red-framed glasses slipping down the sweaty nose of a woman who was pushing multiple elevator buttons in wheezing panic. After several very long minutes, the groaning elevator car started to move again, accompanied by a chorus of sighs. When the doors opened onto the second floor, all of us rushed out into the light, no matter our original destination, exhilarated by the open air of a nondescript hallway lined with yellowing linoleum.

Such a sense of euphoria among intellectuals is how many modernists envision entrance into the early modern era. It is no coincidence, of course, that someone from the early modern period (in 1827) coined the term *medieval*—or middle era—to denote premodernity, the time when Christianity dominated European culture, when revelation defined ultimate truth. For modernists, inhabitants of the Christian "Middle Ages" were like people trapped on an elevator between two floors: confined to a claustrophobic space of narrow thought, without access to the brilliant art and learning of the classical Greek and Roman floors beneath, nor to the scientific and artistic advances of the modern floors above. One early modernist invented the term *Renaissance,* or "rebirth," for the reappearance of classical values after the intellectual stagnation of the medieval period. And having been trapped in a university elevator, I can attest that being delivered from the confining cubicle into the freedom of the otherwise nondescript second floor felt like a "rebirth."

Ironically, of course, the Middle Ages were filled with brilliant minds, many of which were well acquainted with classical writings. As Paul Johnson notes, medieval masons were far more technologically advanced than the classical Romans, whose heavy reliance on slave labor had precluded architectural innovation.[7] The Romans, it would seem, were trapped in a narrower elevator space than many inhabitants of the late Middle Ages. Furthermore, as a 2004 essay in the *New York Review of Books* argues, "the medieval Church was a leading patron of science; . . . and the medieval curriculum was perhaps the most scientific in Western history."[8] Nevertheless, to this day the word *medieval* is often employed—even by Christians—to designate something intolerably outmoded. Every time the word is thus used, it perpetuates an assumption of modernism: that the Christian medieval period was a dark age—an intellectually confining cubicle—that needed to be escaped.

---

[7]Paul Johnson, *The Renaissance: A Short History* (New York: Modern Library, 2000), pp. 11-12, 89-90.

[8]H. Allen Orr, "A Passion for Evolution," review of *A Devil's Chaplain: Reflection on Hope, Lies, Science and Love,* by Richard Dawkins, *New York Review of Books,* February 26, 2004, p. 17.

Some scholars align the opening of the early modern elevator doors with the invention of the printing press in the mid-fifteenth century, others with the Protestant Reformation sixty years later. The two are closely related, for without the printing press Martin Luther could not have advocated a "priesthood of all believers" based on *sola Scriptura* ("only the Bible") as the source of belief. Before movable type, Bibles—like all books—were too expensive for most people to own; hence only church officials and their scribes, as well as those few who had learned to read (usually the very wealthy), had immediate access to Scripture. This left the interpretation of the Bible, out of necessity, to the hierarchy of the church. Once books became more plentiful, however, middle-class people had greater motivation to work toward literacy and hence to read Scripture on their own.

"On their own" is a key phrase here, for the individualism it implies developed into the independence of interpretation that marks "the modern"—and still influences twenty-first-century views of progress. For example, in the 2004 film *The Day After Tomorrow,* several people escape from cataclysmic weather conditions by sequestering themselves in the New York City Public Library, where they have to burn books to keep warm. A librarian holds on to a Gutenberg Bible, one of the first large books printed with movable type, refusing to throw it into the fire. When someone asks him about his reverence for Scripture, he explains that he does "*not* believe in God"; he asserts that he protects the book because it represents how the printing press initiated "the Enlightenment," the time when humans started thinking on their own. For this film character, as for many modernists, the Gutenberg Bible (published 1456) symbolizes—quite ironically—an advance beyond reliance on the Bible.

Reinforcing the early modern development of independence in reading was the Renaissance emphasis on perspective in art. While most medieval images look two-dimensional—flat characters often painted on gold-leaf surfaces—early modern paintings look three-dimensional, such that each painting seems to reflect what an individual might see if standing in a particular spot: objects farther away from the eye look small compared to those that are close to the viewer. Take, for example, the famous *Mona Lisa* (1503-1507): the woman appears near to us, filling the canvas, while the mountains and river in the background look far away. It thus seems "realistic" in comparison to a medieval picture of a two-dimensional Virgin and Child seeming to float on a background of glittery gold. The truth of the medieval painting, however, is based not so much on the authenticity to the viewing eye as on the authenticity of the story—a story so precious to a community of believers that it warrants gold for its depiction. "Realism" of perspective is not as important as the reality of the story to those who believe it.

The elevation from the premodern to the modern, then, is regarded as the transition from valuing a commonly shared, precious story to celebrating the individual reader/viewer who has her own viewpoint. Indeed, when we look at the *Mona Lisa* we have a sense that if we could get to one side, we might see her profile—a different perspective. But this creates a problem: which perspective is most "true"?

In *The Flight to Objectivity,* Susan Bordo argues that the development of perspective in painting contributed to the modern emphasis on objectivity. Worried about the potential for relativism that individualized perspective implies, philosophers in the early modern period asserted that all thinking individuals can ascertain objective truth on their own. Belief in objectivity was an escape from worries about relativism. This is what René Descartes meant in 1637 by the famous phrase *cogito ergo sum:* "I think, therefore I am." After doubting all the truth claims of individualized perspectives, he asserted that one can rely on reason to achieve universal, objective knowledge.[9]

In contrast, then, to the premodern belief that ultimate truth is revealed by God and mediated through the church (about which one subsequently employs reason), truth for the modern thinker is objectively perceived by the unaided human brain. Reason begins to take precedence over revelation; rational analysis starts to supersede the authority of the church. Descartes plays "a central role," as Bordo puts it, in "a historical movement away from a transcendent God as the only legitimate object of worship to the establishing of the *human intellect* as godly, and as appropriately to be revered and submitted to—once 'purified' of all that stands in the way of its godliness."[10] Hence, while the premodern Christian says that belief precedes understanding, as in Anselm's famous aphorism (inspired by Augustine) *credo ut intelligam* ("I believe in order to understand"), the modern era begins to switch it around, saying, "I must understand in order to believe." The

[9]Susan R. Bordo, *The Flight to Objectivity: Essays on Cartesianism and Culture* (Albany: State University of New York Press, 1987), pp. 69-73.

[10]Ibid., p. 81. For Descartes's suspicions about Christianity, also see Ray Linn, *A Teacher's Introduction to Postmodernism* (Urbana, Ill.: National Council of Teachers of English, 1996), p. 4.

trouble is, once reason is turned into the preeminent source of knowledge, it erodes reliance on faith, which is "the assurance of things hoped for, the conviction of things not seen" (Hebrews 11:1).

Going Up: The Enlightenment

Significantly, things *seen* became the basis of John Locke's famous *Essay Concerning Human Understanding* (1690), which some identify, rather than Descartes's *cogito,* as marking the beginning of "the Enlightenment"—in contradistinction to the "Dark Ages" of the Christian medieval period. For Locke the mind is a *tabula rasa,* or erased slate: a clean blackboard in the classroom of life. At birth the blackboard is entirely empty: humans are born with no innate ideas—including any ideas about or intuitions of God. Instead, knowledge comes through the sensations and observations of lived experience: pictures of what we call "empirical" reality which are etched onto the mental blackboard of the brain. The mind then draws connections among these images in order to come up with new perceptions and ideas.

Locke's emphasis on the empirical nature of knowledge contributed to eighteenth-century skepticism about Christianity, for Christ's resurrection cannot be proved with data available to the senses. Pushing Locke's empiricism to its logical extreme, David Hume (1711-1777) argued against miracles, saying, "No testimony for any kind of miracle has ever amounted to a probability, much less a proof."[11] Hume, in fact, defined the self as nothing more than a "bundle of perceptions," defying Descartes's assertion that reason, by itself, can ascertain truth.

In reaction to Hume, Immanuel Kant (1724-1804) synthesized the empiricism of Locke with the rationalism of Descartes, arguing that the human mind gives meaning to the perceptions it internalizes: knowledge is dependent on categories in the mind that interact with empirical data. One might compare Kant's view of the mind to the coin-sorting machines often found in American supermarkets—the ones that roll similar denominations into colorful paper-wrapped logs. Like unsorted coins poured into one of those machines, a wealth of empirical data enters our minds as we experience life. In fact, we can't evaluate each coin, each "thing-in-itself," until it enters the space of the brain. But then, like the channels in a coin machine that cause

---

[11]David Hume, "On Miracles," in *Enquiries Concerning Human Understanding and Concerning the Principles of Morals* (Oxford: Clarendon, 1975), p. 127.

quarters to drop into one slot, nickels in another, dimes in a third, mental categories channel coins of cognition so as to make sense of them—no pun intended (well, OK; maybe a little intention). Furthermore, like the channels in American coin machines, these rational categories are the same for every human, so that the ideas that result, like rolls of organized coin, will have universal value. Like a coin machine, then, the mind does not need human intervention (like the teaching of the church) to produce rolls of truth; reason, with the help of intuition and imagination, can function independently with the empirical data it receives. Kant therefore defined *enlightenment* as "the courage to use your own intelligence."[12]

Like Kant, Voltaire (1694-1778), a leader of the French Enlightenment, argued that an understanding of universal morality can be reached through reason independent of any reliance on revealed religion. Unlike Kant, however, he viciously attacked institutional Christianity, calling for all reasonable people to *ecrasez l'infame!* or "crush the infamous thing!" Many intellectuals like him in this so-called Age of Reason became deists, believing that God created the universe but then withdrew and allowed it to function according to natural laws. Though they didn't eliminate God from the universe, they placed the Creator at a distance—as a cosmic coin-machine maker whose service contract had run out. Fortunately, the brain can run on its own, as human will carefully tunes the mechanisms of the mind.

This, then, became the primary dogma of eighteenth-century Enlightenment thinkers: reason eliminates the need to believe the miraculous. For the French, as Gertrude Himmelfarb puts it, reason "was implicitly granted the same absolute, dogmatic status as religion."[13] Though Himmelfarb argues that the Enlightenment took a different form in America, Thomas Jefferson was enough of a deist to believe that Christian doctrines like the Trinity were "an engine for enslaving mankind," and he would have been happy to take scissors to the Bibles of all Americans in order to cut out passages about mir-

---

[12]Immanuel Kant, "What Is Enlightenment?" in *The Philosophy of Kant*, ed. Karl J. Friedrich (New York: Modern Library, 1993), p. 145. Stanley Grenz identifies "the shift to radical individualism" during the Enlightenment with Kant, who "believed that the burden of discovering truth is ultimately a private matter, that the knowing process is fundamentally a relationship between the autonomous knowing self and the world waiting to be known through the creative power of the active mind." See *A Primer on Postmodernism* (Grand Rapids: Eerdmans, 1996), p. 80.

[13]Quoted in Jonathan Clark, "Light Sources," review of *The Roads to Modernity: The British, French and American Enlightenments*, by Gertrude Himmelfarb, *Times Literary Supplement*, November 12, 2004, p. 3.

acles and Christ's divinity.[14] Assuming that religion was not consonant with authentic intellectual endeavors, he thought about prohibiting the study of Christianity at the University of Virginia and asserted the need for a "wall of separation" between private faith and public learning. His architectural metaphor of a "wall" is consonant with the neoclassical buildings he designed for the nation's Capitol, modeled on classical styles that predated between-the-floors medievalism.

It would be foolish, of course, to entirely dismiss Enlightenment rationality. As Richard Hughes has noted, many "Enlightenment thinkers grounded their moral vision squarely in a religious framework," and therefore scholars "must be careful not to reject the Enlightenment out of hand."[15] After all, the Enlightenment emphasis on reason led to human rights reforms and democratic governments at a time when all too many leaders of the church supported regimes that oppressed their citizens and violently suppressed dissent. Voltaire's disgust with the Christian church was not unwarranted.

Nevertheless, like postmodernists, I have a problem with the Enlightenment emphasis on intellectual autonomy: the idea that humans can ascertain pure, objective, universal truth on their own. Not only did it generate disdain for Christianity, but eventually it led intellectuals to abandon even deism. In 1810 the not-yet-famous poet Percy Bysshe Shelley collaborated on a pamphlet titled "The Necessity of Atheism," which argued that since God's existence could not be proven on empirical grounds, atheism was the only intellectually viable response. In this he echoed the philosopher at the center of the French Enlightenment, Denis Diderot, who had made a similar argument in the late 1740s.

Of course, since the majority of people want to "yeeve it in there," conserving intact paradigms, Diderot was imprisoned for his views and Shelley was expelled from Oxford University. But in a kind of intellectual trickle-down effect, more and more thinkers became dissatisfied with the intellectual stuffiness of those who unreflectively protected the status quo. While philosophers were the ones who did most of the undermining of Christianity in the eighteenth century, it was scientists in the nineteenth century who demolished the Christian edifice for the English-speaking world.

---

[14]Quoted in Michael Massing, "America's Favorite Philosopher," review of *American Jesus: How the Son of God Became a National Icon,* by Stephen Prothero, *New York Review of Books,* December 28, 2003, p. 7.

[15]Richard Hughes, *How Christian Faith Can Sustain the Life of the Mind* (Grand Rapids: Eerdmans, 2001), p. 16.

The Ushering In of Science

James Usher (often spelled Ussher) was a professor of divinity at Trinity College, Dublin, and chancellor of St. Patrick's Cathedral during the first decade of the seventeenth century. In the 1640s he moved to England, where he wrote his most famous work, *Annales Veteris et Novi Testamenti,* which presented a historical chronology for biblical incidents. Based on his reading of all the "begats" in the Bible, along with the stated ages of Old Testament patriarchs, Usher systematically reinforced time frames suggested by earlier Christian leaders to conclude that the world was created on October 23, 4004 B.C.—at 9:00 a.m., no less.

Usher's intellectual edifice was influenced by modernist styles. It reflected the early modern impulse to submit Scripture to reason more than it harmonized with early church tradition, which regarded a literal six-day creation as unnecessary to Christian orthodoxy. One of the preeminent fathers of the Western Church, St. Jerome (c. 340-420), had no trouble with the idea that the Genesis account might be allegorical, for he considered Moses to be writing in "the manner of a popular poet." He himself was following a tradition established by the Christian theologian Origen (185?-254?), who disdained purely literalist readings of Scripture: "The deepest religious (theological) meaning of every text is to be found in its nonliteral, spiritual meaning." Early Protestants maintained this premodern view of biblical truth; John Calvin (1509-1564) did not think that authority of Scripture would be injured if the book of Job, for example, turned out to be fiction rather than history.[16]

However, as the modernist "flight to objectivity" increased its cultural visibility, many Protestants booked passage on the flight, believing that it took them to Usher's house, where the Bible was scientifically accurate and historically objective. Usher's schema became the reigning construction of human history for these Christians: a house of faith into which they moved all their beliefs. Problematically, by the early nineteenth century Usher's construction seemed to be a house built on the sand. And scientists were more interested in the sand, convinced that as the rains came down and the floods went up, ancient life forms were deposited there. Due to the Age of Reason's Industrial Revolution in England, coal was being excavated and canals were

---

[16]For comments by Jerome and on Calvin, see C. S. Lewis, *Reflections on the Psalms* (New York: Harcourt Brace, 1958), p. 109. On Origen, see Luke Timothy Johnson, *Scripture and Discernment: Decision Making in the Church* (Nashville: Abingdon, 1996), p. 48.

being dug to transport the coal, exposing fossils in the sedimentary layers.

People had been excavating fossils, of course, for centuries. Though early Greeks had believed that "they were remains of once-living animals," the medieval church either denied that fossils were once organic or followed Tertullian (160?-230?) to say that these life forms were deposited by Noah's flood.[17] Social interest in fossils, however, didn't develop until the nineteenth century. And I mean "social": British gentlemen would go out on digging parties, in top hats no less, to hammer away at chalky cliffs. Though this sounds delightfully quaint—good material for *Masterpiece Theatre*—the discoveries they made were all but. Amateur geologists were digging up evidence, literally, that called into question what most conservative Christians considered biblical truth: that the earth was created in 4004 B.C. For many, Bishop Usher's house had developed a major structural flaw.

Of course, not all Christians felt the need to shore up Usher's house. Take the Reverend William Buckland, a professor at Oxford University who used to search for fossils wearing his academic gown, looking, we presume, like a college graduate right after commencement digging for gold. Buckland argued that "nowhere did the Bible suggest that God made Heaven and Earth on the first day, but merely 'in the beginning,'" which could have lasted for "millions upon millions of years."[18] Nevertheless, vocal conservatives held on to Usher's young earth, arguing that fossils are remnants from Noah's flood, not the result of millennial processes. Problematically for the flood theory, which is based, of course, on the Genesis account in which God destroys disobedient humans, no human remains were discovered among the most ancient life forms unearthed by geologists.

This greatly troubled those Victorian intellectuals who wanted to believe Usher's interpretation of the Bible. John Ruskin, an influential art historian and cultural critic, complained in 1851, "If only the Geologists would let me alone, I could do very well, but those dreadful hammers! I hear the clink of them at the end of every cadence of the Bible verses."[19] The year before, Alfred, Lord Tennyson had published *In Memoriam*, a long poem about the death of his best friend, in which appear the famous lines "'Tis better to have loved and lost / Than never to have loved at all." But much of the poem is

---

[17]Marjorie Hope Nicolson, *Mountain Gloom and Mountain Glory: The Development of the Aesthetics of the Infinite* (New York: W. W. Norton, 1963), p. 148.

[18]Quoted in Bill Bryson, *A Short History of Nearly Everything* (New York: Broadway, 2003), p. 75.

[19]Quoted in introduction to *The Norton Anthology of English Literature: The Victorian Age*, ed. M. H. Abrams and Stephen Greenblatt, 7th ed. (New York: W. W. Norton, 2000), 2B:1051.

about another loss: loss of confidence in a benevolent God. Geologists were unearthing evidence that whole species—or "types"—had gone extinct, and sensitive souls wondered why God would bring into existence creatures only to let them die out. Tennyson therefore writes,

Are God and Nature then at strife,
    That Nature lends such evil dreams?
    So careful of the type she seems,
So careless of the single life, . . .

"So careful of the type?" but no.
    From scarped cliff and quarried stone
    She cries, "A thousand types are gone;
I care for nothing, all shall go."[20]

It was in this context that Darwin published his theory about evolution in 1859, calling it *On the Origin of Species by Means of Natural Selection, or the Preservation of Favoured Races in the Struggle for Life*. People, evidently, were ready for it: the book sold out all 1,250 copies of its first edition in one day.

It is on this day that some scholars mark the transition from the early modern to the modern era. Though the idea of evolution had been around for a long time (Darwin's grandfather wrote about it in the 1790s), Darwin was able to provide a mechanism—natural selection—that was backed up by geological discoveries. Evolution, therefore, was not the "discovery" of one man; indeed, a contemporary of Darwin, Alfred Wallace, came up with a theory of natural selection almost simultaneously. It was an assumption motivated, it would seem, by the modernist belief in progress. Geological findings could now be interpreted as advancement rather than loss. As Darwin writes in *On the Origin of Species,* "Hence we may look with some confidence to a secure future of great length. And as natural selection works solely by and for the good of each being, all corporeal and mental endowments will tend to progress towards perfection."[21] God was no longer necessary.

Unfortunately, rather than assessing how reason might reconcile the evidence of geological data with Scripture, many Christians made a fortress out

---

[20]From secs. 55-56 of Alfred, Lord Tennyson, *In Memoriam A. H. H.,* in *The Norton Anthology of English Literature: The Victorian Age,* ed. M. H. Abrams and Stephen Greenblatt, 7th ed. (New York: W. W. Norton, 2000), 2B:1250-51.

[21]Charles Darwin, *On the Origin of Species,* in *The Norton Anthology of English Literature: The Victorian Age,* ed. M. H. Abrams and Stephen Greenblatt, 7th ed. (New York: W. W. Norton, 2000), 2B:1685.

of the house of Usher. Ironically, though they conceived of themselves as protecting the Bible from science, what they were protecting was a human construction: Usher's *interpretation* of the Bible. They built up a wall of separation that kept fossil evidence, let alone the theory of evolution, from entering the Usher house.

While scientists were chipping away at this wall, an approach to the Bible called "higher criticism" brought in a battering ram. Developed primarily in Germany, the higher criticism, which questioned the authorship and historicity of Scripture, was being translated into English by Victorian intellectuals. In addition to undermining the literalism of a seven-day creation and Noah's flood, higher critics argued that even the miracles of the Gospels had their origin in secular myths.

With the authority of the Bible undermined, many Victorians came to the conclusion that assent to Bible-believing Christianity necessitated anti-intellectualism, and they sought authority elsewhere. Some, like the brilliant John Henry Newman, reasserted the authority of the traditional Anglican Church, believing that "Evangelicals . . . played into the hands of the Liberals."[22] Eventually Newman converted to Roman Catholicism, endorsing a premodern Christianity that predated the Protestant emphasis on *sola Scriptura* and the individualized readings it can generate.

By the end of the century, however, Newman's "Liberals" had won out and were glorying in the authority of science. Darwin's friend Thomas Henry Huxley coined the term *agnostic* in 1869 to designate what he considered the only intellectually respectable approach to the existence of God. Any "assertion which outstrips evidence," he said, "is not only a blunder but a crime." In other words, since there is no empirically verifiable evidence either for or against the existence of God, it is criminal to make an assertion either way. In his essay "Agnosticism and Christianity," Huxley asserted that belief in "things which are incredible"—like the resurrection—"is an abomination."[23]

Agnosticism Institutionalized

As we have seen, attacks on the supernaturalism of Christianity had been

---

[22]John Henry Cardinal Newman, *Apologia Pro Vita Sua*, in *The Norton Anthology of English Literature: The Victorian Age*, ed. M. H. Abrams and Stephen Greenblatt, 7th ed. (New York: W. W. Norton, 2000), 2B:1132.

[23]Thomas Henry Huxley, "Science and Culture" (1880) and "Agnosticism and Christianity" (1889), in *The Norton Anthology of English Literature: The Victorian Age,* ed. M. H. Abrams and Stephen Greenblatt, 7th ed. (New York: W. W. Norton, 2000), 2B:1565, 1568.

going on for a long time. What distinguishes the modern from the early modern period is the widespread nature of the doubt. While Shelley was expelled from Oxford University in 1810 for criticizing Christianity, by 1871 the same university had decided to eliminate its religious exams, considering them inappropriate for a university degree. Also in 1871, Darwin published *The Descent of Man,* in which he explicitly argued that humans evolved from an ancestor of the ape. Though his *On the Origin of Species* had sent shock waves throughout England in 1859, *The Descent of Man* elicited little furor.

The same thing happened with the work of David Friedrich Strauss, an influential purveyor of the German higher criticism. His book *The Life of Jesus,* which treats the Gospels as myth rather than history, generated hurricanes of controversy in 1835. By 1872, a far more radical book in which Strauss seeks to replace Christianity with Darwinian science—*The Old Faith and the New*—barely stirred the waters. More and more people were abandoning the ship of Christianity for the lifeboat of evolution.

And this was happening outside England as well. In the United States, the Englishman who coined the phrase "the survival of the fittest," Herbert Spencer, was treated like a saint by industrialists, who believed that Darwin's theories justified their economic successes. John D. Rockefeller asserted that "the growth of a large business is merely the survival of the fittest." And Andrew Carnegie, having been introduced to Spencer's social Darwinism, exultantly pronounced, "That light came in as a flood and all was clear. Not only had I got rid of theology and the supernatural, but I found the truth of evolution. . . . Man was not created with an instinct for his own degradation, but from the lower he had risen to the higher forms. Nor is there any conceivable end to his march to perfection."[24] Capitalism harmonized with the "survival ethic" of social Darwinism much better than it did with the ethics of shared resources, forgiveness and grace found in the New Testament. As Graham Sumner, professor of political and social science at Yale, put it in 1883, "Millionaires are a product of natural selection."[25]

These supporters of social Darwinism believed that humanity had evolved the intuitions necessary to interpret life-sustaining morality apart from Christian ethics. Huxley explains, "The causes which have led to the development of morality in mankind, which have guided or impelled us all the way from the savage to the civilized state, will not cease to operate be-

---

[24]Quoted in James Burke, *The Day the Universe Changed* (Boston: Little, Brown, 1985), p. 271.
[25]Ibid., p. 272.

cause a number of ecclesiastical hypotheses turn out to be baseless."[26]

It is no surprise, then, that scientific hypotheses about human nature were replacing those of ecclesiastical Christianity. Marx explained behavior in terms of economics and Sigmund Freud in terms of the unconscious. Both theories were based in a materialist philosophy: the idea that everything that exists is either matter or a product of matter.[27] It is no coincidence that we call Marx's discipline "political science" and Freud's "behavioral science." The word *science* validated the authenticity of their scholarship; science was the elevator that led to the highest truth.

Modernist Alternatives to Christianity

Many Victorian intellectuals worried about the elevation of science over faith. Without religious hope, an empirically verifiable world had "neither joy, nor love, nor light, / Nor certitude, nor peace, nor help for pain," as cultural critic Matthew Arnold wrote in his famous poem "Dover Beach" (c. 1851). Though, like many, he sorrowed over the loss of Christian assurances, Arnold regarded Christianity as hopelessly outdated. In 1867 he said of all "religious organizations," "Do not let us deny the good and the happiness which they have accomplished; but do not let us fail to see clearly that their idea of human perfection is narrow and inadequate, and that . . . the Protestantism of the Protestant religion will never bring humanity to its true goal." The goal, for Arnold, is the truth. But the godless elevator of science taking us there can seem like a dark and lonely place. Hope had to be placed elsewhere. And Arnold placed it in the "sweetness and light" of Culture, by which he meant the arts, especially literary art, which ministers to "our instinct for conduct, our instinct for beauty." He believed that eventually all of "mankind will discover that we have to turn to poetry to interpret life for us, to console us, to sustain us." This led to one of the basic characteristics of modernism: an elitist distinction between capital-*C* Culture, commonly pronounced "Cul'-cha," and lowercase "culture," made up of the middle-class masses (Arnold called them "philistines") who are insensitive to the power of art. These philistines hold on to Christianity out of sheer

---

[26]Huxley, "Agnosticism and Christianity," 2B:1569.

[27]Jacques Barzun notes that Freud offered psychoanalysis "as a physiological science fulfilling the same demands of material verification as any other; to him, Id, Ego, and Superego were organs functioning like the nerves and the brain." See *From Dawn to Decadence: Five Hundred Years of Western Cultural Life, 1500 to the Present* (New York: HarperCollins, 2000), p. 663.

inertia, failing to recognize the sweetness and light of Cul-cha.[28]

Though Arnold and Huxley disagreed about which was more important—science or art—both men trusted in human progress and contributed
to what has been called "secular humanism": the assumption that humans
will continue to evolve as long as they educate themselves in the truth of
science and the enlightenment of art. It is no coincidence that the words *scientist* and *aesthete* were coined during the nineteenth century. Both provided identities other than "Christian" with which to define the self. And in
the 1880s, the decade in which *aesthete* appeared, the word *modernism* was
employed for the first time to denote a mindset rather than a mere innovation. Not coincidentally, it is in the 1880s that art historians date the beginnings of capital-*M* Modernism.[29]

Twentieth-Century Modernism

Whereas in Victorian England many intellectuals despaired over the fact that
they could not sustain intellectual integrity in the house of Christianity, in
the next century more and more intellectuals were celebrating the house's
fall, rejoicing that humankind had progressed beyond the need for religion.
Though World War I sullied this joy, most continued to repudiate Christianity. Even the young C. S. Lewis, whose self-proclaimed atheism was molded
by the modernism of his schooling, asserted soon after the war that he
"never sank so low as to pray" while in the trenches.[30]

After the Great War, many modernist intellectuals jumped onto a philosophic bandwagon called "logical positivism," which directed philosophers
to apply logic only to facts they are "positive" about—facts that are scientifically provable. According to logical positivists, who had their heyday from
the 1920s into the 1960s, the only statements one might call "true" are those
that are empirically verifiable. Therefore all statements about unseen realities—things that can't be tested, like the existence of God—are merely

---

[28]Matthew Arnold, *Culture and Anarchy* (1868), "Literature and Science" (1883) and *The Study of
    Poetry* (1880), in *The Norton Anthology of English Literature: The Victorian Age*, ed. M. H.
    Abrams and Stephen Greenblatt, 7th ed. (New York: W. W. Norton, 2000), 2B:1529, 1555, 1535.
[29]A writer in a popular British journal compared "the spirit of modernism" with "medievalism" in
    1887 *(OED)*. Clement Greenberg identifies the origins of Modernism with Edouard Manet at the
    start of the 1880s, while Arthur C. Danto identifies its origin with Vincent Van Gogh and Paul
    Gauguin toward the decade's end. See Arthur C. Danto, *After the End of Art: Contemporary Art
    and the Pale of History* (Princeton, N.J.: Princeton University Press, 1997), pp. 7-8.
[30]Quoted in David C. Downing, *The Most Reluctant Convert: C. S. Lewis's Journey to Faith*
    (Downers Grove, Ill.: InterVarsity, 2002), p. 11.

"pseudo-statements": they have no "positive" meaning.

An influential literary critic in the 1920s, I. A. Richards, even applied logical positivism to the analysis of literature. Admitting that poetry and fiction offered only "pseudo-statements," he nevertheless asserted that the pseudo-statements of literary art are far more beneficial to humanity than the "pseudo-statements" of Christianity. In a book called *Science and Poetry*, published in 1926, he wrote,

> Countless pseudo-statements—about God, about the universe, about human nature . . . about the soul, its rank and destiny—have suddenly become, for sincere, honest and informed minds, impossible. For centuries they have been believed; now they are gone, irrecoverably. . . . [However], if we can contrive to believe poetry, then the world seems, while we do so, to be transfigured.[31]

Richards thus puts a positive spin on Arnold's idea that true intellectuals—at least the honest ones—can no longer believe Christianity. Richards's views reflect those of many other British scholars, some of whom argued in 1921 that "literature is not just a subject for academic study, but one of the chief temples of the human spirit, in which all should worship."[32]

Cultural critic Jacques Barzun actually dates the beginning of "popular Modernism" to the "victory won by the religion of art in the early 1920s." He wryly comments, "The message first uttered in the early 1800s, 'art for art's sake,' finally conveyed to the literate its true sense: 'art for life's sake.'" Significantly, Théophile Gautier (1811-1872), the man who coined the phrase "art for art's sake" *(l'art pour l'art)*, was the first to use the word *modern* as an adjective of adulation.[33]

The Modernist Trinity: Art, Science and Poetry

The famous English painter John Constable (1776-1837) reflected the early-nineteenth-century validation of science by pronouncing, "I hope to show that our profession as painters is *scientific* as well as poetic."[34] By the end of the century, the French Impressionists regarded paintings themselves as scientific documents recording the way light and color operate on the eye.

---

[31]I. A. Richards, *Science and Poetry* (New York: W. W. Norton, 1926), pp. 71-73.
[32]Quoted in Chris Baldick, *The Social Mission of English Criticism, 1848-1932* (Oxford: Clarendon, 1983), p. 97.
[33]Barzun, *From Dawn to Decadence,* pp. 713-14.
[34]Quoted in Helen Gardner, *Gardner's Art Through the Ages,* 10th ed., ed. Richard G. Tansey and Fred S. Kleiner (Fort Worth, Tex.: Harcourt Brace, 1996), p. 952.

Claude Monet (1840-1926) painted multiple canvases of the same object—a bridge, a cathedral or a haystack—to scientifically demonstrate the optical differences rendered by light at various times of day.

By the twentieth century, as Barzun notes, the "irresistible lure of scientism" infected all the arts, evidenced by the employment of the term *experimental* to positively describe innovations in music, poetry and painting. The Surrealist movement of the 1920s assumed a "scientific" posture by emphasizing the unconscious as a motivator, thus taking a "psychological" approach to art.[35]

In architecture, designers combined science and art to create buildings that were the first to be called "Modernist." The "Modern Movement," according to Charles Jencks, "was in architecture a Protestant Reformation putting faith in the liberating aspects of industrialisation and mass-democracy."[36] When architect Walter Gropius founded the Bauhaus movement in 1919, he regarded it as a "cathedral of the future"; in 1923 he proclaimed its doctrine: "art and technology—a new unity." He called for all the visual arts to participate in this unity in order to create a new religion: "Together let us desire, conceive, and create the new structure of the future, which will embrace architecture and sculpture and painting in one unity and which will one day rise toward heaven from the hands of a million workers like the crystal symbol of a new faith."[37]

Intellectuals who did not commit to this faith were regarded with contempt. After the famed Modernist poet T. S. Eliot converted to Christianity in 1927, for example, Virginia Woolf disdainfully wrote, "Tom Eliot may be called dead to us from this day forward. He has become an Anglo-Catholic, believes in God and immortality, goes to church. . . . There is something obscene about a living person sitting by the fireside and believing in God."[38]

During World War II, however, Woolf committed suicide. The war all but eliminated hope that the modernist trinity was aiding the progress of humanity. Nevertheless, modernists did not return to hope in Christ. Instead, absurdism became the new vogue. Jean-Paul Sartre, emphasizing the mean-

---

[35]Barzun, *From Dawn to Decadence,* pp. 720-31.

[36]Charles Jencks, *What Is Post-modernism?* (New York: St. Martin's, 1986), p. 31.

[37]Walter Gropius, "Programme of the Staatliches Bauhaus in Weimar," in *Programmes and Manifestoes on Twentieth-Century Architecture,* ed. Ulrich Conrads, trans. Michael Bullock (London: Lund Humphries, 1970), p. 25.

[38]Quoted in Robert Craft, "The Perils of Mrs. Eliot," *New York Review of Books,* May 23, 2002, p. 30.

inglessness of human life, advocated existentialism, a philosophy that pushes to its logical extreme the modern trust in human autonomy. He suggested that if there is no God to establish universal value—no "essence" that precedes human existence—then one's individual existence must create one's essence. In other words, a person must create his own unique meaning, define his own morality and then live it to the best of his ability. For Sartre, this is being "a man of good faith." And the art of such a person reflects the essential meaninglessness—the absurdity—of the life into which he is born. What existentialists shared with more hopeful modernists was a contempt for the philistine, who lived a conventional workaday life, experiencing neither the agony of despair nor the ecstasy of art.

Barzun summarizes the artistic temperament of the first half of the twentieth century with the following:

> The attack on authority, the ridicule of anything established, the distortions of language and objects, the indifference to clear meaning, the violence to the human form, the return to the primitive elements of sensation, the growing list of genres called Anti-, of which the root principle is "Expect nothing," have made Modernism at once the mirror of disintegration and an incitement to extending it. And all this was going on long before the moral, sexual, and political rebellions that shook the western world in the 1960s.[39]

These words, rather than describing postmodernism, harmonize with the description of modernism that began this chapter.

From Postwar to Postmodern

With the return of veterans from the European and Pacific fronts came the superficial stability of the 1950s. Cultural philistines in the United States went back to their domestic duties and their Sunday worship, watching *Father Knows Best* and *Leave It to Beaver* on television—the lowbrow version of "art and technology: a new unity." Meanwhile, modernists exchanged existential despair for renewed commitment to the modernist trinity. In a 1953 book so popular that it was reissued in 1958, Kathleen Nott, like Woolf before her, criticized Eliot as well as "stupider" Christian intellectuals like C. S. Lewis and Dorothy L. Sayers. Called *The Emperor's Clothes,* her book argued that Christians are like the brainwashed people in the popular children's fable, believing in realities (the emperor's new clothes) that do not exist. In contrast to

---

[39]Barzun, *From Dawn to Decadence,* p. 727.

those who promote the truth of science and technology, Christians are "engaged in the amputation and perversion of knowledge." Repeatedly invoking the views of Arnold, Nott asserted that "humanism encourages us to look for the empirical and rational steps toward moral conduct, as dogmatic religion does not and cannot."[40]

The attack on traditional religion spread like hot margarine in the noonday sun, until even the pages of *Time* magazine were stained by the grease. In April 1966 the popular weekly devoted a cover story to the "death of God" movement, discussing theologians who, according to Alister McGrath, merely "took their lead from cultural developments." McGrath summarizes the movement as follows:

> In his *Secular Meaning of the Gospel* (1963), Paul van Buren, arguing that the word "God" had ceased to have any meaning, sought to ascertain how the gospel might be stated in purely atheological terms. Belief in a transcendent God was replaced by commitment to a "Jesus-ethic," centered on respect for the lifestyle of Jesus. Thomas J. J. Altizer's *Gospel of Christian Atheism* (1966) refocused the question by suggesting that, while it was no longer acceptable to talk about Jesus being God, one could still talk about God being Jesus— thus giving a moral authority to Jesus' words and deeds, even if belief in a God was no longer to be retained.[41]

Significantly, just as this grease was clogging the religious arteries of the common people, intellectual fiber was being processed in France. In the 1960s several French theorists, who are now identified as "postmodern," started challenging modernist assumptions about art, science and poetry (see appendix).

This does not mean that all Christians at the time had either fallen under the spell of modernism or sequestered themselves in the house of Usher. Christian intellectuals were challenging the modernist mystification of objective reason before postmodernists ever thought to. Strongly influenced by Dutch Reformed political theorist Abraham Kuyper (1837-1920), philosopher Herman Dooyeweerd (1895-1977) started arguing in the 1930s against intellectual objectivity and suggested that all theory is inherently religious, for it is built on unfalsifiable assumptions that must be taken on faith. In the

---

[40]Kathleen Nott, *The Emperor's Clothes* (Bloomington: Indiana University Press, 1989), pp. 68, 31, 40.
[41]Alister McGrath, *Christian Theology: An Introduction,* 2nd ed. (Oxford: Blackwell, 1997), p. 256.

1960s Cornelius Van Til (1895-1987) questioned the autonomy of reason, asserting that humans inevitably argue from their presuppositions.[42] But these thinkers, two among many Christians offering intelligent challenges to modernist rationalism, could not make significant progress on a road posted with "Christians Not Allowed"—as Nott's ticketing of Lewis and Sayers illustrates. It took seasoned travelers on the modernist highway, many of them having commuted for years in the fast lane of godless Marxism, to direct non-Christian attention toward serious cracks in the secularist cement.

One of these was Jean-François Lyotard, who by 1979 had published (in French) *The Postmodern Condition: A Report on Knowledge.* He defined postmodernism as "incredulity toward metanarratives." Sometimes translated as "grand narrative," a metanarrative is an overarching explanation for reality that grounds its truth in universal reason. Lyotard's suspicion toward metanarratives is a reaction against the arrogant confidence of modernists who, thinking they have a special handle on truth, disdain narratives based on faith.[43]

Another postmodern philosopher, Richard Rorty, indicted science a decade later, explaining how "the Enlightenment wove much of its political rhetoric around a picture of the scientist as a sort of priest, someone who achieved contact with nonhuman truth by being 'logical,' 'methodical,' and 'objective.'"[44] For Rorty, all truths, including those of science, are human: intellectual constructions taken as true by groups of people who share the same interpretation of reality.

Today, some scientists—perhaps those most influenced by postmodernism—are willing to admit that fundamental doctrines of science are a matter of belief. In 1994 evolutionary psychologist Robert Wright discussed how scientists have committed themselves religiously to Darwin's famous construct:

---

[42]See Herman Dooyeweerd, *A New Critique of Theoretical Thought*, 4 vols. (Philadelphia: Presbyterian & Reformed, 1953-1958), and Cornelius Van Til, *Defense of the Faith* (Philadelphia: Presbyterian & Reformed, 1967).

[43]James K. A. Smith argues rightly that Christians who establish an incompatibility between postmodernism and Christianity often operate with an inaccurate understanding of Lyotard's word *metanarrative*. For Lyotard, Christianity would be a metanarrative only if its truth claims were proclaimed to be evident through the exercise of unbiased universal reason. See "A Little Story About Metanarratives: Lyotard, Religion and Postmodernism Revisited," in *Christianity and the Postmodern Turn: Six Views,* ed. Myron B. Penner (Grand Rapids: Brazos, 2005), pp. 123-40.

[44]Richard Rorty, *Contingency, Irony and Solidarity* (Cambridge: Cambridge University Press, 1989), p. 52.

The theory of natural selection is so elegant and powerful as to inspire a kind of faith in it—not *blind* faith, really, since the faith rests on the theory's demonstrated ability to explain so much about life. But faith nonetheless; there is a point after which one no longer entertains the possibility of encountering some fact that would call the whole theory into question.[45]

Though many scientists, still molded by modernism, refuse to make this admission, Wright quite disarmingly states, "I admit to having reached this point." He sounds like numerous Christians, including myself, who attest that their faith is reinforced by Christianity's "demonstrated ability to explain so much about life." In fact, for those who have followed Christ for decades, there comes a point after which they no longer entertain the possibility of encountering some fact that would call the fundamentals of Christian orthodoxy into question.

This explains why Lyotard and Rorty regard scientific explanations of reality as similar to religious ones: both must be judged by their internal coherence rather than their correspondence to reality. After all, they would ask, how can one judge a system's correspondence to "reality" if reality is precisely what that system defines? It is like being both inside and outside a house simultaneously: an impossibility!

I will address this "impossibility" in future chapters. For now, I want to direct attention to how these postmodern thinkers unwittingly served Christianity. When Lyotard established scientific rationality as a "language game with its own rules . . . on a par with" other forms of knowledge, he destabilized the idea that only reason and empiricism can access truth. His word *par* allowed Christians to join the intellectual country club as legitimate players in the game of knowledge, for it signaled that all truth claims are situated on presuppositions—rules shared by the players in the language game—that must be taken on faith.[46]

In other words, postmodernism brings us back to the *credo ut intelligam* (I believe in order to understand) of Augustine and Anselm. Thus, while most modernists considered Christian faith as a superstitious human construction doomed to fall, like James Usher's biblical timeline, postmodernists asserted that this modernist idea was itself a human construction. Modernists

---

[45]Robert Wright, *The Moral Animal: Evolutionary Psychology and Everyday Life* (New York: Vintage, 1994), p. 383.

[46]Jean-François Lyotard, *The Postmodern Condition: A Report on Knowledge* (1979), trans. Geoff Bennington and Brian Massumi (Minneapolis: University of Minnesota Press, 1984), p. 40.

were simply ushers at a different house of worship, one that extolled science and art.

Fall of the House of Usher

In Edgar Allan Poe's famous short story "The Fall of the House of Usher," an unnamed narrator discusses his visit to a gloomy, fungus-covered house. Once an elegant mansion, the hoary dwelling now contains the last of the Usher line: Roderick and his twin sister Madeline. Roderick seems obsessed with architecture, painting on canvas an eerie picture of a "ghastly" vault and composing a song titled "The Haunted Palace." When Madeline dies, Roderick's artistic constructions seem to be fulfilled: he buries his sister in a vault similar to what he has painted, only to have sounds from her vault haunt his palace. Roderick, I would suggest, is like the modernist artist so obsessed with the architecture of "the modern" surrounding him that he buries Christianity within it.

In Poe's story, Madeline returns to life, bloody from having fought her way out of the vault. When the horrified Roderick sees her at the door of his library, he dies from terror, followed by an almost supernatural crumbling into ruin of the Usher house. Similarly, to the horror of Roderick-like modernists, when postmodernism exposed that the modernist denial of Christian truth was merely a human construction—a vault inside "the modern" house—it allowed for the return of what modernism had entombed: Christian faith. With the return of faith, the house of modernism fell.

3

The Genius of (Post)Modernism

THE ARTS

I have long been fascinated with how people employ the word *genius*. In movies, a student genius is often depicted as a pointy-headed nerd wearing crooked, duct-taped glasses and picking his nose ("Yeeve it in there, genius"). As I watch such a portrayal, I think, *If he were really a genius he'd be smart enough to assimilate social cues about how to control what's on—as well as what's in—his nose.* In real life, I've heard students say of a professor, "He's such a genius that I can't understand a thing he says." But I'm thinking, *A professor who's a true genius makes extremely difficult ideas accessible to his students.* What, then, do we mean when we describe someone as a genius?

Before the sixteenth century, the word *genius,* which the English appropriated from Latin antiquity, referred to a guiding spirit that governed a person's life—like a genie in a bottle. However, along with the development of the word *modern* in the sixteenth century came the increasing use of *genius* to characterize an individual's disposition or temper of mind: genius was internalized. By the end of the eighteenth-century Age of Reason, genius had developed honorific connotations important to modernism: "native intellectual power of an exalted type, such as is attributed to those who are esteemed greatest in any department of art, speculation, or practice; instinctive and extraordinary capacity for imaginative creation, original thought, invention, or discovery" *(OED).* Modernists celebrated persons of genius who advanced the evolution of society by rising above it in order to generate totally original perceptions. The modernist genius was therefore autonomous, independent of conventional influences and societal restraints. Those who exercised the purest form of genius were artists whose work, unlike that of scientists, was unsullied by practical considerations. For the Modernist, art was infinitely more sacred than science.

It should come as no surprise, then, that postmodernism bubbled up in the arts. In fact, the word *postmodern* was initially employed as a slur by devotees of artistic Modernism.[1] To understand the beginnings of postmodernism, then, we need to think about the Modern art it defied.

Posting Modern Art

You probably know someone who, in response to seemingly random swirls and swaths of color identified with "Modern art," has erupted with "A nine-year-old could have done that!" My father, who disdains abstract art, likes to tell how when he was a young bachelor in the 1940s, he and a friend exposed the fraudulence of abstract expressionism. After squirting mustard and ketchup on a canvas, they tacked a red rubber glove to the surface and then surreptitiously set up their contribution in a San Francisco art show. My father gleefully notes that the "painting" lasted a whole afternoon in the exhibition (although someone else might say, "See! It lasted only one afternoon!").

Of course, my father's parody did not expose abstract expressionism as fake, just as a film parody of hypocritical Christians does not expose Christianity as fraudulent. So also extremist parodies of postmodern rhetoric do not destroy the insights of postmodernism. Instead, these parodies illustrate the power of what they are mocking; after all, one does not make fun of something innocuous or insignificant. (This, at least, is what my mother always told me. When I would run home in tears after boys at school chanted, "Crystal, Crystal, such a pistol, kills you with her breath," she would purr, "Your breath is fine, sweetheart; they say those things because they are intimidated.")

What intimidated many people about Modern art was its obscurity and

---

[1]Though the word *postmodern* was used as early as the 1870s, it wasn't until a century later that the word was applied to the visual arts. Like the word *Christian,* its early uses were dismissive. For example, in 1971, Brian O'Doherty referred to the "angry dumbness" of "postmodern" art in "What Is Post-modernism?" (*Art in America* 59 [1971]: 19). For early uses of the word *postmodern,* see Richard Appignanesi and Chris Garratt, *Introducing Postmodernism* (Cambridge: Icon, 1999), p. 3.

exclusivity: they felt like outsiders rejected by those "in the know." Looking at what appeared to be mere blobs of paint on canvas or else geometrical forms that any ruler-wielding nerd might paint, they couldn't understand what made it "art." For people like my father, true art presents something identifiable, like a landscape with a big tree or a table with small fruit. For them, art is a window on reality, displaying the craft of an artist who beautifully captures the "realism" of a person, place, event or thing.

While Early Modern, or Renaissance, art can be defined as the movement toward increasing "realism" in representation, Modernist art can be defined as increasing contempt for the illusion of "realism." The difference might be explained in part by the invention of photography in the early nineteenth century, for a daguerreotype captured "reality" better than any painter could. In fact, our phrase "take a picture," which we associate with cameras, came from the field of painting: a portrait artist was said to "take a picture" of the person sitting for him. Thus, just as the phrase "take a picture" was eliminated from the rhetoric of painting, which couldn't "take a picture" as well as a camera could, so representational realism was eliminated from the idea of "true" art.

Modernists wanted to draw attention to the artistry on the canvas rather than the subject a painting illustrated—to focus on the window's glass rather than merely looking through it to its subject matter. For them, "realism" distracted from *real* art, which resides in the adept handling of form, line and color. In fact, art history courses taught by Modernists often did not explain the represented subject matter even of traditional paintings. Discussion of a crucifixion scene might focus on expertise in foreshortening, harmony of form, clash of color and tension of line, but never once discuss why someone in the fifteenth century would choose to depict a man nailed to a cross. For the Modernist, all museums, as Arthur Danto notes, "are museums of modern art, to the extent that the judgment of what is art is based on an aesthetic of formalism."[2] In other words, the Modernist emphasis on autonomy became identified with the art object itself. Not being enslaved to representation, "true art" was independent of the reality that surrounded it, just as the artistic genius, not being enslaved to tradition, was independent from surrounding cultural values.

The "first real Modernist," according to Clement Greenberg, the famous

---

[2]Arthur C. Danto, *After the End of Art: Contemporary Art and the Pale of History* (Princeton, N.J.: Princeton University Press, 1997), p. 111.

definer and defender of abstract expressionism, was Kant.[3] Think of the coin-sorting machine analogy from the previous chapter. Kant believed that every mind has similar categories of perception enabling universal judgments—like coin channels that generate rolls of identical value. Modernists like Greenberg assumed this was true even in matters of beauty, and thus regarded haters of abstract art as having deficient sensibilities—like malfunctioning coin machines. People like my father, then, couldn't make sense of what they saw. This, of course, perpetuated Modernist elitism, which assumed that just as a physically disabled person needs a crutch to walk, an aesthetically disabled person needs the crutch of representational "realism." Cultural critic Wendy Steiner parodies the Modernist attitude as follows:

> The public is meant to receive art as manna from the demigod artist and to accept the insult that goes along with it: that they are, by virtue of their status as nonartists and capitalists, incapable of truly understanding high culture. They should consume art, because that is all they know how to do with anything, but leave the judgment of art to its priests.[4]

Many Modernists believed that the common person's dislike of abstract expressionism merely reinforced her or his commonness. Thus, just as Modern art excluded the "realistic" representation of common objects from its canvases, these Modernists excluded the representative common person from the understanding of art.

Posting Modern Literature

The same could be said about Modernist literary art, which boasted styles that baffled the general reader. The French Symbolists, writing in the last decades of the nineteenth century, were abstract expressionists of language, employing obscure metaphors to suggest mysterious emotional states. Their poetry celebrated the autonomy of their personal visions.

The obscurantism of Symbolist poetry influenced English literature in the early twentieth century, explaining not only the difficulty of "The Waste Land" by T. S. Eliot (1888-1965) but also the "stream of consciousness" style employed in novels by James Joyce and Virginia Woolf (both 1882-1941). Symbolist poetry and the stream-of-consciousness novel feature an autono-

---

[3]Quoted in ibid., p. 67.
[4]Wendy Steiner, *Venus in Exile: The Rejection of Beauty in Twentieth-Century Art* (New York: Free Press, 2001), p. 20.

mous narrator who filters everything through an individualized conscious-ness, using unique stylistic components that are daunting to the common person.

Also celebrating autonomy, the phrase "free verse" developed in the first decade of the twentieth century to describe poetry that refused to follow tra-ditional metrical patterns. Modernist poets regarded meter and rhyme the same way Modernist painters perceived pictorial realism and modernist theologians considered Christian doctrine: as intellectual baby food for the immature masses. Things of the past, traditional modes, were impediments to authentic genius. "Make It New," a phrase made famous by the poet Ezra Pound (1885-1972), became the Modernist rallying cry.

For the Modernist, a truly artistic poem, like a painting, is not to "mean" but to "be." It is an intriguing artifact that draws attention not to the outside world but to its own form. Modernist novelist E. M. Forster (1879-1970) dis-tinguished the workaday language of the common person—used for mere "information"—from the lasting language of poetry: "Information points to something else. A poem points to nothing but itself. Information is relative. A poem is absolute; it is eternal and indestructible."[5]

Such emphasis on the nearly sacred autonomy of literary art affected Modernist literary criticism as well. In the 1940s influential critics taught that it was an error to either talk about the intention of the poet or consider the feelings a poem elicited in its audience; they called these errors the "inten-tional fallacy" and the "affective fallacy."[6] Literary art was to be celebrated not for its "message" but for its "autonomous structure," as the famous critic Northrop Frye declared in 1957. He asserted, "In literature, questions of fact or truth are subordinated to the primary literary aim of producing a structure of words for its own sake."[7]

Nonautonomous Autonomy

Ironically, this reiterated emphasis on autonomy in painting and literature shows that Modernists were not autonomous! All the people who used such language were performing a script of their day. What postmodernists call "discourse"—the assumptions and values that are embedded in language

---

[5]E. M. Forster, *Two Cheers for Democracy* (New York: Harcourt, 1951), p. 82.

[6]See W. K. Wimsatt Jr., *The Verbal Icon: Studies in the Meaning of Poetry* (Lexington: University of Kentucky Press, 1954), pp. 3-40.

[7]Northrop Frye, *Anatomy of Criticism: Four Essays* (Princeton, N.J.: Princeton University Press, 1957), p. 74.

and perpetuated by culture—molded their perception and behavior.

What I have just done is an example of "deconstruction," a popular component of postmodernism that will be explained more thoroughly below. For now, all you need to know is that deconstruction is about identifying hidden contradictions in someone's philosophy—not due to logical errors but due to the vagaries of language. When Modernists celebrate the idea of autonomy, for example, they use a word that is encoded with centuries of assumptions about human progress. Hence, their word *autonomy* is not autonomous: it is the reflection of cultural values.

The postmodern deconstruction of Modernist autonomy sends *genius* back to its premodern definition: an external spirit that guides human thought. Only, for the postmodernist, the spirit is "the spirit of the age" rather than a spirit in a bottle. The spirit of a new age began haunting the arts during the "Radical Sixties."

The Brillo-iant 1960s

When most people hear the term "the sixties" they think of long-haired, flower-adorned hippies protesting the war in Vietnam. As a child growing up near San Francisco, I went from worry about communist attacks to fear over what might explode in Haight-Ashbury (which, ironically, is where my father lived when he and his friend made their rubber-glove "painting" over a decade earlier). Not until the late 1980s did I realize that the most significant revolution of the 1960s had little to do with tie-dye or sit-ins. The "establishment" being protested was much more fundamental than America's military-industrial complex. The protest was over a long-established model of intellectual autonomy that had shoved Christianity out the door.

The revolution was most easily apparent in the visual arts. In 1962 Andy Warhol displayed an oil painting that precisely reproduced multiple Campbell's Soup labels. Two years later he exhibited *Brillo Boxes* at the Stable Gallery in Manhattan (see figure 3.1).

Not only were the images representational, looking exactly like soup-can labels and packing boxes for Brillo soap pads, they signified things commonly used by the common man—or at least the common woman (it was the early 1960s, remember). Warhol's *200 Campbell's Soup Cans* and his *Brillo Boxes* thus represented more than soup and the cleaner of pans that cooked it; they represented a kind of art that defied Modernism's exclusivity. In fact, it was called "Pop art," in reference to its subject matter, which was

Figure 3.1. Andy Warhol's *Brillo Boxes* (Digital image © The Museum of Modern Art/Licensed by SCALA/Art Resource, NY)

taken from the popular culture of the common person: images of advertise-
ments, movie stars, comic strips. Warhol defended Pop art in 1963: "How
can you say any style is better than another? You ought to be able to be an
Abstract Expressionist next week, or a Pop artist, or a realist, without feeling
that you have given up something."[8] With this emphasis on pluralistic possibilities for true art, we see the stirrings of postmodern thought. Greenberg,
the high priest of abstract expressionism, was appalled. Borrowing Arnold's
word for the uncultured—*philistines*—he attributed the demise of artistic
standards to "philistine taste," "middlebrow demands" and "the democrati-
zation of culture under industrialism."[9]

Of course, my middlebrow father did not think Warhol's soup cans and
Brillo boxes qualified as art either. However, when I told him that Warhol,
like other Pop artists, was challenging the elitism of abstract art, making fun
of the limited definition of artistic legitimacy that "modern art" allowed, he
was delighted. After all, he and a friend had tried to do the same with ham-
burger condiments and a rubber glove. In fact, without knowing it, they had
made a postmodern gesture when they named the piece *Golden Foot*, drawing attention to the artifice of language as well as of visual form.

The difference is that Pop artists, trained in the tenets of Modernism, understood what it was they were challenging. They helped initiate what has
been called "the end of art," which really means the end of a certain story
about art. It is the end of the Modernist myth that art, like science,
progresses toward greater levels of sophistication as innovative, autonomous individuals (people of genius) learn from and advance beyond their
predecessors.[10]

Postmodernism in the Visual Arts

After Warhol and other Pop artists challenged the exclusivity of abstract expressionism, art allowed for the return of traditional forms. Portraiture and
still life paintings, which Modernists had reviled as inauthentic, slowly came
to be respected once again. Of course, throughout the Modernist period
there had been painters who produced portraits and other kinds of "realism": dolphins leaping out of shiny seas, deep-hued sunsets behind palm

---

[8]Quoted in Danto, *After the End of Art*, p. 37.
[9]Quoted in Eleanor Heartney, *Postmodernism* (Cambridge: Cambridge University Press, 2001),
    p. 12.
[10]See Danto, *After the End of Art*.

trees. But "true" artists—that is, High Modernists—disdained such "realist" art as crass commercialism, pictures to satisfy the lowbrow tastes of the uncultured philistine masses. In reaction, some postmodern artists produced "Super Realism": paintings that look like and even directly imitate photographs.

Because photography strongly influenced the development of Modernism, a return to photographic realism was a kick of sand in the face of the Modernist bully. As early as 1966, for example, Malcolm Morley painted on a large canvas an exact replica of the *SS Amsterdam in Front of Rotterdam* as it appears on a picture postcard. Rather than create something new in fulfillment of Pound's dictum "Make It New!" Morley copied something old, something that was itself a copy: a photograph of a real boat that the common person could own by purchasing a picture postcard. He thus subverted not only the Modernist sanctification of originality but also its elitist elevation of art above the "masses."

Many postmodern paintings, while engaging traditional styles of realism, simultaneously draw attention to their own artifice, to the fact that "realism" is not real. For a good example, look at the painting on the cover of this book: a 1983 oil on canvas by Carlo Maria Mariani called *La Mano Ubbidisce all'Inteletto (The Hand Obeys the Understanding)*. The figures look quite "realistic," reminding us of classical Romans with their togalike drapings and laurel-leaf crowns. But the high seriousness of the subject matter is broken when we notice that the figures are painting each other. This type of humorous playfulness disgusted Modernists, who took very seriously the responsibility of art and genius to elevate culture.

Making fun of the Modernist mystification of art's autonomy, Mariani's painting directs attention to what is outside its form: the painter painting it. However, by having the traditional figures paint each other, Mariani implies that tradition itself paints the picture. In other words, because cultural values mold human perception of life and art, no art is autonomous; tradition—even when one rebels against it—guides the artist's hand because it shapes his understanding of reality. Vision, then, even for the artist, is situated—something Mariani implies by placing each figure on a different geometrical form: they see each other according to the foundational shapes on which they are situated.

Though Pop artists in the 1960s did not think of themselves as "postmodernists," what they set into motion had become so identifiably "postmodern" by the 1980s that in 1987 Boston's Institute of Arts initiated a "critical over-view of postmodernist practices." One of the artists featured in the show, Jeff Koons, didn't just paint or construct images of everyday objects; he put the actual objects on display. His *New Shelton Wet/Dry Double Decker* (1981) was an installation made up of two vacuum cleaners placed in clear Plexi-glas boxes.[11]

Advocates of postmodernism therefore argue that postmodern art, unlike abstract expressionism, is egalitarian, destroying the barrier between high and low culture, between Cul-cha and everyday culture. They would note that an Ivy League graduate student could have a meeting of the minds with an inner-city gang member about the merits of Nike running shoes, but probably not about the Nike of Samothrace (the statue commonly called "the Winged Victory"), and that both the privileged and the impoverished could probably discuss MTV images of Madonna but not Renaissance paint-ings of the Madonna. By focusing on images from common culture—from teenybopper commodities to television commercials—postmodern art im-plies that the creativity in a bicycle momma is as interesting as that in New York's MOMA (Museum of Modern Art).

Postmodern Poetry: Falling Fallacies

Just as postmodern painters resurrected traditional styles, postmodern poets resurrected traditional forms of poetry. Writing rhymed verse in defiance of "free verse," these artists, called "the New Formalists," returned to poetic forms like the sonnet, villanelle and sestina.

The Modernists' "intentional fallacy" was challenged by "confessional po-etry" in which writers talked explicitly about traumas in their lives. In fact, in defiance of Modernist elitism, postmodern poets worked to return poetry "to the people," seen most dramatically when Robert Pinsky, U.S. poet lau-reate in 2000, asked everyday Americans of all ages to mail him their "favor-ite poem," even if they knew it had no pretensions to be "great art." Pinsky placed these poems into the permanent holdings of the Library of Congress as a record of what all Americans, not just "artists," valued.

---

[11]Stuart Sim, ed., *The Routledge Companion to Postmodernism* (New York: Routledge, 2001), p. 295. In 1917 Marcel Duchamp did something that anticipated Koons's vacuum cleaners; under a pseudonym he submitted a urinal, which he called *Fountain,* to an art exhibition. The American Society of Independent Artists, true to its Modernist sensibilities, rejected the piece, but when it was discovered that a Modernist "genius" had created it, *Fountain*—although only in photographic form—became famous.

The distinctive mark of postmodern poetry, however, is that it has no distinctive mark. Similar to Warhol in his encouragement of pluralistic art forms, postmodern poetry encourages a multiplicity of approaches. One approach, which some people regard as most fully "postmodern," is called L=A=N=G=U=A=G=E poetry. Just as its oddly typed descriptor draws attention to the individual components that make up the word *language*, its poetic form draws attention to the individual components of language: words. By arranging words in odd sequences, breaking them away from any sense of recognizable grammar, L=A=N=G=U=A=G=E poets, like postmodern theorists, call attention to the idea that language is arbitrary: it is an artificial product of human beings.

Novel Postings

Challenges to Modernism were also apparent in the novel—so much so that by 1965 Leslie Fiedler, a famous literary critic, was singing the praises of "post-Modernist literature," and in 1969 he published the statement "We are living, have been living for two decades, through the death throes of Modernism and the birth pangs of Post-Modernism."[12]

Anti-Modernist elements in the novel have taken several forms. Often postmodern novels subvert the linearity of progress that Enlightenment thinkers value(d) so highly. Sometimes the protagonist will not make any progress, and it may even be hard to figure out who the protagonist is supposed to be. Many times the novel's story line itself, containing unexplained jumps in time, location or perspective, does not progress in a linear fashion: the narrative does not "evolve" toward a clear-cut resolution.

Challenging the modernist trust in autonomous objectivity, the postmodern novel sometimes has the narrator misinterpret the things she describes. Or, to achieve the same effect, a novel might have multiple narrators who report the same events in radically different ways. Of course, earlier literary artists had used similar effects, but the postmodern author leaves it ambiguous as to which is the "correct" view.

Another genre, "magical realism," defies logical positivism, wherein only empirically verifiable events can be considered "true," by including supernatural elements in a "realistic" setting. Influenced by the 1960s novels of Latin American writers Gabriel García Marquez, Carlos Fuentes and Octavio

---

[12]Quoted in Hans Bertens, *The Idea of the Postmodern: A History* (New York: Routledge, 1995), p. 30.

Paz, magical realism was given a postmodern spin by English writers Salman Rushdie and Angela Carter, who use unexplainable events to challenge the way cultures conceptualize "the normal." This postmodern openness to the invasion of everyday reality by supernatural forces explains the popularity of television shows like *Touched by an Angel* and *Buffy the Vampire Slayer.*

Several characteristics of postmodern fiction are manifest in the novels of Kurt Vonnegut. As early as 1961, with the publication of *Mother Night,* Vonnegut defied the linear storytelling of the traditional novel. His most famous novel, *Slaughterhouse-Five* (1969), combined quotations from historical texts about the bombing of Dresden during World War II with a fictional tale that included space creatures establishing contact with a U.S. soldier at Dresden. Vonnegut even inserts himself into the novel's depiction of Dresden, saying, "I know. I was there"—which is true. Vonnegut did, indeed, witness the aftermath of the U.S. attack on Dresden. The novel thus challenges our sense of the distinction between fiction and history as it forces the reader to question which parts to believe. The "Tralfamadorian" space creatures claim the ability to see all moments at once, which seems outrageous until we realize that historians make a similar claim as they write "true" accounts of things that occurred before they were born. In the 1960s, Vonnegut thus anticipated the postmodern challenge to modernist objectivity.

Another 1969 novel that foreshadowed postmodern strategies is John Fowles's *The French Lieutenant's Woman.* Reminding us of the traditional novel, Fowles's story is set in 1867, a time when the novel genre was at its height. But then he inserts himself—writing a century later—as a character in the novel, along with digressions and footnotes that read more like a history text than a fictional story. Furthermore, just as he disrupts easy distinctions between fiction and history, he disrupts his own narrative closure by providing several possible endings. In defiance of the "autonomous structure" of art so valued by Modernists, Fowles thus enables readers to become part of the creative process as they choose which ending they prefer. Repudiating "the affective fallacy," Fowles—like many postmodern writers to follow—considers the emotional effects on the reader to be integral to a novel's meaning.

Responding Readers

An emphasis on the reader, in fact, is key to postmodern views of literature.

While Modernist critics wanted to keep the work of art as autonomous as the "genius" who created it, most postmodern critics focused attention on what surrounded the artwork. In fact, they replaced the word *art* with the term *text,* in recognition that literary forms are not the works of autonomous genius; they are instead the compositions of many cultural voices, woven together as in a textile: the text is textured.

In 1972, Wolfgang Iser published *The Implied Reader,* establishing that readers are necessary to complete a text. His emphasis on "Indeterminacy and the Reader's Response" (the title of one of his essays) influenced one of the most vocal postmodernists of our time, Stanley Fish. In a famous book titled *Is There a Text in This Class?* (1980), Fish asserts that authors do not create literary art, readers do. By this he does not imply that someone can read into a poem whatever she wants; such an assumption reeks too much of modernist individualism. Instead, "interpretive communities" establish the meaning of a text, reading it according to the assumptions, values and goals of their particular subculture.

For example, take the text of the hit song "Bridge over Troubled Water," released by Simon and Garfunkel in 1970. Its refrain went, "Like a bridge over troubled water, I will lay me down." Starry-eyed adolescent girls considered the song to be "soooo romantic." But in my Sunday school class (I had graduated to the Purple Room) we came up with another interpretation; we heard in the lyrics an expression of Christ's sacrifice for us as he laid down his life on the cross. The song really did mean this to us, whether Simon and Garfunkel intended it or not; our "interpretive community" had created a profoundly spiritual song.

The idea of "interpretive communities" explains the multiplicity of Christian denominations. Throughout history, different Christian groups have read different meanings in Scriptures such as Paul's account of the Last Supper:

> The Lord Jesus on the night when he was betrayed took a loaf of bread, and when he had given thanks, he broke it and said, "This is my body that is for you. Do this in remembrance of me." In the same way he took the cup also, after supper, saying, "This cup is the new covenant in my blood. Do this, as often as you drink it, in remembrance of me." (1 Corinthians 11:23-25)

Though ancient doctrine about transubstantiation is far more subtle than most Protestants realize, over time medieval interpretive communities came to read Jesus' statement "This is my body" as literal: the bread actually transforms into Christ's flesh as it is consumed during the Eucharist. Most Protestant communities, however, read Christ's statement as metaphoric: Communion is merely a symbolic "remembrance" of his sacrifice. Some Lutheran communities split the difference, replacing transubstantiation with "consubstantiation": the idea that Communion bread and wine maintain their substance as wheat and grape products, but they also mystically invoke the essence of Christ's flesh and blood once consumed.

The same biblical text has plural meanings, and all of them are "true" to the interpretive communities that assert them. While modernists pointed to diverse interpretations such as these as evidence that Christianity was not "objectively" true, the postmodern Fish asserts that we must honor the truth claims of each community and, furthermore, encourage each community to stay committed to its version of the truth.

The Death of the Author

While Fish, the famous promoter of "Reader Response Criticism," emphasizes the conditions under which a text is read, other postmodernists emphasize the conditions under which a text is written. For them, a text is always textured with threads of other texts: ideas, images, values, metaphors that surround the author. Writers therefore do not have complete control over their ideas or the way they say things.

In *Huckleberry Finn*, for example, Mark Twain establishes the dignity, integrity and compassion of the runaway slave, Jim. However, writing the novel in the 1880s, Twain also reflects attitudes of his time toward blacks, seen when Jim acts less savvy than his adolescent companion, Huckleberry Finn. Some people therefore call the novel "racist," while others consider it an indictment of racism. Rather than asking "Why can't Twain make up his mind?" postmodern critics note that, despite his awareness of the horrors of slavery, Twain is inevitably shaped by the white discourse of his day. This is demonstrated most fully in the name "Nigger Jim," which makes readers today wince, for we have been molded by a different kind of language. So it's not a question of either-or—either Twain *is* or he is *not* a racist—but of both/and: sometimes the novel is racist, other times it challenges racism. Both attitudes, of course, were part of the culture in which Twain was situated, and both affected the way he thought.

Aware of how culture affects both the expression and the reception of art, the postmodern critic thus calls into question the modernist sanctification of autonomous "genius." Postmodern critic Roland Barthes, in fact, generated lots of hoopla in the 1960s when he referred to "the death of the author." Barthes, of course, did not think that authors were clever cadavers writing from their coffins—Madeline Usher not withstanding. He was using hyperbole, the way Warhol used Brillo boxes, to combat the modernist sanctification of originality. For Barthes, the Modernist author— the one who could transcend culture and "Make It New!"—was dead. In contrast to the autonomous author of Modernism, Barthes asserted that various strands of language—culturally embedded ideas, constructs, images, phrases—speak through the author, who weaves them together into a linguistic tapestry. As he puts it in his essay "The Death of the Author," it is "language which speaks, not the author." The author, then, simply becomes another kind of reader: a reader of multiple linguistic codes embedded in language. Barthes closes his essay characterizing this writing reader as "someone who holds together in a single field all the traces by which the written text is constituted. . . . The birth of the reader must be at the cost of the death of the Author."[13]

Significantly, the very same year Barthes rerouted the Modernist "author" to the postmodern mortuary—1968—Michel Foucault drove up in a hearse, pronouncing the death of the author in an essay entitled "What Is an Author?" This "coincidence" goes to show that even the ideas of postmodern thinkers are not "original." The fact that two men come up with the same construct at the same time—as when Charles Darwin and Alfred Wallace formulated the theory of natural selection separately but simultaneously— proves to the postmodernist that texts are what they call "intertextual": they echo each other because they have been molded by concepts embedded in the language of their culture.

Julia Kristeva coined the word *intertextuality* in 1969, saying that "any text is constructed as a mosaic of quotations; any text is the absorption and transformation of another."[14] In other words, a work of art is not an "autonomous structure"; it contains concepts, constructs, paradigms, ideas, phrasing that are manifest in other texts—whether the writer intended them to be there or not. The author does not "originate" ideas; the discourse of her culture does.

One way to illustrate intertextuality is through a phenomenon you have

---

[13]Roland Barthes, *Image—Music—Text*, trans. Stephen Heath (London: Fontana, 1977), pp. 143, 148.

[14]Julia Kristeva, *Desire in Language: A Semiotic Approach to Literature and Art*, ed. Leon S. Roudiez, trans. Thomas Gora, Alice Jardine and Leon S. Roudiez (New York: Columbia University Press, 1980), p. 66.

probably noticed: no matter how hard parents try to come up with "original" names for their children, they often end up following cultural trends. I notice this as a teacher. One year I'll have so many Ashleys that I can't keep them straight; a couple of years later the favored name is Amanda. And time and time again, these students with duplicate names tell me that their parents thought they were coming up with something unique. My parents, as well, worked hard to come up with unusual names for their children, including that of my sister, Karen (the one with me under the dining-room table). However, my sister usually had at least three or four other Karens in her classes; one time another Karen even shared my sister's last name. This is a good example of how Foucault believes "discourse" works: people end up being influenced by culture even when they try to resist it.

For a more artsy example, think once again of the Simon and Garfunkel line "Like a bridge over troubled water, I will lay me down." It is highly unlikely that the non-Christian duo intended their audiences to hear references to Christ in their song. However, as they developed their lyrics, "lay me down" obviously struck them as the perfect way to communicate sacrificial love. Clearly, this phrase in their "original" song is not original. "Lay me down" has power because of cultural associations that the singers probably didn't consciously think about.

First, there is the tender resonance of the trustful child's prayer: "Now I lay me down to sleep; I pray the Lord my soul to keep." Second, there is a two-thousand-year-old story so thoroughly embedded within Western discourse that people of all religions know about it: Christ laid down his life for human salvation. In fact, Jesus repeats the phrase "lay down my life" four times in only three verses of John's Gospel (10:15, 17-18). Finally, even among atheists, John 15:13 has achieved the status of a universal profundity: "No one has greater love than this, to lay down one's life for one's friends."

The postmodernist acknowledges that these texts, essential to the discourse of Western culture, inevitably influence the way artists think and write, totally apart from their intentions. "Bridge over Troubled Water" is thus intertextual. Furthermore, its status at the top of the charts for weeks on end was intertextual, as diverse audiences either subconsciously or consciously heard the echo of significant cultural texts in the song.

Literary Deconstruction

With the Modernist ideas of "originality" and "genius" called into question, works of literature became subject to deconstruction, a mode of philosophic analysis that Jacques Derrida introduced in the "Radical Sixties."[15] American literary critics were especially enamored, turning Derrida's idea into a reading technique that became as trendy on American campuses as disco dancing. Professors and students ("Stayin' Alive, Stayin' Alive") scoured famous literary works for inconsistencies, showing how an author makes assertions that are undermined either by something elsewhere in the narrative or by the connotations of the words the author employs to make her point.

Let me illustrate deconstruction with something from everyday life. Consider, for example, a "prolife" demonstrator who kills a doctor by blowing up an abortion clinic; the statement "I'm prolife" is undermined by his actions. The deconstruction occurs through an analysis of what "prolife" means in his context; for him, "prolife" really means "antiabortion." There is a discontinuity between the actual words and their signified referent.

On the other end of the political spectrum, take a "liberal" who says, "I'm a Democrat because I care for the poor and the environment," but who is so overextended on her credit cards, paying for her gas-guzzling SUV, that she never donates time or money to people in need. Her statement "I care for the poor and the environment" boils down to "I feel good about myself by voting with a party whose rhetoric foregrounds poverty and ecology."

How is this different from old-fashioned hypocrisy? you might ask. I would respond that hypocrisy usually implies that people realize their actions do not fit their words. In contrast, for both scenarios above, the speakers earnestly believe what they say—"I am prolife" or "I care for the environment"—not realizing that their statements don't fully correspond with reality. These people think they are using language, when really language is using them. In other words, they echo phrases that reflect cultural values with which they identify.

Deconstruction as a trendy literary technique has all but died out, largely because it was not particularly illuminating. Based primarily on fanatical searches for textual inconsistencies, this kind of deconstruction often echoed the Modernist emphasis on textual autonomy—the only difference being that the worshipful Modernist looked at the literary work as a "Verbal

---

[15]In one amazing year, 1967, Derrida published (in French) three works: *Of Grammatology, Writing and Difference* and *Speech and Phenomena,* all of which challenged the philosophic tradition of modernism. The phrase "to deconstruct," however, was used by French literary critics before Derrida. See Kevin Hart, *Postmodernism: A Beginner's Guide* (Oxford: Oneworld, 2004), p. 114.

Icon" (the name of a 1954 book of criticism) while the iconoclastic decon-
structionist surveyed a work only for its insufficiencies. Both perpetuated
the Modernist mystification of genius. In the first instance the creator of the
Verbal Icon was the genius, whereas in the second the wily deconstructor
was the genius.[16]

Significantly, Derrida did not intend deconstruction to be a "technique"
at all. For him texts deconstruct themselves *because they are not autonomous*. Instead, texts reflect inconsistencies embedded in the culturally generated language out of which they arise. Deconstruction is more a philosophical issue than a literary one for Derrida; this issue, still relevant today,
will be discussed more fully in chapter five.

Architecture: The Razing and Raising of Postmodernism

The movement from Modernism to postmodernism in the visual and verbal
arts is writ large in the field of architecture. In 1965, not long after Andy Warhol produced *Brillo Boxes,* architect Robert Venturi published "A Justification
for a Pop Architecture." His justification came after he designed "one of the
first buildings to make the bold move away from the cubes and right angles
of most Modernist architecture."[17] The anti-Modernist architecture he inspired was first called "postmodern" by "the acknowledged guru of Post-
Modernism," Charles Jencks, with whom I had a conversation in the late
1980s.[18] At the time, I was troubled by phenomena I inaccurately assumed
were nihilistic, and Jencks was the first theorist to inform me, in a gentle
buttoned-down way, of the benevolent possibilities of postmodernism—
largely due to its attitude toward Modernism.

In his famous 1977 book *The Language of Post-modern Architecture,*
Jencks correlates the undermining of Modernism with a literal undermining:
the 1972 destruction of worker housing in St. Louis, Missouri. Built in the
1950s according to the Modernist "International Style," the multistory Pruitt-
Igoe complex was so impersonal that tenants of the identical concrete slab
apartments did not care for them—in either sense of "care for." The build-

---

[16]Christopher Norris described this kind of reading technique as "deconstruction on the wild
side," discussing the work of Geoffrey Hartman and J. Hillis Miller. See *Deconstruction: Theory and Practice* (New York: Methuen, 1982), pp. 92-99.
[17]The design was for a house in Philadelphia. See Lucy Peel, Polly Powell and Alexander Garrett, *An Introduction to Twentieth-Century Architecture* (London: Quantum, 1996), p. 101.
[18]The statement about Jencks is by Ada Louise Huxtable and is quoted in Bertens, *Idea of the
Postmodern,* p. 57.

ings, having become a haven for derelict activities, became so derelict themselves that it was cheaper to blow them up than to repair them or rectify the activities within them.[19] (In a bit of gruesome irony, the razed buildings had been designed by the same architect responsible for the Twin Towers of the World Trade Center, blown up by terrorists on September 11, 2001.)

Modernists, of course, did not intend to build ugly, impersonal buildings. Quite the opposite, in fact: they desired to improve a world that no longer had any need for religion. For Modernist architects, technology, not God, would save humanity. So they designed edifices that looked technologically advanced: huge rectangles of steel and glass. It is no coincidence, I think, that the mysterious black obelisk in the film *2001: A Space Odyssey* (1968) looks like a paradigmatic Modernist edifice: Manhattan's Seagram Building, conceptualized by Mies van der Rohe in 1921 and built in the 1950s (see figures 3.2 and 3.3 on pp. 97 and 98).

In the opening scene of the film, when the monolithic black structure mysteriously appears among a group of apes, they begin to use tools, implying that the structure symbolizes evolutionary energy. Similarly, the sleek linear lines of Modernist architecture symbolized evolution: the progressivism of "original" individuals who surmounted outmoded ideas. Architectural decoration, in fact, was disdained; like religion, it was considered superfluous, something that weak-minded philistines relied on to brighten their shallow lives. Modernist architects believed that people, like buildings, needed to get rid of the fluff that impeded clear, objective perception.

In contrast, postmodern architecture alludes to the past, sometimes reviving old styles in what some call "Radical Traditionalism." Many times the allusions to tradition are quite playful. For example, Philip Johnson, who coined the term "International Style" to describe the work of architects like Mies van der Rohe, designed the AT&T Corporate Headquarters in New York (completed in 1979) to look like a huge chest of drawers in the eighteenth-century Chippendale style. Just as Pop artists created images accessible to the common person, Johnson's design put "a cosy domestic gloss on a form of architecture [the International Style] that had grown remote and authoritarian."[20]

Often, postmodern architects combine styles from various historical

---

[19]Charles Jencks, *The Language of Post-modern Architecture*, 4th ed. (London: Academy, 1984), p. 9.
[20]Heartney, *Postmodernism*, p. 11.

Figure 3.2. Mies van der Rohe's Seagram Building (Ezra Stoller/Esto Photographics)

Figure 3.3. Obelisk from *2001: A Space Odyssey* (Julia Tenney)

periods, usually with exaggerated decorative flourishes, to remind us that different eras build constructions differently and that no one era is "better" than another. Echoing the intertextuality of literature, postmodern buildings are, to coin a term, interarchitextual. Repudiating the Modernist celebration of original genius summarized by Pound's "Make It New," postmodernism, like Christianity, makes the past relevant to contemporary lived experience, as though to say that the Enlightenment did not get any closer to objective truth than did the Christian Middle Ages.

In sum, the postmodernist asserts that, like postmodern buildings constructed out of images from antecedent architectural styles, thought is constructed out of antecedent concepts, ideas, practices and knowledge. Of course, even this postmodernist idea is not "original." As one genius put it several millennia ago, "What has been is what will be, / and what has been done is what will be done; / there is nothing new under the sun. / Is there a thing of which it is said, / 'See, this is new'? / It has already been, / in the ages before us" (Ecclesiastes 1:9-10).

4   The Antifoundational Foundations of Postmodernism

W hen Charles Jencks suggested that "Modern Architecture died" in 1972 with the razing of foundations in St. Louis, he provided an apt analogy for postmodernism in general. For despite the fact that there are as many kinds of postmodernism as there are of Christianity, one attitude unifies most postmodernists: the desire to raze foundations. This, in fact, is what disturbs Christians about postmodernism. How can we welcome postmodern "antifoundationalism" while also singing with certitude "The Church's one foundation / Is Jesus Christ her Lord"? Isn't antifoundationalism antithetical to the truth of Christianity? Before I discuss specific postmodern theorists, I need to grapple with this very significant issue.

Fighting Foundationalism

More than "The Church's One Foundation," I grew up singing "Onward Christian Soldiers," relishing the drumlike beat of "marching as to-oo war." Even better was a song that allowed our entire Junior Church congregation to slide off our cold folding chairs in the Blue Room, the girls with accompanying squeaks of petticoated flesh on metal, in order to throw ourselves into full-body movements. We would swing our arms and rowdily stomp our feet while singing, "I may never march in the infantry," and then "ride in the cavalry" while bobbing up and down with arms extended before us holding pretend reins. The bobbing stopped when we took aim with the next phrase, "shoot the artillery," one eye closed as we held left arms in air like rifles, right fingers pulling fantasy triggers next to our (incipient) biceps. After several more gestured phrases, we gleefully shouted the closing line of the refrain: "But I'm in the Lord's army!"

We honed our battle techniques through Sunday school "sword drills" inspired by Ephesians 6:17: "Take the helmet of salvation, and the sword of the Spirit, which is the word of God." No one pointed out that the "sword" could not possibly be the Bible as we knew it; after all, when Paul wrote to the Ephesians, there was no New Testament, which for us was the part that contained the truth of salvation. Instead, seated on the edge of our chairs with trusty "swords" perched in our laps, we held our breaths until the teacher yelled out a Bible reference: "Revelation 21:11." Gulping air, we'd madly surf through the thin pages of our Bibles, and the first person to find the verse leaped (or squeaked) off the chair in order to exultantly read the passage aloud to the remaining lackluster soldiers.

Early in my walk with Jesus, then, I developed a distinct sense that the Christian life was a combat zone and that I needed to be vigilant; Christians were surrounded by enemies far more subtle than those wanting to bomb me out from under my dining-room table. Today many Christians still feel as if they are in a combat zone, the enemy of their adult faith being postmodern attackers of foundations. What I have discovered since my sword drill days, however, is that foundationalists who wear philosophic boxing gloves to battle antifoundationalists are often shadow boxing: what they think they are fighting is in actuality foundationalism, only under a different guise.

Defining Foundationalism

Some people define foundationalism as the existence of indubitable, universal axioms that all intellectually honest individuals—no matter when and where they live—can perceive apart from empirical proof. Derrida called this kind of foundationalism "a metaphysics of presence": certain foundational truths are so fully apparent, so "present" to the consciousness of any perceiver, that they provide knowledge no thinking person would question.[1] This kind of truth does not need to be transmitted through scientific discovery, philosophic formulation or divine revelation. It is self-evident.

In contrast, others define foundationalism as the commitment to founda-

---

[1]Jacques Derrida, *Of Grammatology*, trans. Gayatri Chakravorty Spivak (Baltimore: Johns Hopkins University Press, 1976), p. 49.

tional *beliefs* on which people build a worldview that explains reality. They *believe* their perceptions about the world to be universally true. Unlike the first group, these foundationalists make no claims about "invincible certainty."[2]

Modernists appropriated the first definition, which can be traced back to pre-Christian philosophers such as Plato (427-347 B.C.) and his student Aristotle (384-322 B.C.). In fact, during the early years of Christianity, Platonists criticized the new religion because it emphasized belief in Christ rather than certitude in Ideal Forms that provide the foundation for all perception. In other words, Platonists considered Christians to be nonfoundationalists!

Traditional Christianity, then, at least during its first thirteen hundred years, operated by the second definition of foundationalism, articulated most famously by Augustine: "Understanding is the reward of faith. Seek therefore not to understand in order that you may believe, but to believe in order that you may understand."[3] Augustine, quite appropriately, seems to reflect a New Testament view of foundations, which repeatedly identifies Truth with Jesus Christ, a person to believe rather than an Idea obvious to all rational people.

With the demise of medieval assumptions about the centrality of belief, however, early modern philosophers reasserted ancient pagan certainty about autonomous reason. Aristotle's assumption that "mental experiences . . . are the same for all"[4] was echoed not only in Descartes's *cogito,* which eliminated possibilities of doubt, but also in Kant's coin-machine mind, which posited uniform categories of perception for all.

The edifice of Enlightenment truth was thus constructed on a foundation of empirical stones mortared together with reason. Though its seventeenth-century architects kept Christ as a cornerstone, builders in the eighteenth century spread the mortar of reason over the cornerstone, covering Jesus up. Remodelers in the nineteenth and twentieth centuries chipped away at the cornerstone, eventually prying Christ out of the foundation altogether. For

---

[2]Robert C. Greer, *Mapping Postmodernism: A Survey of Christian Options* (Downers Grove, Ill.: 2003), p. 237. Greer aligns Derrida's "metaphysics of presence" with foundationalism as I do. Philosophers tend to call the first kind of foundationalism "strong" or "classical" and the second "soft" or "modest." See John R. Franke, "The Nature of Theology: Culture, Language and Truth," in *Christianity and the Postmodern Turn: Six Views,* ed. Myron B. Penner (Grand Rapids: Brazos, 2005), p. 210.

[3]Quoted in Diané Collinson, *Fifty Major Philosophers: A Reference Guide* (New York: Routledge, 1987), p. 28.

[4]From *De interpretatione,* quoted in Greer, *Mapping Postmodernism,* p. 237.

them, Jesus was not a solid stone because his miracles defy reason and his claims cannot be empirically proved. By the end of the twentieth century, however, postmodern building inspectors starting digging away at the mortar of reason, creating a space to replace the stone which the builders had rejected (Mark 12:10).

Defining Antifoundationalism

Postmodern antifoundationalists are really anti, or against, *modernist* foundationalism; they are against the idea that indubitable truth can be objectively perceived by reason alone. For them, as for Augustine, truth is built on foundational beliefs—beliefs that precede any kind of thought. Foundations, they readily admit, are necessary to build any kind of knowledge. But this is different from modernist foundationalism. Indeed, Stanley Fish, one of the most famous antifoundationalists of our time, acknowledges that if foundationalism is defined as "holding some foundational beliefs," then all humans are foundationalists.[5]

The postmodern Fish becomes even more like the premodern Augustine when he attests that the only means to "absolute certainty" is through "revelation (something I [Fish] do not rule out but have not yet experienced)."[6] Enlightenment foundationalists, of course, disdain the idea of revelation, deeming it superfluous (not to mention superstitious), since for them unaided reason can access truth on its own. Postmodern antifoundationalism, in contrast, allows for revelation as a "foundational belief" for people of faith.

It is therefore ironic that during the reign of modernism, many Christians moved into the Enlightenment house, aligning foundational truth not with a personal God, manifest in Christ and revealed through the Scriptures, but with impersonal self-evident universals. A good number of Christians still reside there, proudly mounting their cornerstone on a wall, hiding under the dining-room table when postmodernists arrive with eviction notices. Such Christians seem to be modernists as much as Christians, sometimes throwing as much energy into defending the modernist foundation as they spend proclaiming the love of Christ.

---

[5]J. Judd Owen, *Religion and the Demise of Liberal Rationalism* (Chicago: University of Chicago Press, 2001), p. 146.
[6]Stanley Fish, *There's No Such Thing as Free Speech* (New York: Oxford University Press, 1994), p. 113.

In my experience, this Enlightenment house has many mansions, or apartments,[7] occupied by at least five different kinds of modernist Christians who sometimes pound on the walls when they become incensed by the noise coming from their Christian neighbors.

In Modernist Mansion #1: Demythologizers

In one apartment are members of many mainline churches that in the early to mid twentieth century chose to decorate their residences with the anti-supernatural assumptions developed during the Enlightenment. Influenced by the higher criticism of the nineteenth century, these modernist Christians "demythologize" their Scriptures, as when theologian Rudolf Bultmann pro-claimed in 1941, "We cannot use electric lights and radios and, in the event of illness, avail ourselves of modern medical and clinical means and at the same time believe in the spirit and wonder world of the New Testament."[8] Because it is not "modern" to believe in a literal resurrection, which defies both reason and scientific verifiability, these modernist Christians assert a figurative resurrection: Christ is resurrected in those followers who practice his teachings. When they say that Christ was God incarnate, they mean that the man Jesus incarnated the unfallen characteristics that God intended for all human beings: characteristics endorsed by Enlightenment thinkers, such as liberty, equality and fraternity.

These modernist Christians helped motivate my interest in postmodern-ism, for though I admired their ethical commitment to resurrect Jesus in their actions, often recognizing my own inadequacy in comparison, I still wanted to believe in a literal, historical resurrection—for two reasons. First, if Jesus didn't miraculously arise from his tomb, Christianity became, for me, simply one attractive ethical system among many competitors. Second, since there is no way anyone can *prove* that the resurrection did or *did not* occur (the desire for proof itself reflecting a modernist mindset), all I can do is take on faith the Gospels, trusting that the Holy Spirit guided the church fathers who canonized them and interpreted them through their creeds. Belief in a literal resurrection—as opposed to the metaphoric or "poetic" rendition of demy-thologizers—was foundational to Christianity very early on. To identify my-

---

[7]See John 14:2 KJV. To this day in England, the King James word *mansions* sometimes means "apartments."

[8]Rudolf Bultmann, "New Testament and Mythology: The Problem of Demythologizing the New Testament Proclamation," in *New Testament and Mythology and Other Basic Writings*, ed. and trans. Schubert M. Ogden (Philadelphia: Fortress, 1984), p. 4.

self as a Christian, then, is to identify with a cornerstone assumption held by myriad Christians for over two millennia.

Of course, modernist Christians in Mansion #1 might legitimately protest that the church also believed, and defended, some pretty wacky ideas for nearly that long—like Ptolemy's view of the heavens, in which the earth was at the center of the universe. This protest is modernist because it trumps something that is not empirically verifiable—Christ's divine nature and miraculous resurrection—with science. However, the ancient creeds do not make scientific claims. They present a statement of belief formulated, sometimes amid contentious debate, by followers of Christ attempting to come up with the shared foundations of their faith.

I therefore rejoiced when postmodernism started undermining modernist foundations, not only by dissolving the antisupernatural mortar of reason holding together the "evidence" of science but also by implying that *all* worldviews are based on unprovable axioms. Thanks to postmodernism, as I have already discussed, Christians were invited to once again sit at the intellectual table (rather than under it). Of course, modernist scholars resent—sometimes viciously—this invitation, and many postmodernists feel like withdrawing the invitation, largely due to Christians in the next apartment of the modernist house.

In Modernist Mansion #2: Fundamentalists

While Christian demythologizers destabilize the architecture of Christianity by cutting extra doors to allow easier access for modernists, fundamentalists guard their one and only door, allowing only those who have the right password to come inside. People who do not use the correct phrasing—such as "I have a personal relationship with Jesus" (even though that phrase appears nowhere in Scripture)—or who cannot identify a specific moment when they were "born again" are left out in the cold (or perhaps I should say "in the heat").

I thoroughly understand this position, having served for many years as a vigilant door monitor myself. After all, in Sunday school I gleefully sang "One door and only one, and yet its sides are two; I'm on the inside, on which side are you?"—a song based on Christ's words "I am the door: by me if any man enter in, he shall be saved, and shall go in and out, and find pasture" (John 10:9 KJV). Only now do I realize that my focus was more on the password than on the door, placing the power of salvation on human language rather than the work of Christ. Furthermore, I totally overlooked a later verse that was part of Christ's same parable: "I have other sheep that do not belong to this fold. I must bring them also, and they will listen to my voice" (John 10:16). This statement can be interpreted a number of different ways, but it clearly implies that the "inside" and "outside" of Christ's fold are not as clear-cut as "password" thinking implies.

I held onto password Christianity until I started studying the Anglo-Catholic writer Dorothy L. Sayers, whose BBC radio plays about the life of Jesus brought many people into the fold in the 1940s. Admiring her well-educated defense of Christian orthodoxy, I was shocked when I read her repeated assertions that she never had a "conversion experience"; how could she get inside without the right password? Furthermore, she, like her friend C. S. Lewis, enjoyed smoking and drinking—behaviors not allowed in my Christian mansion. Nevertheless, my admiration of Sayers and Lewis—who were disdained by fundamentalists and modernists alike—won out, and I began to wonder whether fundamentalist Christians borrowed the design of their mansion door from modernists.

Indeed, like the modernists I encountered in grad school (see chapter one), many fundamentalists consider it impossible to be a Christian and an intellectual simultaneously. The big difference, of course, is that Enlightenment intellectuals say "Christian" with a sneer of disdain, whereas fundamentalist Christians often say "intellectual" with a sneer of defiance. During the first half of the twentieth century, scientific modernists and fundamentalist Christians seemed to stand on opposite sides of the same door. But the door wasn't Christ; it was logical positivism, which asserted that only scientifically verifiable statements can be considered "true." Seeming to agree with modernists that only science is worthy of reasoned assent, fundamentalists argued (and many still do) for the scientific accuracy of the Bible. They turned Scripture into a collection of positivistic statements and went to incredible lengths to explain away textual discrepancies, as when Harold Lindsell, in the 1970s, worked to reconcile the fact that "Paul in I Corinthians reports that '23,000 fell in a single day' while the account in Numbers 25:9 says '24,000.'"[9]

Even to this day, rather than simply *believing* the Bible to be the Word of God, fundamentalists invoke science to "prove" the Bible's truth. When, for example, they work to find "empirical evidence" that a dyspeptic whale

---

[9]Harold Lindsell, *The Battle for the Bible* (Grand Rapids: Zondervan, 1976), p. 167.

could indeed burp up an undigested Jonah,[10] fundamentalists unwittingly imply that empiricism has a greater truth claim than Scripture. And their commitment to a literal six-day creation—to prove the Bible's scientific accuracy—has motivated numerous expeditions to find Noah's Ark. Mimicking Charles Darwin, these raiders of the lost ark are in search of scientific data to explain fossil evidence; however, while the modernist Darwin wanted to prove godless natural processes deposited the fossils, these modernist Christians want to prove that the Genesis flood deposited the fossils. They stand on opposite sides of the same door.

Ironically, then, when Christians argue for the scientific accuracy of the Bible they are conceding that science has ultimate ownership of the truth; they are signing their house of faith over to a modernist landlord. Before the development of modernism, Christians did not feel the need to defend the Bible as though it were a scientifically formulated life-saving document, for they assumed that it is Christ who saves us, not the Bible. This is not to say that medieval Christians did not develop their own passwords. Fallen human nature repeatedly wants to substitute human language and behavior for Christ. It is also not to say that fundamentalists are deficient Christians. Like the demythologizers in Mansion #1, many put me to shame with their dedication to following Christ. My criticism is directed, instead, to the notion of an "inerrant" Bible.

It is no coincidence that the concept of biblical "inerrancy" developed in nineteenth-century England almost simultaneously with Darwin's idea of natural selection: both were influenced by Enlightenment empiricism. Ironically, then, when fundamentalists think they are protecting Christianity by arguing that the Bible contains no scientific or historical inaccuracies, they assert a view of Scripture that is more modernist than traditional. They show a commitment to the canons of scientism more than to orthodox faith. Fundamentalists today might be shocked to discover that Christians believed in the literal death and resurrection of Christ for nineteen hundred years without having to insist on biblical inerrancy. The concept of an inerrant Bible did not appear until the 1820s, and, like evolution, it did not become widespread for at least a century.[11]

---

[10]For an overview of reputed evidence for the scientific accuracy of the book of Jonah, see Edward B. Davis, "A Whale of a Tale: Fundamentalist Fish Stories," *Perspectives on Science and Christian Faith* 43 (December 1991): 224-37.

[11]For a brief history of biblical inerrancy, see D. W. Bebbington, *Evangelicalism in Modern Britain: A History from the 1730s to the 1980s* (London: Unwin Hyman, 1989), pp. 81-91.

In Modernist Mansion #3: Cultural Conservatives

In the third apartment of modernist Christianity are those who have resisted not only the antisupernatural assumptions of the demythologizers but also the anti-intellectual impulses of fundamentalism. I admire them greatly; they are well educated and articulate, their mansion walls lined with the "great books" of the Western canon. But I worry when some begin complaining that, due to postmodern "multiculturalism," students no longer know the "classics."

As a professor of English literature, I value the "classics" myself, regarding *Middlemarch* by George Eliot (1872), *Jane Eyre* by Charlotte Brontë (1847) and *Pride and Prejudice* by Jane Austen (1813) to be far superior in artistry and insight to most bestsellers of our day. In fact, I feel tremendous satisfaction quoting the definition of "bestsellers" in *The Oxford Companion to American Literature:* "Seldom of great literary significance, such works are often ephemeral and dependent upon temporary tastes and interests."[12]

Nevertheless, postmodernism has made me aware that "literary significance" is itself contingent upon historical contexts. Along with their peers, J. R. R. Tolkien and C. S. Lewis thought it a waste of time to teach Shakespeare, let alone Austen, Brontë and Eliot. After all, they asserted, students should be able to read these "easy" works on their own. Education instead should focus on Greek and Latin so that students can read the "real" classics: Homer and Virgil, Sophocles and Terence (despite all the naughty bits). Ironically, even the heroic parts of Homer's *Odyssey* are often inimical to Christian orthodoxy.[13] Thus, not only do pagan "classics" undercut Christian perspectives, but many of the so-called classics considered necessary today for a quality school curriculum were once dismissed by an earlier generation as superfluous.

Furthermore, when Christians extol with evangelistic fervor the "great books" advocates E. D. Hirsch and Allan Bloom, I get a bit uncomfortable, for these writers perpetuate the Modernist sanctification of art. All too often, those who preach the educational necessity of the "classics" do so assuming the demise of Christianity. For them, only the humanities can save humanity.

---

[12]James E. Hart, ed., *The Oxford Companion to American Literature*, 4th ed. (New York: Oxford University Press, 1965), p. 75.

[13]Daniel Ritchie, author of *Reconstructing Literature in an Ideological Age: A Biblical Poetics and Literary Studies from Milton to Burke* (Eerdmans 1996), makes this point during an interview on *Mars Hill Audio Journal* 69 (July/August 2004).

George Sampson, for example, wrote in his *English for the English*, "What the teacher has to consider is not the minds he can measure but the souls he can save." Like other Modernists, Sampson believed that the study of English literature "is not a routine but a religion. . . . It is almost sacramental."[14] Cul-cha replaces Christ as cornerstone for many advocates of the "classics."

If anything, Christians should be advocates of "multiculturalism," wanting to understand how and why people of other cultures think and act the way they do. If God loved the whole world enough to send Christ to save it, Christians should want to immerse themselves in contemporary literature in order to understand how the good news is relevant to all people. Furthermore, U.S. Christians should be especially hesitant to proclaim the superiority of Western culture since "Christianity is rapidly becoming a non-Western religion, with Evangelical Protestants comprising only about 3-4% of the world population of Christians."[15]

In Modernist Mansion #4: Two Kinds of Objectivists

The last mansion in the Enlightenment edifice is occupied by individuals much to be respected: Christian academics who, having been trained by modernists in grad school, can often hold their own with the best minds in their discipline. The scholars in this mansion take two forms:

* those who clothe their Christianity with modernist designs
* those who alternate between modernist and Christian styles, keeping their clothing in separate closets

I have encountered this second kind of Christian scholar most often in the sciences. Drilled by empiricist captains, they follow orders to be "totally objective"—which usually translates to the idea that Christianity is irrelevant, if not inimical, to their discipline. Their faith, like their Sunday suit, is therefore closeted until they take off their uniform of scientific inquiry. Though many of these scholars teach at secular institutions where they are discouraged from ever wearing Christianity on their sleeve, I had my first contact with separate-wardrobe-Christians on a Christian college campus: in the 1970s I overheard a psychology professor state, "I'm a behaviorist on weekdays and a Christian

---

[14]Quoted in Chris Baldick, *The Social Mission of English Criticism, 1848-1932* (Oxford: Clarendon, 1983), pp. 100-101.

[15]Joseph Huffman, "Faith, Reason and the Text: The Return of the Middle Ages in Postmodern Scholarship," *Christian Scholar's Review* 29 (1999): 298 n. 51.

on the weekends." Even in 2005, while discussing the "intelligent design" court case that was taking place ten minutes from my house, I overheard a Christian science teacher from a local high school say that scientists are "pure" in their analysis of evolution while nonscientific Christians are "prejudiced" against it. Bringing Christianity into a discussion of science was, to her, about as appropriate as wearing a football helmet at the opera.

Modernist scholars of the other kind, rather than divorcing their intellectual work from their Christianity, employ modernist paradigms to argue for the legitimacy of Christianity. I highly value their desire to make Christianity intellectually tenable, but sometimes it seems as if they're trying to dress Jesus in a top hat and spats while turning the truth of Christ into the well-dressed propositions of modernist fashion. Some of these Christians can be so steeped in Enlightenment paradigms that rather than "The Church's one foundation is Jesus Christ her Lord," their refrain sounds like "The Church's one foundation is the objectivity of truth." For them, an Enlightenment paradigm props up the cornerstone of Christ.

When Christians think like this, argues philosopher James K. A. Smith, "the human person is *reduced* to a (primarily or essentially) rational animal, and truth is reduced to an affair of reason"—a reductionism that is "unbiblical."[16] Even Christian philosophers wary of postmodernism recognize the problem with such modernist Christianity. As theologian Kevin Vanhoozer argues, "The truth of Christianity is not like the universal truth of reason. The cradle of Christian faith is a story rather than a system."[17]

Truth of the Christian Story

The story with which we identify ourselves, of course, is presented in the

---

[16]James K. A. Smith, "Who's Afraid of Postmodernism? A Response to the 'Biola School,'" in *Christianity and the Postmodern Turn: Six Views,* ed. Myron B. Penner (Grand Rapids: Brazos, 2005), p. 219. Smith parallels this kind of thinking with "Christian philosophy that is devoted to analytic philosophy, a revised foundationalist epistemology, a classical evidentialist apologetics . . . and a biblicist notion of propositional revelation" (p. 226). For other Christian critiques of the "objectivity of truth," see Philip D. Kenneson, "There's No Such Thing as Objective Truth, and It's a Good Thing, Too," in *Christian Apologetics in the Postmodern World,* ed. Timothy R. Phillips and Dennis L. Okholm (Downers Grove, Ill.: InterVarsity Press, 1995), and Rodney Clapp, "How Firm a Foundation: Can Evangelicals Be Nonfoundationalists?" in *The Nature of Confession: Evangelicals and Postliberals in Conversation,* ed. Timothy R. Phillips and Dennis L. Okholm (Downers Grove, Ill.: InterVarsity Press, 1996), pp. 81-92.

[17]Kevin J. Vanhoozer, "Pilgrim's Digress: Christian Thinking on and About the Post/Modern Way," in *Christianity and the Postmodern Turn: Six Views,* ed. Myron B. Penner (Grand Rapids: Brazos, 2005), p. 84.

Bible. And according to that story, Jesus did not identify truth with a prop-osition to be believed but with a person—himself—to be trusted: "I am the way, and the *truth,* and the life. No one comes to the Father except through me" (John 14:6). Reinforcing these statements, Paul says of Christ, "For surely you have heard about him and were taught in him, as *truth* is in Jesus" (Ephesians 4:21), and John refers to "the *truth* that abides in us and will be with us forever" (2 John 2).

Just as the performance of the embodied Christ is the truth of our salva-tion, our performance in response confirms that truth. Jesus tells his disci-ples, "If you continue in my word, you are truly my disciples; and you will know the *truth,* and the *truth* will make you free" (John 8:31-32). The letters of St. John reiterate the importance not of "knowing" the truth but of "walk-ing in the truth" (2 John 4; 3 John 3-4): "If we say that we have fellowship with him while we are walking in darkness, we lie and do not do what is true" (1 John 1:6); and "Whoever says, 'I have come to know him,' but does not obey his commandments, is a liar, and in such a person the truth does not exist" (1 John 2:4). Truth is something we *do* in loving response to the Truth Incarnate.

The performance of the body is so foundational to Christian belief that Paul made it a point to emphasize the resurrection of believers' bodies (see 1 Corinthians 15). He did so in order to argue against an antibody philoso-phy that had infiltrated the church. Influenced by Plato, this pagan philoso-phy (which developed into Gnosticism by the second century) regarded the body as a mere prison of the mind or soul.

Gnostic Foundationalism

Despite Paul's arguments against proto-Gnostic tendencies in the early church, the historic map of Christianity is crisscrossed with repeated detours into Gnostic thought. The most dismal, dead-end detour developed during the patristic period, when Christian ascetics would torture their bodies—wearing prickly hairshirts, whipping their backs, sometimes even following the example of Origen (185?-254?) by castrating themselves—in an attempt to defy their physical impulses.

Contemptuous of such Christian practices, modernists nevertheless de-veloped their own brand of Gnosticism when they established that the mind could reach disinterested truth totally apart from the body. This seems to be Descartes's point in his *cogito,* where he implies what I've added in parentheses: "(I can transcend the positionality of my body when) I think, therefore I am."

When Christians like Descartes started traveling the modernist road, they gassed up on an unleaded form of Gnosticism to drive their belief: a belief that was as much about the godlike power of the mind as it was about the truth of Christ. As Susan Bordo notes about Descartes, "The godly intellect is on the way to becoming the true deity of the modern era." Even to this day, argues famous literary critic Harold Bloom, religion in the United States—from the Southern Baptists to the Mormons—is fueled by Gnosticism.[18]

St. Paul, in contrast, so believes in the importance of the body that he exhorts Christians to be in fellowship with other bodies, and he compares the body of the church with parts of the human body:

> Indeed, the body does not consist of one member but of many. If the foot would say, "Because I am not a hand, I do not belong to the body," that would not make it any less a part of the body. And if the ear would say, "Because I am not an eye, I do not belong to the body," that would not make it any less a part of the body. If the whole body were an eye, where would the hearing be? If the whole body were hearing, where would the sense of smell be? But as it is, God arranged the members in the body, each one of them, as he chose. If all were a single member, where would the body be? As it is, there are many members, yet one body. The eye cannot say to the hand, "I have no need of you," nor again the head to the feet, "I have no need of you." On the contrary, the members of the body that seem to be weaker are indispensable, and those members of the body that we think less honorable we clothe with greater honor, and our less respectable members are treated with greater respect; whereas our more respectable members do not need this. But God has so arranged the body, giving the greater honor to the inferior member, that there may be no dissension within the body, but the members may have the same care for one another. If one member suffers, all suffer together with it; if one member is honored, all rejoice together with it. (1 Corinthians 12:14-26)

In this passage, which engages seven more verses than I quoted, Paul gives the most extended metaphor in all his writings, perhaps because he seeks to establish two important concepts:

1. Rather than becoming autonomous believers, Christians are to act as interdependent performers, all participating in the body of Christ.

---

[18]Susan Bordo, *The Flight to Objectivity: Essays on Cartesianism and Culture* (New York: State University of New York Press, 1987), p. 81; Harold Bloom, *The American Religion: The Emergence of the Post-Christian Nation* (New York: Simon & Schuster, 1992).

2. Rather than submitting to the Gnostic privileging of soul and mind over body, Christians are to recognize the importance of all parts of the body, both literal and figurative.

Paul would be quite dismayed at the contamination of Christianity by the Gnosticism of modernism, which severed the mind from the body to such an extent that the head—the organ of reason—proclaimed to the feet, "I don't need you!"

Christian Nonfoundationalism

The efficacy of reason itself is a matter of belief. And postmodernists were not the first to recognize this. In 1943 Sayers explained to a non-Christian correspondent,

> One act of faith must, indeed, be made before one can accept Christianity: one must be prepared to believe that the universe is rational, and that (consequently) human reason is valid so far as it goes. But that is an act of faith which we have to make in order to think about anything at all. . . . Admittedly, we cannot prove that the universe is rational; for the only instrument by which we can prove anything is reason, and we have to assume the rationality of things before we can trust or use our reason.[19]

Or, as stated by Anselm over eight centuries earlier, *credo ut intelligam:* I believe in order to understand. To deny that belief precedes knowledge is to duplicate the assumptions of modernists, who assume belief to be a deficient mode of understanding.

In 1976, Christian philosopher Nicholas Wolterstorff explicitly challenged modernist foundationalism in a remarkable little book he called *Reason Within the Bounds of Religion,* a title that reversed the emphasis of Kant's famous work *Religion Within the Bounds of Reason Alone.* Indicting Christians who have appropriated modernist foundations in their desire for "indubitable" truth, Wolterstorff argues that all truth, including scientific truth, is built on assumptions that must be taken on faith:

> Foundationalism is a normative theory. And though I shall argue that no one who has professed to be a foundationalist has ever followed the norm to which he subscribes, yet overall the acceptance of foundationalism by Western scholars has profoundly affected their theorizing. In the case of those scholars

---

[19] *The Letters of Dorothy L. Sayers,* vol. 2, *1937 to 1943: From Novelist to Playwright,* ed. Barbara Reynolds (New York: St. Martin's, 1997), p. 401.

who were Christians, its acceptance has repeatedly served to confuse and intimidate them in their theorizing. Only if the sting of foundationalism is plucked will the infection subside.

As a plucky plucker of the foundationalist sting, Wolterstorff, like St. George battling the dragon, takes action in the name of Christ. Rallying Christian scholars to his aid, he seeks to conquer the dragon of modernism that continues to attack the foundations of a house not made with hands. Rather than capitulate to scientism, Wolterstorff argues that "the religious beliefs of the Christian scholar ought to function as control beliefs within his devising and weighing of theories."[20]

Following this charge, numerous Christian intellectuals have celebrated the subversion of modernist foundationalism by postmodern thinkers.[21] As Stanley Grenz noted in 2000, "Scholars today have embarked on a quest to uncover a nonfoundationalist, or, as some prefer, a postfoundationalist approach. Viewed from this perspective, we might say that the intellectual world lying 'after modernity' is a realm 'beyond foundationalism.'"[22] John Franke provides a helpful explanation of "beyond foundationalism":

> If we must speak of "foundations" for the Christian faith and its theological enterprise, then we must speak only of the triune God who is disclosed in polyphonic fashion through scripture, the church, and even the world, albeit always in accordance with the normative witness to divine self-disclosure contained in scripture. Put another way, nonfoundationalist theology means the end of foundationalism but not "foundations."[23]

Beyond Foundationalism: Radical Orthodoxy

In the 1990s, a group of Christian scholars in England began conceptualizing

---

[20]Nicholas Wolterstorff, *Reason Within the Bounds of Religion,* 2nd ed. (Grand Rapids: Eerdmans, 1999), pp. 34, 70.

[21]A notable movement in this regard is the "postliberal narrative theology" generated by Hans Frei and George Lindbeck. Evangelicals have written so much about Frei and Lindbeck that I do not discuss them in this book. Instead, I would refer readers to two books cited above: Robert Greer's *Mapping Postmodernism,* and *The Nature of Confession* edited by Phillips and Okholm. For other significant Christian engagements with nonfoundationalism, see Edith Wyschogrod, *Saints and Postmodernism: Revisioning Moral Philosophy* (Chicago: University of Chicago Press, 1990); and Merold Westphal, *Overcoming Onto-theology: Toward a Postmodern Christian Faith* (New York: Fordham University Press, 2001).

[22]Based on a paper Grenz delivered in 2000, these words appear in Stanley J. Grenz and John R. Franke, *Beyond Foundationalism: Shaping Theology in a Postmodern Context* (Louisville, Ky.: Westminster John Knox, 2001), pp. 28-29.

[23]Franke, "Nature of Theology," p. 118.

what they named Radical Orthodoxy: a return to orthodox Christianity before it was tainted by modernist foundationalism. For "radically orthodox" scholars, the "modern" era began in the thirteenth century when John Duns Scotus (1265?-1308) "attempted to argue for knowledge of God" apart from revelation and thus established perceived truth as a more solid foundation than dogma. This kind of foundationalism, based on reason, "elevated a neutral account of being above the distinction between the Creator and his creatures."[24] Duns Scotus thus led the way for human reason to supersede divine revelation in the pursuit of truth. As a result, rather than humbly submitting to a God who transcends all human knowledge, early modern foundationalists, as we have seen, sanctified the human mind in the assumption that reason can reach indubitable, objective, universal truth on its own.

Taking a stand against such modernist autonomy, Radical Orthodoxy emphasizes, as did St. Paul, that Christians are all "members of the household of God, built upon the foundation of the apostles and prophets, with Christ Jesus himself as the cornerstone" (Ephesians 2:19-20). The foundation is not indubitable propositional truth but a community of believers with whom Christians should identify: "God's household, which is the church of the living God, the pillar and foundation of the truth" (1 Timothy 3:15 NIV). Depending on how you diagram the grammar of this verse, the foundation of truth is either God or the church—an appropriate ambiguity, since we come to know God through participation with other believers.

The word *participation,* in fact, is key to Radical Orthodoxy. First and foremost, Radical Orthodoxy asserts that all of creation participates with God, for everything created is dependent on its Creator. Conversely, belief in autonomous reason—or modernist foundationalism—is fundamentally "nihilistic," as is any ideology that severs dependence on God. Because all that is within creation—including human creations—participates "in the primal gift of the Creator,"[25] Christians are called to value the body and how it participates in God's creation, manifesting this value through their worship: not only in liturgy, sacrament and art but also by embodying Christ to others. However, for the radically orthodox, the truth in which we participate is not self-evident; it has been revealed to us by the Holy Spirit working through

---

[24]Phillip Blond, "Perception: From Modern Painting to the Vision in Christ," in *Radical Orthodoxy: A New Theology,* ed. John Milbank, Catherine Pickstock and Graham Ward (New York: Routledge, 1999), p. 233.

[25]James K. A. Smith, *Introducing Radical Orthodoxy: Mapping a Post-secular Theology* (Grand Rapids: Baker, 2004), p. 67.

the "household of God." We therefore walk by faith in the truth of revelation, rather than in sight of indubitable foundations.

Though often called a "postmodern theology," Radical Orthodoxy is an attempt to reinstate the theology of significant premodern Christian thinkers without repudiating the contributions of the Reformation or abandoning the important political, social and technical advances of the Enlightenment.[26] Catherine Pickstock, for example, shows how the great Christian philosopher Aquinas (1225-1274), though he encouraged the use of human reason, nevertheless recognized "the situatedness of our manner of knowing": "For Aquinas truth is not at all a matter of detached abstraction, but rather of the specific entry into our minds of certain contingent features and events."[27] In other words, Aquinas recognized that we interpret reality according to how we are placed in it: the positionality of our body. We should not be surprised, then, that postmodern perceptions sometimes echo premodernism, the time when Christianity had cultural dominance in Europe.

Paralleling the Premodern with the Postmodern

A great way to think of the parallel between postmodernism and premodernism was given to me by medieval scholar Joseph Huffman in an essay called "Faith, Reason and the Text: The Return of the Middle Ages in Postmodern Scholarship." Among his many insights, Huffman discusses the transformation of the phrase *bona fide*.[28] Most of us today know the term by its modernist use: "that's a bona fide Picasso painting," or "that's a bona fide zit on your nose." Something "bona fide" has been verified by empirical evidence.

Ironically, *bona fide* is a Latin term that actually means "in good faith" (both words were pronounced with two syllables: bo'-na fi'-de). For premodern Christians, who usually wrote in Latin, something was true if it was

---

[26]Radical Orthodoxy is also critical of postmodernism—primarily when it perpetuates modernist paradigms. For instance, John Milbank thinks that postmodernism is as Gnostic as modernism because both sever material realities from dependence on the transcendent. See ibid., p. 192.

[27]Catherine Pickstock, "Radical Orthodoxy and the Mediation of Time," in *Radical Orthodoxy? A Catholic Enquiry*, ed. Laurence Paul Hemming (Burlington, Vt.: Ashgate, 2000), p. 67.

[28]Huffman, "Faith, Reason and the Text," p. 290. Huffman's essay focuses on attitudes toward texts. For the modernist, a text was bona fide if authentic authorship could be verified; for the premodernist, a text was bona fide if the content accorded with traditional Christian truth, even if the text was a forgery of a famous church father.

bo-na fi-de: if it reflected the orthodox doctrines of Christianity. Foundations, then, were considered genuine not due to the evidence of reason or empirical data but through reasoned identification with the good faith of the Christian community. The truth of Christ was bona fide.

By the eighteenth century, however, *bona fide* had been reduced to simply mean "genuine," and by the twentieth century such genuineness was aligned with empirical verifiability. This etymology shows that Aquinas was right: knowledge of the meaning of *bona fide* is affected by the contingent features and events of our culture, such that most twenty-first-century Christians have replaced the Christian meaning of *bona fide* with the modernist redefinition. Just as the spoken phrase has been reduced from four syllables to three, so also the meaning has been reduced to what can be empirically proven.

Bona Fide Postmodernism: Neopragmatism

Like premodern Christians, postmodern "communitarians" identify foundational truth with the bo-na fi-de of a believing community. The two most famous—also known as postmodern "neopragmatists"—are Stanley Fish, quoted above, and Richard Rorty. Fish and Rorty assert that a community must stand by its bona fide truth, believing it passionately. The difference between them might be explained with the language Robert Putnam employs in his book *Bowling Alone.*[29] Putnam identifies two kinds of communities: bridging and bonding. In Putnam's terms, Fish emphasizes the importance of community *bonding,* where members of a group cling to their distinctions from the rest of culture, feeling separate from it as they proclaim the truth of their particular position. In contrast, Rorty advocates communities that maintain their beliefs while seeking to build *bridges* with groups that think differently, finding language that can emphasize the commonalties among them.

Problems with the postmodern bridging and bonding of Rorty and Fish will be addressed in chapter seven. For now, I'd like to suggest that a truly vibrant Christianity reflects both impulses, communities bonding together for the purpose of mutual edification and growth in order to more effectively build bridges that transport grace to those outside "the household of God."

---

[29]Robert D. Putnam, *Bowling Alone: The Collapse and Revival of American Community* (New York: Simon & Schuster, 2000).

Biblical Foundations

I hope you are convinced by now that foundationalism is tricky business. For, in many people's minds, it is nothing other than the philosophical base for the house of modernism: a tacit trust in the "objectivity of truth"—in contradistinction to the backward "superstitions" of faith. Nevertheless, we can understand its attractions, as the word *foundation* evokes the image of rock-solid stasis. That's why we like the word; we want our truth to stay put.

The New Testament, however, aligns the foundation of Christianity with dynamism, not stasis. Just think of Jesus' parable about the wise and foolish builders:

> Why do you call me "Lord, Lord," and do not do what I tell you? I will show you what someone is like who comes to me, hears my words, and acts on them. That one is like a man building a house, who dug deeply and laid the foundation on rock; when a flood arose, the river burst against that house but could not shake it, because it had been well built. But the one who hears and does not act is like a man who built a house on the ground without a foundation. When the river burst against it, immediately it fell, and great was the ruin of that house. (Luke 6:46-49)

Obviously, someone who calls Jesus "Lord, Lord" believes in him—or at least acknowledges his preeminence. However, according to Jesus, the successful foundation is not simply belief or knowledge; the solid foundation is action.

Paul confirms Jesus' activist foundations in his letters to Timothy. He directs his "loyal child in the faith" how to exhort rich Christians: "They are to do good, to be rich in good works, generous, and ready to share, thus storing up for themselves the treasure of a good *foundation* for the future, so that they may take hold of the life that really is life" (1 Timothy 6:18-19). And later Paul writes, "God's firm *foundation* stands, bearing this inscription: 'The Lord knows those who are his,' and, 'Let everyone who calls on the name of the Lord turn away from wickedness'" (2 Timothy 2:19). The foundation is sealed not by human knowledge but by God's knowledge; it stands firm not simply through confession of belief but in the actions that follow.[30] Hence, when the New Testament repeatedly

---

[30]John confirms Paul's perception: "Whoever says, 'I have come to know him,' but does not obey his commandments, is a liar, and in such a person the truth does not exist" (1 John 2:4).

aligns foundations with the performing body, it implies that foundations move.

Moving Foundations

The idea of moving foundations probably sounds oxymoronic, if not moronic, to anyone who hasn't lived in California. I, however, have experienced several dramatic California earthquakes, including one that turned a hundred-year-old stone grotto on my parents' property into a pile of rubble. I am aware, therefore, that foundations for newer skyscrapers in San Francisco and Los Angeles are placed on rollers, enabling them, during earthquakes, to roll with the movement of the earth rather than crack apart. Their foundations hold strong precisely *because* they move.

Sometimes Christians get so rigidly committed to a certain idea of "truth" as foundational that when the earth, or at least culture, moves under them their faith develops huge cracks—as happened to those Christians endorsing geocentricism. Galileo, as is well known, was tried by church officials because of his "unbiblical" assertion that the earth moved around the sun. Many of his judges used the Bible to support the traditional view they had inherited from the ancients: the sun, moon and stars all move around the earth. However, as their biblical geocentricism became more and more problematic, church teaching as a legitimate foundation for truth was called into question. The foundation cracked when it was discovered that the earth does indeed move.

The same is happening today with Christians who are "young earth" creationists.[31] Though they assume that they are standing firm for their faith with a rock-solid foundation, they don't realize that the Christian house built on such a foundation has such huge cracks in it that no one believing even the most conservative scientific estimates for the world's age would dare to move in. Thus, in the minds of many intelligent design scholars, rather than preserving Christianity, "young earth" creationists are making it intellectually unten(ant)able. Like skyscrapers in California, the house of Christian faith as expressed in the Apostles' Creed will stand

---

[31]I am not indicting the "intelligent design" movement, even though "young earth" creationists usually identify with it. Two of the most intelligent Christian philosophers I have met endorse a form of "intelligent design." Both, however, argue that the earth is far older than "young earth" creationists allow. For a good overview of intelligent design, see William Dembski, *Intelligent Design: The Bridge Between Science and Theology* (Downers Grove, Ill.: InterVarsity Press, 1999).

longer if Christians allow theories about the earth's age to move.

But how far can we allow foundations to move without doing disservice to our faith? Once again, think of San Francisco skyscrapers. Though they are on rollers, this doesn't mean that an earthquake will send a building located on Union Square over to Golden Gate Park several miles away, negotiating streets and sidewalks like a kid on his skateboard. The pit in which the movable foundation stands provides limits.

I would argue that the foundation of Christianity stands in a four-sided pit dug into a bedrock of belief. One side that limits extreme movement is lined with the Bible; another side is lined with church tradition; the third side is a wall of reason; and personal experience (which includes cultural situatedness) makes up the fourth wall.[32] With a movable foundation placed within these four walls, Christianity can withstand cultural earthquakes that present us with new ways of thinking, as when astronomers suggested that the earth orbits around the sun, or biologists suggest that homosexuality may be rooted in prenatal development more than personal choice. Because our foundation is placed on rollers of faith, it can move as we employ reason to assess empirical data in the light of biblical teaching and traditional dogma. But this also means that we need to assess our understanding of the Bible and church tradition by reasoned assessment of science and culture: to keep our foundation intact by allowing it to move.[33]

Significantly, the Bible warns against *unmoving* foundations. In the Gospels we are told that many people had such rigid foundations that they failed to see the Incarnate Truth when he walked and talked among them. In contrast, Christ moved foundations when he healed on the sabbath and rose from the dead. In the early apostolic period Peter moved foundations when he extended Christianity to Gentiles. In 325 the Council at Nicaea moved foundations when it established, with the help of the Roman emperor, that Jesus was "begotten, not made." In 1098 Anselm moved foundations when he redefined atonement as a payment made to God rather than

---

[32]Many readers will recognize in my four walls an echo of the "Wesleyan Quadrilateral," a term Albert Outler coined in the 1960s to describe how Methodist preacher John Wesley (1703-1791) approached theological issues.

[33]In the words of theologian/scientist Alister McGrath, "As any serious historian of Christian thought knows, Christianity is committed to a constant review of its ideas in the light of their moorings in scripture and tradition, always asking whether any contemporary interpretations of a doctrine is adequate or acceptable." See *Dawkins' God: Genes, Memes and the Meaning of Life* (Oxford: Blackwell, 2005), p. 13.

as a ransom required by the devil.[34] In 1517 Luther moved foundations when he posted ninety-five theses about Christianity on the door of Wittenberg Cathedral. In 1882 Elizabeth Cady Stanton moved foundations when she argued, with the aid of the Bible, that Christians should support women's suffrage.[35]

Christians today, then, can sing with confidence "The Church's one foundation is Jesus Christ her Lord," knowing that they join myriad others throughout the last two millennia to confirm that just as our One God is three, so our One Foundation is plural: the body of Christ kept alive in numerous bodies of believers, whose faith is bona fide *because* it moves.

---

[34]For a brief but illuminating history of changes in the doctrine of the atonement, see J. Denny Weaver, "Violence in Christian Theology," *CrossCurrents* 51 (Summer 2001): 151-53.

[35]This may explain why the famous postmodernist Jacques Derrida stated that "Christianity is the most plastic, the most open, religion, the most prepared, the best prepared, to face unpredictable transformations." See "Epoché and Faith: An Interview with Jacques Derrida," in *Derrida and Religion: Other Testaments,* ed. Yvonne Sherwood and Kevin Hart (New York: Routledge, 2005), p. 33.

PART THREE

Situating Influential Postmodern Thinkers

Deconstruction

THE POSTING OF STRUCTURALISM

There was a boy in my ninth-grade English class named Alan May who was somewhat goofy looking, largely due to his weird haircut. I didn't realize that his odd locks were styled after those of a rock star, which made him especially attractive to people more in tune with popular culture than I. To my surprise, numerous girls from class started moaning over the hair-disabled boy during gym; they leaned up against their lockers with dreamy eyes, saying things like "Isn't Alan May gorgeous!" and "Alan May is *so* cool!" In a matter of weeks I had such a crush on Alan May that I couldn't concentrate in class, sneaking glances at the "gorgeous" adolescent every chance I got.

Some might explain away my response as capitulation to "peer pressure." However, I didn't want anyone—especially my peers—to know of the crush; I wasn't trying to "belong," as "peer pressure" implies. Instead, just as rock culture had influenced the hair of Alan and the ensuing sighs of fourteen-year-old girls, so the language of those girls—especially the word *gorgeous*—affected my perception.

The word *gorgeous,* then, is not autonomous, standing on its own with a universal definition. Shaped by culture, the word molds the way people see. If you are not convinced, look at famous paintings of "beautiful" nineteenth-century nudes. You will probably be struck by the billowing corpulence of the figures, as though the painters had confused down pillows with the women's thighs. If those painters were to look at a "beautiful" runway model in our day, they would be appalled by her skeletal limbs; to them she would look as though several elongated string beans had gotten together to wear a bikini. "Beauty" for one society is a cultural oddity to another—something any child who has perused old *National Geographic* magazines can tell you.

This has led some of the more inconsistent postmodernists to argue that there are no universals. But such a statement, being a universal itself, is as problematic as the statement "There is one universal standard of beauty." The very existence of numerous definitions of beauty implies that the love of beauty is innate to humans: it is a universal. However, the different ways various cultures define beauty proves that beauty is shaped by and re-inforced in language. Indeed, before the twentieth century "stout," even "fat," was a compliment when applied to a person,[1] while, in our own day, the nicest thing you can say to a woman who has intentionally lost weight is "How skinny you look!" or even "You look like a string bean!" And every time we use such diction, we reinforce our culture's truth about beauty.

For this reason, postmodernism asserts that language is not innocent—in two senses. First, language does not have universal unchanging meaning, for it is the creation of humans. Second, language has power to mold human vision and action, as when the positive connotations of *skinny* lead to obsessive dieting, if not anorexia/bulimia. I even think the word *skinny* has contributed to the problem with obesity in twenty-first-century America: because the "ideal" weight for women is associated with the word *skinny,* females have given up on attaining the ideal; it's too hard to be ideally "skinny." What we see here is that language has incredible power but is as limited as the humans who use it: the power and poverty of language.

Analysis of the power and poverty of language is the focus of *poststructuralism,* which appeared in France during the late 1960s, right when postmodernism was coming of age in the arts scene. The marriage between postmodernism and poststructuralism was celebrated in 1979 when Jean-François Lyotard, a French poststructuralist, borrowed the term *postmodernism* to describe his project: questioning the language of modernist metanarratives. However, even before this union was made formal, two children were spawned by the growing attachment between poststructuralism and postmodernism: (1) deconstruction, which focused on the poverty and power of lan-

---

[1]Note the following compliment Dorothy Wordsworth wrote in an 1802 journal: "Mary . . . looked so fat and well that we were made very happy by the sight of her." See "The Grasmere Journals," in *The Norton Anthology of English Literature: The Romantic Period,* ed. M. H. Abrams and Stephen Greenblatt, 7th ed. (New York: W. W. Norton, 2000), p. 395.

guage through textual analysis, and (2) cultural studies, which focused on the power and poverty of language through cultural analysis.

Jacques Derrida (1930-2004) was godfather to deconstruction, while Michel Foucault (1926-1984) served in the same capacity for cultural studies. Though both disliked application of the term *postmodernist* to their work, they nevertheless reinforced a basic assumption of postmodernism: the interdependence of knowledge and language. This chapter will employ some of my own experiences of knowledge and language in order to explain both poststructuralism and deconstruction and suggest how they served (my) faith. In the next chapter I will grapple with the "language games" made famous by Foucault and other postmodern theorists.

Fixing Structuralism

Just as postmodernism started as a challenge to Modernist art and architecture, poststructuralism started as a challenge to a philosophy of language called "structuralism." In fact, structuralism operates as a bridge between modernism and postmodernism, undermining faith in autonomous reason and radical individualism. Helping generate "the linguistic turn" in twentieth-century philosophy, structuralism asserted that language shapes the way humans think, but that words themselves are *arbitrary*.

By "arbitrary" structuralists meant that there is no innate, universal connection between a "signifier" and its "signified," between a word and its meaning. Take, for example, the phrase "Oh God!" For earnest believers, the phrase is prayerfully uttered in petition or thanks to our Creator. But for many people in America, the phrase is usually an expletive of derision or delight. The signified meaning of "Oh God!" depends on the speaker's culture and the context in which she is speaking.

Structuralism, which was started by linguists, came to prominence in the field of anthropology as scholars studied how cultures and contexts (rather than the autonomous individual promoted by Kant) give meaning to language. However, like Kant, structuralists assumed that the human mind, no matter the culture, has an innate, universal structure. Think again of the supermarket coin-sorting machine. While Kant saw perceptions of empirical data entering into the coin-machine brain, structuralists instead saw coins of language entering the brain. All humans have the same slots to sort the sense, but because language and customs differ from culture to culture, the resulting rolls of coin, though they had the same tube shape and paper color, had different contents: one culture might have an orange tube of pennies, another an orange tube of pesos or pence. For the structuralist this meant that one culture might worship Allah, another Jehovah, but both faiths were merely orange tubes of religion: while the structure was the same, the content was as arbitrary as the language that entered the coin-machine brain.[2]

Paradoxically, structuralists acted as though all human brains were coin machines except their own. In other words, assuming that they could stand outside of culture in order to analyze it, structuralists reflected the modernist belief that scientific objectivity could explain away faith. In contrast, poststructuralism asserts that there is nowhere to stand outside of our language in order to *objectively* investigate it. Language molds perception—including the perceptions of structuralism *and* poststructuralism, which poststructuralists readily admit. Recognizing the power and poverty of language, poststructuralism implies that all knowledge, including its own, must be taken on faith.

This is what Derrida meant by his eyebrow-raising statement "There never was any 'perception.'"[3] He is using hyperbole to emphasize how our situatedness—our placement in location and time—affects the way we see things. And Christians dare not begrudge him hyperbole, since Jesus often employed it to make his point: "And if your eye causes you to stumble, tear it out" (Mark 9:47). "Whoever comes to me and does not hate father and mother, wife and children, brothers and sisters, yes, and even life itself, cannot be my disciple" (Luke 14:26). Despite the fact that Gospel writers place these sayings directly in the mouth of Jesus, I have encountered very few one-eyed fundamentalists, very few evangelical Christians who denounce "family values." They know that Christ used hyperbole to get our attention and force us to ask exactly what influences our perception: is God the center of our life, or do distractions of the eye, including desires of family and friends, control our behavior? Christ seemed to recognize that the assumptions and values of the culture that surrounds us can be reinforced by those

---

[2]Nietzsche, who influenced poststructuralism, used a coin analogy even before the invention of coin machines. In "On Truth and Lie in an Extra-moral Sense," he says, "Truths are . . . metaphors which are worn out and without sensuous power; coins which have lost their pictures and now matter only as metal, no longer as coins." *The Portable Nietzsche*, ed. and trans. Walter Kauffman (New York: Penguin, 1976), p. 47.

[3]Jacques Derrida, *Speech and Phenomena and Other Essays on Husserl's Theory of Signs*, trans. David B. Allisons (Evanston, Ill.: Northwestern University Press, 1973), p. 103.

closest to us: father and mother, wife and husband, brothers and sisters. Poststructuralism recognizes this as well.

Prestructuralism: Biblical Views of Language

The Old Testament seems to endorse the power and poverty of language. The power is implied by the Third Commandment: "You shall not make wrongful use of the name of the LORD your God, for the LORD will not acquit anyone who misuses his name" (Exodus 20:7). In contrast to the child's jingle "Sticks and stones may break my bones, but words will never hurt me," this commandment seems to acknowledge that words have the power to mold perception. Hence, when people say "Oh God!" in derision or delight they trivialize God and become guilty of perpetuating disbelief in an all-powerful God who is involved with humanity.

The injunction against using God's name in vain relates to God's answer to Moses from the burning bush: "Thus you shall say to the Israelites, 'I AM has sent me to you'" (Exodus 3:14). Though the Hebrew is obscure, many scholars believe that the name of Yahweh, "I AM WHO I AM," can also be translated "I WILL BE WHAT I WILL BE." As though in recognition that language molds perception, God communicates a Self that transcends the limitations of any noun referring to a created entity: a person, gender, place or thing. God is a verb, but not even a verb of identifiable creaturely activity. God's identity as self-sustaining uncaused actuality—the I AM—cannot be understood apart from God's own self-revelation.

The power of language to mold, and hence limit, our understanding of God thus implies its poverty. Language cannot capture the essence of God because it is a human, not a divine, creation. Scripture implies as much when it tells us that Adam named the animals. God did not supply the absolutely "correct" word that might establish a direct correspondence between the signifier *kangaroo* and its referent: a hopping marsupial with its own carry-on luggage. In fact, we would consider it quite presumptuous if a French speaker insisted that her word for "dog," *chien,* was the name preferred by God.

The story of Adam naming the animals implies that language is part of what it means to be human and therefore is good. But the story goes on to describe Adam's fall from innocence, implying that language, though an element of human glory, is sullied by the fallen humans who use it.[4] For the

---

[4]Note Merold Westphal: "The hermeneutics of finitude is a meditation on the meaning of hu-

poststructuralist, language is like the fallen Lucifer: appearing as an angel of light (indeed, how could we function without language?), it insidiously influences the way people think and act.

Here's an example of Luciferian language. When I was a little girl, I loved to color and was especially fond of the Crayola sixty-four-pack—the flip-top box with its built-in crayon sharpener. I learned some lovely names from the colored papers that enwrapped each crayon: chartreuse, magenta, mauve. One of the crayons in that pack—a light pinkish beige—was named "flesh." As a child, I thought nothing of it; after all, my flesh was, indeed, pinkish beige. But today I am disturbed to think of how the word *flesh* on that innocent crayon reflected and perpetuated problematic attitudes of the 1960s. When crayon makers employed the descriptor *flesh* for pinkish beige, they implied that only one color is correctly human. Of course, Crayola wasn't being intentionally racist. Its assumptions were molded like its crayons, embedded in a white-dominated cultural context like crayons in a box. The word *flesh,* then, reflected the assumptions of its time, assumptions perpetuated when children all over America read the worded crayon and identified true, acceptable, culturally condoned "flesh" with pinkish beige. Black and brown crayons were never called "flesh."

Deconstructing Binaries

This deconstruction of the color "flesh" calls attention to the poststructuralism of Jacques Derrida, developed in the late 1960s. Derrida was concerned with the ways language perpetuates certain binary oppositions in Western culture, like white versus black. For example, when someone thinks of herself as "white"—a misnomer, since very few people have truly *white* flesh— she is distinguishing herself from a dark-skinned person: black is what she is not. However, if all humans had the same color of skin, the distinction would not be necessary; then (and only then) would a single-colored crayon named "flesh" be accurate. If all human flesh were "white," it would be just as silly to say "I am white rather than black" as it would be to assert "I am white rather than magenta." There is no need for distinction if the descriptor is universal. Imagine someone saying to you, "I am an air-breathing human." What else is there? You might conclude—at least, if you watch *Star Trek* re-

man createdness, and the hermeneutics of suspicion is a meditation on the meaning of human fallenness." See *Overcoming Onto-theology: Toward a Postmodern Christian Faith* (New York: Fordham University Press, 2001), p. xx.

runs—that the speaker is a disguised space alien unaware that all humans breathe air. You would thus establish a new binary, earthling versus alien, to distinguish yourself from this bizarre creature who made an irrelevant distinction.

Structuralists established binary oppositions as the means by which societies categorize phenomena: one slot in the coin-machine brain channels behavior that was "male" and another "female"; one slot categorizes "the natural" in contradistinction to "the cultural" slot. In fact, the famous structural anthropologist Claude Lévi-Strauss asserted that the categories of "nature" and "culture" were so mutually exclusive that human behavior falls into either one slot or the other, but not both. It was this idea that Derrida challenged in 1966, thus sinking structuralism just as it was getting launched.[5]

Derrida was especially concerned with how binaries tend to be hierarchical, one term regarded as superior to the other. Take the hierarchies perpetuated by Modernists, as surveyed in chapter three:

high culture (Cul-cha)	creative art	individual genius
popular culture	critical analysis	social norms

For Modernists, the term on top embodied an authenticity that would be sullied by any invasion from the realm described by the term beneath it. However, as we have seen, Pop art started challenging these hierarchies in the early 1960s. Later in the decade, Derrida began his own challenge of various binaries established in Western tradition:

white	male	natural	reason	objectivity	thought	speech
black	female	cultural	belief	subjectivity	language	writing

For each of these coupled terms, the top word has, in the West, usually been treated as preferable to the concept underneath it. In fact, the top usu-

---

[5]Derrida challenged the structuralism of Lévi-Strauss at the conference "Critical Languages and the Science of Man," held at the Johns Hopkins University in October 1966. In the published form of the essay, "Structure, Sign and Play in the Discourse of the Human Sciences," Derrida quotes a passage about nature and culture from Claude Lévi-Strauss's *The Elementary Structures of Kinship* (1949). See Jacques Derrida, *Writing and Difference*, trans. with introduction and notes by Alan Bass (Chicago: University of Chicago Press, 1978), p. 283. For the following discussion about binaries, see Jacques Derrida, *Positions*, trans. Alan Bass (Chicago: University of Chicago Press, 1981), p. 41.

ally defines itself in contradistinction to the inferior term, its superiority perpetuated by language.

Take the male-female binary. When I was growing up, a boy who acted
like a girl was described in derogatory terms: sissy, swishy, fairy, flitty. A girl
who acted like a boy, however, was considered cute; the word *tomboy* was
not at all demeaning. (I, who could not catch a softball to save my life,
longed to be a tomboy!) In other words, it was permissible for the inferior
person (female) to act like the superior, but embarrassing when the superior
"lowered" himself by performing female behaviors. Language and behavior
reinforced the hierarchy.

Thus, in the history of Western culture, most of the top terms were perceived as central to being fully human, closer to authentic reality. This explains why for many years neither blacks nor females could vote in America—even after the so-called Enlightenment. We can therefore add to the
above binaries these summarizing distinctions:

center	reality	inside
margin	appearance	outside

In all three lists of binaries, you can see parallels among the lower terms,
such that women, valued for their appearance, were considered "marginal"
in their exercise of the superior traits of reason, objectivity and thought. In
the 1980s, for example, while I was still in grad school, my husband and I
got stopped by a policeman on a mountain road in Colorado. When the officer questioned the speeding driver, who was (ahem) me, I explained that
I didn't notice the speed limit. He replied, "Well, if you women would stop
yak-yak-yakking while you drive, you could think more about what you are
doing!" Ironically, as my husband will attest, of the two of us he is much
more the talker. He, in fact, was the one doing the talking during our drive,
while I merely provided feedback. This officer had categorized me according to the cultural binary.

Many modernist feminists responded to such sexism by inverting the binary, putting females on top—as morally superior—while condemning men
as male chauvinist pigs. But Derrida would say that inverting the binary
merely perpetuates the system as people continue to define themselves by rejecting someone else as inferior—someone who is "other" to themselves and
hence not completely human (as the term "male chauvinist *pigs*" implies).

Instead, Derrida sought to "deconstruct" these binaries—take them apart—by calling into question the clear distinction between them. One way he did this was by pointing out that the dominant term on top gets its meaning by the lower term it rejects. Thus the top term contains a "trace" of what is not itself. In my white flesh versus black flesh example above, "white" needs "black" to establish its superiority; hence, black is a part of white's self-definition. As this illustration shows, binaries contain within them their own deconstruction, as each element reveals a trace of what is other to itself. Technically, then, critics do not "deconstruct" language; they merely expose something that is already there. Nevertheless, as the first sentence of this paragraph indicates, it is hard to talk of this critical exposé without using *deconstruct* as a verb. Even the language of deconstruction contains a trace of something it is not!

The Deconstruction of Sacred and Secular

The history of the word *secular* provides an interesting example of deconstruction. Coming from a Latin term meaning "of an age," *secular* in the thirteenth century meant "in the world" and designated civil affairs. The medieval church therefore employed the word *secular* to describe ordained clergy who went out into the world to preach the gospel (they were "secular"), as opposed to those priests who remained within the confines of monasteries. In other words, the *outside* of monasteries, the "secular," was actually *inside* Christianity. Up through the seventeenth century, *secular* had neither positive nor negative connotations; it merely provided a helpful distinction between the sacred things of the church, which were for all ages and all generations, and things of the current age or generation, which were "secular."

During the Enlightenment, however, a hierarchy developed wherein the secular was established as superior to the sacred: secular/sacred. By 1851, in the midst of the Victorian faith crisis, the word *secularism* had been coined to describe the "doctrine that morality should be based solely on the regard to well-being of mankind in the present life, to the exclusion of all considerations drawn from belief in God or in a future state" *(OED)*. For many Victorians, the "secular" should have no trace of the "sacred." However, as my chapter on the history of modernism demonstrates (chapter two), the secular humanist disdain for religion contained a trace of what it rejected, for it made reason sacred and turned art into a kind of religion. The "outside" of the secular was actually "inside" it.

Unfortunately, many Christians responded by inverting the modernist binary, so that anything "secular" was evil: sacred/secular. To this day, there are some Christians who refuse to read C. S. Lewis because he smoked cigarettes and drank alcohol: his involvement with such "secular" activities destroys any Christian insights that he might offer. Other Christians, however, demonstrate the deconstruction of sacred and secular when they share their faith over a beer (or write books celebrating postmodernism *and* Christian faith).

Significantly, scholars today often describe postmodernity as "postsecular."[6] The binary opposition between sacred and secular has been deconstructed with the recognition that many modernists treat their secularist values as sacred and many religious people protect as sacred something that originated in secular culture.[7] In both cases, "the outside is the inside," to quote Derrida.[8]

Deconstructing Plato

Derrida's early work was especially concerned with the last two binaries in the second chart above: the hierarchies of thought over language and speech over writing. He discusses the pre-Christian philosopher Plato, who assumed that attentive humans could conceive pure ideas in their minds, which they then put into language. Language was therefore a deficient but necessary tool for expressing Idea. Even more deficient, however, was writing, which was another step removed from pure Idea. Writing, for Plato, was a sign of weakness: not only did it demonstrate an inability to remember ideas but also "a writing cannot distinguish between suitable and unsuitable readers."[9]

---

[6]See, for example, Kevin Hart, *Postmodernism: A Beginner's Guide* (Oxford: Oneworld, 2004), pp. 10-12. Tyler Roberts notes that "Derrida's 'turn to religion' involves a complex effort to deconstruct settled oppositions between the religious and the secular, as well as between the theological and philosophical." See "Sacrifice and Secularization: Derrida, deVries, and the Future of Mourning," in *Derrida and Religion: Other Testaments*, ed. Yvonne Sherwood and Kevin Hart (New York: Routledge, 2005), p. 274.

[7]Missionary Elisabeth Elliot, for example, generated a great deal of controversy in the 1960s when she indicted Christian missionaries for inserting American cultural values into their messages about Christian truth. In the same year that Derrida first challenged structuralism, she published a novel deconstructing an extant binary between the sacred and the secular. See *No Graven Image: A Novel* (New York: Harper & Row, 1966).

[8]Derrida puts an *X* over the word "is" in order to avoid making a universalist statement. See *Of Grammatology*, trans. Gayatri Chakravorty Spivak (Baltimore: Johns Hopkins University Press, 1974), p. 44.

[9]Plato *Phaedrus* 275e, trans. W. Hamilton (Harmondsworth, U.K.: Penguin, 1973), p. 97.

Plato's paradigm can be illustrated with the movie *Multiplicity* (1996). A character played by Michael Keaton has himself cloned so he can better handle his hectic schedule. Having a clone, he can finally be in two places at once—quite literally. But soon his clone decides he wants a clone, as does that clone-of-a-clone, and each clone is not quite as sharp as its predecessor. Thus the original Michael Keaton character is superior to all subsequent expressions of himself, which get further and further removed from his original form.

Similarly, Plato believed that all the realities of the sensible world get their qualities from corresponding Ideal Realities in a higher realm; in other words, things in the world function as clones of Ideal Form. Though thought can conceive of Ideal Forms, when someone puts that thought into speech a somewhat less-exact clone is created. Writing down speech generates an even more imperfect clone. Finally, using writing to create fiction is so far removed from Ideal Form that Plato bans it from his scheme for a utopian republic. Fiction, for Plato, is comparable to Michael Keaton's clone-of-a-clone-of-a-clone, who drools, trips and blathers like a lobotomized drunk—far removed from its Origin.

Derrida challenges the very notion of pure origins, deconstructing the superiority of thought to language and speech to writing by establishing that the "outside" elements (language and writing) are actually part of the "inside" (thought and speech). This is just a complicated way of saying what I've reiterated here: that language shapes thought, that our speech is "always already" (one of Derrida's favorite phrases) molded by "writing." In other words, the way we speak reflects traces—as though already written—of what we don't say: supplementary elements of language that shape thought before it is given voice. That which seems marginal—as writing seems to thought—is actually central to the phenomenon that seems to originate it. Through deconstruction, the "original" center is "decentered."

Derrida's terms are significant. *Deconstruction* is not the same as *destruction*. *De-centering* differs from *displacement*. Derrida is not out to *destroy* all binaries or to *displace* Western philosophy with nihilism. In his famous essay challenging structuralism, "Structure, Sign and Play in the Discourse of the Human Sciences," Derrida asserts that "we cannot do without the concept of the sign, for we cannot give up this metaphysical complicity without also giving up the critique we are directing against this complicity."[10] In other words, we need faith in the power of language in order to articulate the poverty of language. Derrida therefore borrows the idea of "unbuilding" (deconstruction) from the philosopher Edmund Husserl (1859-1938), in order to take apart assumptions that philosophers—especially modernist philosophers—take for granted.

Nevertheless, just as some Christians turn biblical guidelines into legalisms—the very thing the apostle Paul taught against—some postmodernists turn language or culture into an absolutist dictator that controls everything we do and say—the very thing Derrida warned against. Those postmodernists who regard language as deterministic, such that it entirely negates free will, merely invert the binary, placing language over thought and writing over speech. Hence, in my opinion, they deserve the disdain of the leftist critics who attack them.[11] Derrida, in contrast, neither destroyed nor inverted binaries; he demonstrated their inherent deconstruction, showing how each term contains a trace of the other. The "outside" is "always already" part of the "inside."

Deconstructing Modernism

Significantly, Derrida inspired a form of postmodern architecture called "Deconstructivism," which was exhibited at New York's Museum of Modern Art in 1988.[12] Deconstructivist architecture destabilized the relationship between "inside" and "outside," using unusual materials built into odd angles and forms to create confusion as to whether you were looking at part of the inside or the outside of the building, or even whether the building were finished. Deconstructivist architecture has not caught on, largely because it is so unremittingly ugly. Like a bunch of Dr. Frankensteins, its practitioners discovered that a fascinating idea could appear monstrous when actualized.

---

[10]Derrida, "Structure, Sign and Play," p. 281.

[11]Some of the most famous leftist attackers of postmodernism are Alex Callinicos (*Against Postmodernism: A Marxist Critique,* 1989), Fredric Jameson (*Postmodernism, or the Cultural Logic of Late Capitalism,* 1991), Christopher Norris (*What's Wrong with Postmodernism?* 1990, and *The Truth About Postmodernism,* 1993) and Terry Eagleton (*The Illusions of Postmodernism,* 1996).

[12]At the entrance to the show was a statement that defied the sleekly geometric, autonomous form of Modernist buildings: "Pure form has indeed been contaminated, transforming architecture into an agent of instability, disharmony and conflict." See Lucy Peel, Polly Powell and Alexander Garrett, *An Introduction to Twentieth-Century Architecture* (London: Quantum, 1989), p. 106.

Though Derrida advised architect Peter Eisenman on Deconstructivist designs, he is better remembered for his deconstruction of *intellectual* edifices: the binaries of Western tradition. Notice how three of the binaries listed in my chart above are especially relevant to modernism:

natural	reason	objectivity
cultural	belief	subjectivity

As we have seen, modernists assumed they could achieve objectivity through autonomous reason. And once the power of reason became the dominant term in the modernist binary, it led to a repudiation of Christianity. Indeed, if *reason* is the *natural* way to discover *objective* truth, belief is unnecessary. Faith, for the modernist, becomes a matter of subjective desire: the psychological (if not psychotic) need to identify with the conventional beliefs of a particular religious culture.

Derrida, along with other poststructuralist thinkers of the 1960s (most notably Roland Barthes and Michel Foucault), challenged these modernist hierarchies by pointing out how

1. culture molds our sense of the natural
2. trust in reason is a kind of belief
3. a subject's language shapes her sense of "objective" truth

In each case, a trace of that which is "outside" the natural, the reasonable or the objective is actually "inside" it. Following are some examples.

Natural/Cultural

Most people assume that it's only "natural" to ooh and ah over the Alps. After all, we hang pictures of snow-capped peaks on our walls and plan vacations to soak up gorgeous Swiss sights. The poststructuralist does so as well, but might, in addition, point out how often Americans, when hiking to the Matterhorn, say of the mountain, "It's just like the one at Disneyland!" Perception of the Matterhorn's significance is molded by culture. But there's better proof than this that the "natural"—an emotive response to Alpine beauty—is actually "cultural."

For me, the discovery was a shock. While studying the English Romantic writers, who wrote between 1789 and 1830, I read essays by earlier eighteenth-century authors against whom the Romantics defined themselves. One of these so-called Neoclassical writers referred to the "terrible" Alps and

dismissed the Swiss as "besotted" with their mountains, "silly" for considering them beautiful. After further research, I discovered that this opinion was
not the idiosyncrasy of a nearsighted dolt. In the seventeenth century, the
Christian poet John Donne (who is responsible for the antimodernist phrase
"No man is an island") referred to mountains as "warts" on "the face of the
earth."[13] His opinion was shared by most of his peers, who described mountains with such metaphors as "tumours," "blisters" and "pimples." One seventeenth-century visitor to Switzerland wrote that the Alps looked "as if nature had here swept up the rubbish of the Earth"; another described the
Swiss mountains as "one of the most irregular, mis-shapen scenes in the
world." Furthermore, this disgust for mountains was not limited to the English. When one of the kings of France had a chateau built in the Alps for his
mistress, he did not include any windows facing the mountains. And he
equipped his carriage with shades so he could block out distressing views
of those horribly angular peaks. In the seventeenth century, such actions
were only "natural" because mountains were considered "unnatural": "unnatural Protuberances upon the Face of the Earth," as Cambridge professor
Henry More put it.[14]

So what happened? Why do we see mountains so differently today?

Nature changed because culture changed.

As Marjorie Hope Nicolson explains, "During the first seventeen centuries
of the Christian era, 'Mountain Gloom' so clouded human eyes that never for
a moment did poets see mountains in the full radiance to which our eyes have
become accustomed." This is due, in part, to Jewish and Christian expositors
of the Bible who held that mountains resulted from human sin. For some it
was the Fall of Adam and Eve, for others the sin in Noah's day, that had led
to mountainous "Ruins upon Ruins in monstrous Heaps." The Alps, then, as
"ruins of a broken world," demonstrated the ugliness of human depravity;
they were warts, pimples and boils on the once beautiful skin of the Earth.

According to Nicolson, things started to change when seventeenth-
century telescopes revealed that mountains exist where humans don't:

---

[13]John Donne, "The First Anniversary," in *The Variorum Edition of the Poetry of John Donne*,
ed. Gary Stringer (Bloomington: Indiana University Press, 1995), 6:13.

[14]I thank sculptor Ted Prescott for the information about the king of France, a story he learned
from Hans Rookmaaker. The quotations about seventeenth-century distaste for mountains all
come from Marjorie Hope Nicolson, *Mountain Gloom and Mountain Glory: The Development
of the Aesthetics of the Infinite* (New York: W. W. Norton, 1963), pp. 76, 35, 42, 62, 116. Nicolson, by the way, was an early fan of C. S. Lewis.

on other planets. Though untouched by human sin, astronomical bodies are as "pock-marked" as earth. This discovery, along with early modern emphasis on reasoned analysis of empirical data, destabilized theological explanations for irregularities on Earth's face. This allowed for mountains themselves to become the empirical data of geological exploration, and descriptions of them in the eighteenth century turned more and more to appreciative, if still intimidated, awe. (Remember that our word *awful* is etymologically related to the word *awe*.) By the early nineteenth century, a distinguishing characteristic of the Romantic poets was their reverential awe; they proclaimed the glories of mountains in ways that seem most "natural" to us.[15]

Modernists would tend to explain this transition from "mountain gloom" to "mountain glory" as a casting aside of superstitious religious culture in order to freely embrace "natural" perceptions, and they might quote from Nicolson's book *Mountain Gloom and Mountain Glory:* "What men see in Nature is a result of what they have been taught to see—lessons they have learned in school, doctrines they have heard in church, books they have read." Nicolson, however, provides evidence that followers of the Romantic poets were no less "learned" in their perceptions of mountains than medieval Christians had been: "As the [nineteenth] century went on, the traveler, armed with . . . the poems of Wordsworth, Byron, and Shelley, gazed at the Alps . . . and felt, or thought he felt—or pretended to feel—as . . . Wordsworth actually had felt": ecstasy over the majestic beauty of mountains.[16] Nicolson thus demonstrates a deconstruction of the modernist privileging of "natural" perception over religious "cultural" authority. The "natural" is colored by the "cultural," such that even nature is not "natural": it is inevitably defined by the grammar of cultural values.

Reason/Belief

Derrida, of course, was not the first person in the twentieth century to challenge the primacy of reason over belief; he and his fellow poststructuralists were simply the first people to get widespread respect for it—at least from the secular academy. At the height of modernism, Christian scholars were questioning the legitimacy of modernist "rationality"—largely because it was used to dismiss their faith.

---

[15]Ibid., pp. 3, 72-112, 278, 206, 131, 186-87.
[16]Ibid., pp. 3, 372-73.

In the 1930s, for example, Christian philosopher Herman Dooyeweerd argued in his magnum opus, *A New Critique of Theoretical Thought*, that rational thinking is based on pretheoretical assumptions that are religious in nature; for him there is no such thing as religiously neutral "reason."[17] Not long afterward, detective fiction writer Dorothy L. Sayers published a book called *Begin Here* (1940), in which she describes "the Modern Era" as the time in which "Reason" became the "supreme object of human devotion," worshiped in "the sacred name of progress." Sayers challenged this sanctification of reason and progress by arguing that faith—exactly what modernists placed outside of reason—is very much a part of it: modernists had faith that reason could lead them to the truth.[18] The outside (faith) is "always already" part of the inside (reason).

Sayers's friend C. S. Lewis expressed similar skepticism about the modernist elevation of reason over faith. In a 1946 essay called "'Bulverism,' or the Foundation of Twentieth Century Thought," he notes how both Marxists and Freudians, in their pretense of scientific objectivity and rational progressivism, dismiss Christianity as "ideologically tainted." But then he goes on to argue that "Freudianism and Marxism are as much systems of thought as [is] Christian theology":

> The Freudian and the Marxian are in the same boat with all the rest of us [Christians], and cannot criticize us from the outside. They have sawn off the branch they were sitting on. If, on the other hand, they say the taint need not invalidate their thinking, then neither need it invalidate ours. In which case they have saved their own branch, but also saved ours along with it.[19]

What Marxists and Freudians consider "outside" their systems—belief—is actually inside them. By repudiating Christian belief, they destroy their own tree. Lewis, in contrast, challenges the hierarchy of reason over faith in order to save the tree.

Inspired by Lewis and Sayers, this book you are reading right now (assuming you haven't yet thrown it against the wall) celebrates deconstruction of the reason/faith binary. I need to emphasize this point, because my reiterated disdain for Enlightenment reason might lead you to think I am en-

---

[17]For a helpful overview of Dooyeweerd's thought, see Brian Walsh and Jon Chaplin, "Dooyeweerd's Contribution to a Christian Philosophical Paradigm," *Crux* 19 (1983): 8-22.
[18]Dorothy L. Sayers, *Begin Here: A War-Time Essay* (New York: Harcourt Brace, 1941), p. 66.
[19]C. S. Lewis, "Bulverism," in *God in the Dock: Essays on Theology and Ethics*, ed. Walter Hooper (Grand Rapids: Eerdmans, 1970), p. 272.

dorsing unreflective fideism (blind faith). But I do not want to invert the hierarchy, turning faith into something that repudiates reason (the way Enlightenment reason repudiated faith). I like how theologian Kevin Vanhoozer acknowledges deconstruction within the reason/faith binary:

> *I believe in reason.* Reason is a God-designed cognitive process of inference and criticism, a discipline that forms virtuous habits of the mind. *I reason in belief.* Reasoning—giving warrants, making inferences, analyzing critically—does not take place in a vacuum but in a fiduciary framework, a framework of belief.[20]

Objectivity/Subjectivity

With the deconstruction of the reason/faith binary comes the deconstruction of objectivity over subjectivity. This is what really worries people. The destabilization of objectivity allows any bizarre opinion to go unchallenged. If a man says, "The moon is a big gooey ball of Gorgonzola cheese," and we protest, he can simply retort, "Well, it is true *for me!* Truth, after all, is subjective!"

But this is not what postmodernism asserts. Such a definition of subjectivity presupposes the modernist notion of radical individualism. The postmodernist, however, does not say that every person sees what he wants to see, that all truth is "subjective." If anything, some postmodernists go to the opposite extreme, asserting the "death of the subject." This hyperbole means the same thing that Derrida means by "there never was any 'perception'": humans are not autonomous subjects entirely in control of their perception. Instead, they are *subjected to* the language of their culture, which shapes the way they see things. Language molds subjectivity, as when I was molded to see Alan May as gorgeous and "flesh" as pinkish beige. For the postmodernist, all seeing comes from a certain standpoint, and depending on where and when you are standing—York in the seventeenth century or New York in the twenty-first century—you will see things differently. They call this standpoint your "subject position." Subjectivity for the postmodernist, then, is not individualistic; it is corporate, reflecting a community's model of truth.

While some postmodernists therefore assert that there is no objective truth "out there" to be discovered, such a conclusion does not harmonize

---

[20]Kevin J. Vanhoozer, "Pilgrim's Digress: Christian Thinking on and About the Post/Modern Way," in *Christianity and the Postmodern Turn: Six Views,* ed. Myron B. Penner (Grand Rapids: Brazos, 2005), p. 87.

with deconstruction. To eliminate the idea of objective truth altogether merely inverts the hierarchy, such that subjectivity trumps all possibility of objectivity. Deconstruction of the binary, in contrast, exposes how the outside is part of the inside, and vice versa: our subjectivity operates in response to objective truths, but our knowledge of those truths is always implicated by the models that shape our subject positions.

C. S. Lewis, who believed in objective truth, also recognized that we understand most truths according to our culture's interpretive models. In lectures he gave at Cambridge University in the 1950s, later published as *The Discarded Image*, Lewis discusses how the Christian culture of the medieval period interpreted the universe according to a certain "Model" that turned out to be wrong. Modernists, in reaction, established that scientific reason had enabled humans to progress beyond superstitious belief to objective truth. Lewis deconstructs this concept of scientific objectivity by asserting that modernism simply supplies another "Model"—a "construction" he calls it—of truth:

> In every age the human mind is deeply influenced by the accepted Model of the universe. . . . We can no longer dismiss the change of Models [from the premodern to the modern] as a simple progress from error to truth. No model is a catalogue of ultimate realities, and none is a mere fantasy. Each is a serious attempt to get in all the phenomena known at a given period, and each succeeds in getting in a great many. But also, no less surely, each reflects the prevalent psychology of an age almost as much as it reflects the state of that age's knowledge.[21]

Lewis here sounds much like Thomas S. Kuhn, who has been compared to the postmodern Michel Foucault. Kuhn argued in 1962 that scientific "discoveries" occur not due to the autonomous genius of individual scientists who rise above culture, as modernists argued, but due to "paradigm shifts": changes in the *models* under which scientists operate and which shape the way they see reality. And he defines a scientific paradigm as a "constellation of beliefs."[22]

Similar to postmodernists versed in deconstruction, neither Lewis nor Kuhn denies the existence of factual "evidence." They simply assert that the *interpretation* of evidence is not purely "objective." Contemplating the fu-

---

[21]C. S. Lewis, *The Discarded Image: An Introduction to Medieval and Renaissance Literature* (Cambridge: Cambridge University Press, 1971), p. 222.

[22]Thomas S. Kuhn, *The Structure of Scientific Revolutions*, 2nd ed. (Chicago: University of Chicago Press, 1970), p. 175.

ture "death" of the model under which his culture was currently operating, Lewis states, "The new Model will not be set up without evidence, but the evidence will turn up when the inner need for it becomes sufficiently great. It will be true evidence. But nature gives most of her evidence in answer to the questions we ask her."[23] And the questions we ask depend on the way we see reality: the subjectivity of our subject position. As Lewis scholar David C. Downing puts it, "Like Derrida, Lewis emphasizes that all analysis is situated, that there is no position of utter objectivity from which one may think about thinking itself."[24]

Other Lewis scholars might brandish Lewis's essay "The Poison of Subjectivism" as a sword to disembowel this argument. But it must be remembered that Lewis wrote "The Poison of Subjectivism" during the height of modernism, when the word *subjectivity* meant something quite different. In fact, postmodern theorists would agree with Lewis's assertion in "The Poison of Subjectivism" that it is a "fatal superstition" to believe that humans "can create values, that a community can choose its 'ideology' as men choose their clothes."[25] Such a "superstition" reflects the modernist belief in the autonomy of reason and radically free choice. In contrast, the poststructuralist would say that the language and practices of our culture not only guide our choice in clothes but also mold our values.

Even in *The Abolition of Man*, which argues for unchanging moral values, Lewis describes "objective value" as a "*doctrine*," a "*belief* that certain attitudes are really true, and others really false."[26] This belief includes the idea of a God whose very essence defines the good and the true—a standard above and beyond the subjectivity of language. As Lewis puts it in "The Poison of Subjectivism,"

> God neither obeys nor creates the moral law. The good is uncreated; it never could have been otherwise; it has in it no shadow of contingency; it lies, as Plato said, on the other side of existence. It is the *Rita* of the Hindus by which the gods themselves are divine, the *Tao* of the Chinese from which all realities proceed.[27]

---

[23]Lewis, *Discarded Image*, pp. 222-23.
[24]David C. Downing, "C. S. Lewis Among the Postmodernists," *Books & Culture*, November/December 1998, p. 37.
[25]C. S. Lewis, "The Poison of Subjectivism," in *Christian Reflections*, ed. Walter Hooper (Grand Rapids: Eerdmans, 1967), p. 73.
[26]C. S. Lewis, *The Abolition of Man* (1947; reprint, New York: Macmillan, 1973), p. 29, emphasis mine.
[27]Lewis, "Poison," p. 80.

Notice how Lewis acknowledges that people of different cultures—Platonists, Hindus and Buddhists—perceive some "objective" standard beyond their language but describe it, and hence *see* it, only through the language in which they are situated. Objectivity is "always already" subjected to language.

Biblical Deconstruction

C. S. Lewis and Dorothy L. Sayers sound, at times, like advocates of deconstruction because they were well-educated not just in the Bible but in how Christians for two millennia have interpreted the Bible. They were aware that anti-Roman zealots of Christ's day assumed their long-anticipated Messiah would invert extant hierarchies through revolutionary means: placing the Jew over the Roman, the pauper over the priest, the downtrodden over the dignitary. But Jesus offered, instead, deconstruction, destabilizing binaries that privileged male access to God over female, priest over publican, Jewish over Samaritan, law over grace.

Despite Jesus' teaching and example, letting go of binary hierarchies did not come easy for his followers. Simon Peter had to be put "into a trance" in order to get him to renounce binaries of his culture. The tenth chapter of Acts recounts Peter's vision of a "large sheet coming down" to earth. Lumped together in the sheet were animals usually kept separate from each other in Peter's culture, some distinguished as "clean" and others as "unclean." After hearing the Lord's voice tell him three times to disregard the distinction between clean and unclean, Peter finally realized that the binary oppositions of clean and unclean, circumcised and uncircumcised, Jew and Gentile, were to be dismantled (cf. Acts 10:45). In the imagery of his vision, that which had once been considered "outside" the sheet of acceptability was now "inside."

Peter's experience was a dream compared to the waking nightmare of Paul. Before his conversion, the then-named Saul helped execute Christians in order to protect a binary important to his identity:

<u>following the God of Abraham</u>
following the Christ of Nazareth

He, like many Jews, probably thought disciples of Jesus were trying to invert the binary, establishing Jesus as more important than the God of Abraham, Isaac and Jacob. Such fears should make us very sympathetic to Saul's position. According to Christian tradition, however, followers of Christ were recognizing a deconstruction, rather than inverting the either-or binary. By asserting that to follow Jesus was to continue to follow the Hebrew God, early Christians established that the "outside" of God—Jesus—was always already "inside."

Saul, however, was so adamant about the truth of his position that God had to put him into more than a Peter-like trance. It's as though Saul had to experience deconstruction in the body before he would release his white-knuckled grasp of the Jewish/Christian hierarchy. Sure enough, his Damascus Road experience deconstructed a clear distinction between darkness and light, between blindness and sight. For, upon seeing the light, he went blind (Acts 22:11). And only when he was in darkness could he see Christ's truth. Significantly, Derrida discusses Saul's blinding in *Memoirs of the Blind,* first published in 1990.[28]

Having experienced, in the flesh, a deconstruction between blindness and sight, Paul developed a strong sense that the "new self" in Christ does not perpetuate binary hierarchies, either by legalistically adhering to them or by iconoclastically inverting them. As he tells the Galatians: "There is no longer Jew or Greek, there is no longer slave or free, there is no longer male and female; for all of you are one in Christ Jesus" (Galatians 3:28). He slightly changes the list for the Colossians: "There is no longer Greek and Jew, circumcised and uncircumcised, barbarian, Scythian, slave and free; but Christ is all and in all" (Colossians 3:11). That which is outside ourselves, Christ, has come inside ("in all"), encouraging the deconstruction of problematic distinctions.

Battle for the Binary

Ironically, since the time of Peter and Paul, all too many antagonisms among Christians have resulted from rigid adherence to binary oppositions. The medieval church reinstated Saul's Jewish/Christian binary by inverting it, condoning an anti-Semitism that has marred Christianity for centuries. Ignoring another New Testament deconstruction, medieval attitudes toward the sacraments sometimes seemed to privilege law over grace, a hierarchy especially abused in the granting of indulgences (purchasing a quicker passage through Purgatory) and simony (gaining positions in church leadership for a fee). Practices like these generated Martin Luther's

[28]Jacques Derrida, *Memoirs of the Blind: The Self-Portrait and Other Ruins,* trans. Pascale-Anne Brault and Michael Naas (Chicago: University of Chicago Press, 1993), pp. 116-17.

protest against excesses in the church, manifest especially in his desire to undermine the works/faith binary: to *re*-form it.

Ironically, some Christian reformers in the sixteenth and seventeenth centuries suspicious of the works/faith and faith/works binaries—the Anabaptists—were persecuted by Roman Catholics and Protestants alike. Their gruesome deaths, recounted in *The Bloody Theater or Martyrs' Mirror of the Defenseless Christians Who Baptized Only upon Confession of Faith, and Who Suffered and Died for the Testimony of Jesus, Their Savior, from the Time of Christ to the Year A.D. 1660,* illustrate the extreme measures to which people go to protect their binary constructions.

The story of Dirk Willems in *The Martyrs' Mirror* provides an apt illustration of the Anabaptist refusal to follow an either-or binary. Running across a frozen lake to escape a persecutor, Willems heard his antagonist fall through the ice behind him. Rather than thinking in terms of good/bad, self/other, authentic believer/hypocritical Christian (and thus praising God that his tormentor was destroyed), Willems turned to help his enemy (see Luke 6:27).

Figure 5.1, a woodcut from *The Martyrs' Mirror,* pictures Willems on top

Figure 5.1. A woodcut of Dirk Willems from *The Martyrs' Mirror* (Lancaster Mennonite Historical Society)

of the ice, as if on the top level of a binary, lending a hand to pull his submerged assailant up to his level. Because of this act of grace, Willems was captured by the rescued man, who, refusing to renounce his clear-cut binary of true believer (himself) over apostate Christian (Willems), led his savior to his death. (Sound familiar?)

As Willems shows, honoring the deconstruction of binaries is not easy. Most people like clear-cut, indisputable distinctions between good guys and bad guys, saved and unsaved, sheep and goats. Because of this, many Anabaptists today seem to have returned to the works-over-grace hierarchy: Old Order Mennonites and the Amish are so committed to orthopraxis (right actions) that they will "shun" members of their group who break the rules. In the twentieth century, one Amish woman was shunned for putting pockets on her dress, a man for putting tires on his tractor.

I run the same kind of risk. Delighted with how postmodernism has served my faith, I get close to inverting the modernist hierarchy of reason over belief, making Enlightenment humanists sound like wicked witches seeking to destroy the ruby slippers of faith. My intention, however, is to return us to a place where faith and reason are interdependent, one not eschewing the other. To get there, however, the great Oz of unbiased autonomous reason must be exposed as illusionary; for when it comes to thought, there is always already a human behind the curtain.

Maintaining binaries—sometimes by inverting them—is so easy that many of Derrida's followers strayed from deconstruction by stumbling into "political correctness." Welcoming his message that those traditionally marginalized by dominant culture—gays, blacks, women—should be given voice, these followers missed Derrida's point and merely inverted the hierarchy, repudiating straight white males. As postmodern theologian Mark C. Taylor stated in his obituary for Derrida, "Betraying Mr. Derrida's insights by creating a culture of political correctness, his self-styled supporters fueled the culture wars that have been raging for more than two decades and continue to frame political debate." In contrast, Derrida argued that "it is necessary to recognize the unavoidable limitations and inherent contradictions in the ideas and norms that guide our actions, and do so in a way that keeps them open to constant questioning and continual revision. There can be no ethical action without critical reflection."[29]

---

[29]Mark C. Taylor, "What Derrida Really Meant," *New York Times,* October 14, 2004, p. A29.

Divining Deconstruction: The Religious Implications

You may feel uncomfortable right now, thinking that I've turned deconstruction into a religious enterprise. But I didn't have to; Derrida did so before me—much to the chagrin of those hardcore modernists who attacked deconstruction early on. One of Derrida's most respected commentators, John Caputo, explains that "deconstruction comes down to an affirmation or hope or invocation which is a certain *faith* . . . in something that pushes us beyond the sphere of the same, of the believable, into the unbelievable, that which exceeds the horizon of our pedestrian beliefs and probabilities."[30]

Even Christian intellectuals who are suspicious of postmodernism often value deconstruction. Kevin Vanhoozer calls deconstruction "the single most helpful contribution of postmodernity to Christian thinkers," due to its "radical protest against oppressive systems of thought."[31] Rather than relishing a backward-looking position of protest, however, Derrida, especially in his later years, emphasized a forward-looking position of trust: trust that deconstruction might open us up to "the other," trust that there is Justice beyond the limitations of language.[32]

Although deconstruction is about faith in an "Event" that surpasses all understanding—what Derrida calls "the messianic"—he does not endorse any particular religion. Nevertheless, his sense that *in the beginning was the word*—in so far as words mold thought—provides an anchor for the ark of Christianity, which had been put to sea during the reign of modernism.[33] For in addition to establishing that the Word precedes human reason, Christian orthodoxy asserts that "the Word was with God, and the Word was God. He was in the beginning with God. All things came into being through him, and without him not one thing came into being. What has come into being in him was life, and the life was the light of all people" (John 1:1-4).

[30]John Caputo, *The Prayers and Tears of Jacques Derrida: Religion Without Religion* (Bloomington: Indiana University Press, 1997), p. 64.
[31]Vanhoozer, "Pilgrim's Digress," p. 80.
[32]Derrida writes, "Justice remains, is yet, to come, *a venir*, it has an, it is *a venir*, the very dimension of events irreducibly to come." See Jacques Derrida, "Force of Law: The 'Mystical Foundation of Authority,'" in *Deconstruction and the Possibility of Justice*, ed. Drucilla Cornell, Michel Rosenfeld and David Grey Carlson (London: Routledge, 1992), p. 27. Derrida's "turn to religion" has been charted in two volumes by Hent de Vries: *Philosophy and the Turn to Religion* (Baltimore: Johns Hopkins University Press, 1999), and *Religion and Violence* (Baltimore: Johns Hopkins University Press, 2002).
[33]Derrida actually said, "In the beginning is hermeneutics," meaning that the word, even the beginning word, must be interpreted; truth is never self-evident. See Derrida, *Writing and Difference*, p. 67.

Christians, therefore, are not called to protectively cling to words that re-inforce cultural hierarchies. They are called to follow the Word: a Person who, in living flesh (and probably not pinkish beige flesh), challenged easy distinctions between inside and outside, between the sheep and the goats.

6   Building Truth

THE CULTURAL CONSTRUCTION
OF KNOWLEDGE

W hen I first learned about deconstruction, I was not overly threatened, perhaps because I was reared in a house where the outside was quite insistently part of the inside. The 1881 edifice in which I grew up—the one with the infamous dining-room table—was filled with Old World charm and New World life forms. At night, before we turned out the light, my sister and I would count the daddy longlegs on the ceiling, checking their location in the morning. If I awoke before dawn, my eyes met the hypnotic stare of a ghostly barn owl perched on a tree limb outside my window. It and its brood resided in the large palm tree by the dining-room door, the house serving as their well-stocked rodent pantry. In the still of the night we could often hear the clicking claws of critters scurrying inside the walls. Once, rummaging in a little-used drawer built into the dining-room wall, I uncovered the perfectly preserved skull of a squirrel. The most pernicious pests, however, were the bees in the attic. Delighted when we no longer heard the steady buzz above our heads, family members were dismayed when honey from the abandoned honeycomb started dripping down bedroom walls.

This continual visitation of unwelcome creatures generated childhood nightmares in which scary figures invaded my house. In one dream, a mad scientist in a white lab coat chased me out of my brother's bedroom. As I ran down the stairs, cellar doors opened before me, exposing the skeletons of my parents. Awaking at that moment, I jumped out of bed, turned on the light and paced the room till dawn, terrified of sleep.

I still have architectural dreams, but now I am the invader, wandering around or through a building, enjoying the aesthetics of its construction. I survey edifices in my waking life as well, taking advantage of historic house tours, both official and unofficial. On my jogs through the Pennsylvania countryside, when I come upon owners of a centuries-old farmhouse who happen to be working in their garden, I often stop to chat in the hope that they will invite me in for a peek. Even my dissertation—for a Ph.D. in English—builds on my dreams, as it examines the ways characters in fiction and poetry respond to architecture.

This persistent edifice complex, I am arguing, helped break down my initial resistance to postmodernism. Building on my interest in postmodern architecture, I started to study postmodern theorists. After several years of excruciatingly difficult reading, I came to realize that the postmodern emphasis on the "cultural construction of knowledge" awakened intellectuals from the dream of modernism: the dream that science and art had successfully replaced Christ as the salvation of humanity.

You, however, may regard my reference to the "cultural construction of knowledge" as too much like my childhood nightmare—a disturbing concoction of a brain disconnected from reality, providing only a skeletal image of truth. Let me affirm right now that I do believe the absolute truth of a God who transcends all cultural constructions.

"But how is that possible?" some wonder as I chase them down new stairs of thought. Keeping a wary eye on the cellar door, they query, "How can you believe that knowledge is culturally constructed but also hold on to absolute truth?" That, of course, is what this book is about, and if readers object that I can't logically support a paradox, all I can answer is that, as a Christian, I have committed my life to following paradox: I believe in Jesus Christ, who, though fully human, remained fully God, who died and yet lives. Thus, just as theologians work to make sense of these paradoxes, so this book works to make sense of absolute truth in relation to competing constructions of knowledge. This chapter offers one way to understand a postmodern view of cultural constructions, suggesting how it might serve Christian faith.

A History of the Cultural Construction of Knowledge

As we have seen, Enlightenment modernists assumed that universal truth could be ascertained by anyone, anywhere, through an intelligent exercise of unbiased reason. Because of this assumption, many concluded that people of non-European cultures explained reality oddly because their reasoning abilities were only "primitive." The modernist remedy, of course, became "the white man's burden": to educate primitives in European thought processes so that they could "logically" discover the truth on their own. (And as we have seen, one of the "truths" modernists "discovered" was that Christians perceived reality in primitive ways.)

Scholars in the social sciences challenged such Enlightenment assumptions as early as the 1930s. Rather than seeing "primitive" peoples as deficient in their reasoning abilities, anthropologists suggested that natives of non-European cultures both perceived and processed reality differently from Europeans. The mode of reasoning that one culture considered "logical" might be considered "illogical" in another. In 1937, E. E. Evans-Pritchard published his research on the Azande, concluding that these Sudanese people employ a rationality at variance with Western forms of reasoning. Four years later, Benjamin Whorf's study of Hopi Indians in America argued that the very language in which a native speaks affects the way she reasons.[1] In other words, rather than endorsing an evolutionary view of culture in which so-called primitive tribes have yet to evolve "authentic" rationality, these anthropologists were arguing for relative rationalities—decades before the word *poststructuralism* pursed the lips of postmodern theorists.

Around the same time, philosophers started challenging the logical positivism of high modernism: the philosophy positing that only language about scientifically verifiable facts can be considered "true." In 1935 Karl Popper argued that scientific facts are themselves molded by the theoretical assumptions of the scientific community and hence can be doubted. In the same decade Ludwig Wittgenstein, whose *Tractatus Logico-Philosophicus* (1921) was celebrated by logical positivists, started questioning his own positivism. While in the *Tractatus* he argued that certain kinds of language conform to the structure of reality, he later turned this assumption on its head. In *Philosophical Investigations* he argued that reality conforms to the way we use language, that reality is defined by our "language games."

Two ways to talk about the construction of knowledge thus developed around the same time. The social construction of knowledge was made famous in the social sciences when Peter Berger and Thomas Luckman pub-

---

[1]Paul O'Grady, *Relativism* (Montreal: McGill University Press, 2002), pp. 151-52, 132-33.

lished their 1966 book *The Social Construction of Reality: A Treatise in the Sociology of Knowledge.*[2] It was Wittgenstein's concept of "language games," meanwhile, that fueled much of the early work of poststructuralist theorists. In order to understand how postmodernists conceptualize the cultural construction of knowledge, then, we must consider Wittgenstein's famous idea.

Playing Wittgenstein's Games: Jean-François Lyotard

Jean-François Lyotard discusses Wittgenstein near the start of his watershed book *The Postmodern Condition:*

> What [Wittgenstein] means by [language games] is that each of the various categories of utterance can be defined in terms of rules specifying their properties and the uses to which they can be put—in exactly the same way as the game of chess is defined by a set of rules determining the properties of each of the pieces, in other words, the proper way to move them.[3]

To give other words for Lyotard's "other words," Wittgenstein does not mean that reality is merely whatever we want it to be—that one day we choose to "play" life as a football game and the next day as a volleyball tournament, or that one day we decide to play by the rules of young earth creationism and the next by those of evolution. Instead, Wittgenstein means that the way we perceive reality—whether following the assumptions of fundamentalist Christianity or scientific materialism—is molded by the way language works in those different arenas; we can't step in and out of language at will.

A football player, for example, functions according to the rules of the game, not only acting but also *willing* his actions according to the boundaries of those rules. In the middle of a game, a quarterback will not suddenly decide, *I want to play volleyball now!* and proceed to toss the pigskin up in the air with his fingertips and spike it onto the bent-over backs of the opposing linemen. If he did, he wouldn't be playing football anymore; it wouldn't be the same reality, because the rules of football are what define the reality. Similarly, it wouldn't be Christianity anymore if someone said, "I am a Christian but I don't believe in God." I use this example because there are people who say this. But they are playing by "rules" different from those

---

[2]Peter Berger and Thomas Luckman, *The Social Construction of Reality: A Treatise in the Sociology of Knowledge* (Garden City, N.Y.: Doubleday, 1966).
[3]Jean-François Lyotard, *The Postmodern Condition: A Report on Knowledge,* trans. Geoff Bennington and Brian Massumi (Minneapolis: University of Minnesota Press, 1984), p. 10.

of orthodox Christianity, which assumes the existence of God. As Lyotard puts it, "If there are no rules, there is no game."[4]

Nevertheless, a football player can suggest a "new play" that no one has ever thought of before, as long as it harmonizes with the existing rules of the game. Sometimes a new play gains such popularity that those with authority over the game decide to change the rules. This happened when the National Football League decided to initiate a new rule: rather than being able to kick one-point field goals only after touchdowns, professional teams now have the option of going for a two-point conversion by running or passing the ball into the end zone.

So also the "language game" of Christianity changed in the sixteenth century after Luther challenged the rules of the Roman Church, suggesting, among other things, that the diction of "indulgences" and "penance" resulted in problematic behavior. Luther, of course, was trying to change the rules from within; it's just that rather than playing a "Hail Mary," he was emphasizing the play of "grace" in a radical new way. Ultimately, however, Luther was forced to define Protestant Christianity as a different language game from Roman Catholicism, even though the two shared many of the same rules of faith.

Playing Wittgenstein's Games: Richard Rorty and Michel Foucault

Postmodernist Richard Rorty also borrows Wittgenstein's phrase "language games," asserting that philosophy itself is a kind of "language game." In contradistinction to analytic philosophy, which operates under the assumption that a rigorous employment of both reason and language can get one closer to the truth, Rorty believes that philosophic analysis has its own biased rules—something Christians should consider, since it was the rigorous employment of "unbiased" cognitive philosophy that dismissed Christianity as intellectually untenable. Rorty, who achieved his fame as a philosopher, has moved away from it, saying that an analysis of poetic principles in language—especially metaphor—gets us closer to the way people define truth.

For Michel Foucault, one of the major influences on postmodern thought, even one's sense of self is a result of language games. Throughout his career he was to ask, "What are the games of truth by which man pro-

---

[4]Ibid.

poses to think his own nature when he perceives himself to be mad; when he considers himself to be ill; when he conceives himself as a living, speaking, laboring being; when he judges and punishes himself as a criminal?"[5] He therefore rigorously studied the language games of different historical periods in order to argue that definitions of sickness, insanity and criminality, varying from culture to culture, define selfhood differently. He ended his famous 1969 book *The Archaeology of Knowledge* by addressing those Enlightenment humanists who think that reason has allowed them to be autonomous individuals: "You may have killed God beneath the weight of all that you have said; but don't imagine that, with all that you are saying, you will make a man that will live longer than he."[6] In other words, humans cannot be "human" apart from the language games with which they define "the human." This is what he meant when he talked about "the death of the self."

Foucault and the (Post)structuring of Culture

With "the death of the self," Foucault became one of the major postmodern architects of the cultural construction of knowledge. In books written from 1961 until he died in 1984, he analyzed how societies in different eras defined, in radically different ways, madness versus reason, sickness versus health, criminal punishment versus rehabilitation, and sexual propriety versus deviance. From his historical research he concluded that "power produces knowledge."[7]

Foucault did not mean by this that "all knowledge is made up by people with power"—that exceptional individuals can rise above their culture to effect widespread change. Such an assumption better caricatures aspects of modernism than Foucault's postmodernism. Indeed, the modernist emphasis on the power of genius to shape culture sometimes generated what sound like conspiracy theories: tales of social constructions built by the powerful few. Certain Marxists, for example, suggested that the bourgeoisie willfully perpetuate an ideology that keeps workers in their place, with Christianity functioning as an "opiate" that anesthetizes any impulses toward

---

[5]From Foucault's *The Use of Pleasure* (1984), quoted in Alan Ryan, "Foucault's Life and Hard Times," *New York Review of Books,* April 8, 1993, p. 12.

[6]Michel Foucault, *The Archaeology of Knowledge,* trans. A. M. Sheridan Smith (New York: Pantheon, 1972), p. 211.

[7]Michel Foucault, *Discipline and Punish: The Birth of the Prison,* trans. Alan Sheridan (New York: Viking, 1979), p. 27.

revolt. Some modernist feminists explicitly blamed men for conspiring against females by willfully withholding the vote, and they often asserted that the Christian emphasis on wives' submission was employed to keep power in the hands of white males.

The Foucauldian poststructuralist, in contrast, assumes that "cultural constructions" are not willfully erected by power-hungry people. They are instead empowered by "discourse," the shared assumptions of a society that are embedded in and transmitted through language. Rather than attacking males, therefore, poststructuralist feminism analyzes an era's "construction" of gender—one entered into by both males and females alike—discussing how and why different eras define the capabilities of women differently.

Victorian doctors, for example, argued that women's minds cannot function as well as men's because women have less blood available to nourish their brain (due to their monthly cycle). Similarly, some Victorian doctors argued that adolescent girls must avoid all competition, both academic and athletic, for it would injure their reproductive systems.[8] Despite the outrageousness of these views, the postmodern critic does not express outrage toward Victorian doctors and dismiss them as sexist so much as analyze what it was about their culture that nurtured and sustained such ideas. So also they would argue that the hesitancy about women's suffrage in England and America was not a male conspiracy to keep women under their thumb so much as a reflection of cultural constructions that the majority of people, both male and female, regarded as "true."

Christians need to think more earnestly about the cultural construction of knowledge, remembering that followers of Christ in one era used the Bible to "reasonably" argue against women's suffrage, while equally earnest disciples in the next used different verses to "reasonably" argue the opposite.[9] To help with this thinking process, I want to share my earliest encounter with the word *construction*.

---

[8] See Janet Oppenheim, *"Shattered Nerves": Doctors, Patients and Depression in Victorian England* (New York: Oxford University Press, 1991), pp. 190, 254.
[9] At the suffragists' convention of 1886, a Mrs. Meriwether pronounced, "We can overwhelm [ministers] with arguments for woman suffrage—with Biblical arguments." In contrast, a Christian bishop in the early twentieth century used Jesus' words to argue against the vote for women. See Susan B. Anthony and Ida Husted Harper, *History of Woman Suffrage* (Rochester, N.Y.: Susan B. Anthony, 1902), 4:76; and Lovat Dickson, *H. G. Wells: His Turbulent Life and Times* (New York: Atheneum, 1969), pp. 221-22.

Constructive Towers of Knowledge

In grammar school I enjoyed working with construction paper, relishing the brilliant colors that could be cut and pasted on top of each other. Only now do I realize that the word *construction* referred to the fact that the stiff paper might be rolled and folded into shapes that hold their form, at least if you used enough of that tasty white paste.

Imagine yourself with a large sheet of construction paper that you cover with written statements of things your parents reiterated throughout your childhood: *Share your toys. A soft answer turns away wrath. Don't bite your fingernails—or playmates. Think of all the starving children in* _____ *[name the country of your parents' choice].* In your mind, roll the paper into a tube, with the writing on the inside, and tape it upright onto a piece of cardboard, so that it looks like a tower. Finally, think of the movie *Honey, I Shrunk the Kids* and imagine yourself inside that construction-paper tower, surrounded by the statements of your parents. These statements mold your existence; they are the truths that gave shape to your childhood reality. Neither you nor your parents made the statements up; what is written on the construction-paper walls reflects the values of their cultural affiliations. If you were to remain in that tower, you would assume that all these statements reflect absolute, universal truth, for that is all you know: the construction of discourse that surrounds you defines the good, the true and the beautiful.

Of course, sometimes the statements of your family tower, rather than spoken, are implied by the practices of your parents. Foucauldian theorists therefore refer as well to the "discursive practices" that mold perception. Take, for example, my father's experience as a young boy. Because his parents had moved into separate bedrooms after he was born, he was appalled the first time he visited a friend's house and discovered that her mother and father slept not only in the same room but also in the same bed! Attempting to gently inform the girl about the deviance of her parents' behavior, he pointed out that at school males and females had separate bathrooms and were not allowed to undress in front of each other. In other words, he was able to explain the "correctness" of his parents' sleeping arrangements by the rules of culture—a tower of language that surrounded his own family's tower.

To understand this, you need to imagine that the construction paper of your tower is actually transparent, like a plastic tube, so that the statements written on it are clearly perceived, but you can nevertheless see out beyond the words that encircle you. Our family towers of truth are embedded in larger cultural towers of truth that we can read beyond our family values, and to which we often appeal to justify the way our family does things. Our thinking is therefore formed by transparent language towers surrounded by larger towers, which are themselves surrounded by transparent towers and so on. Think of one person's tower constructions according to figure 6.1—a bird's-eye view of various constructions that affect our perceptions, though not always embedded in this order.

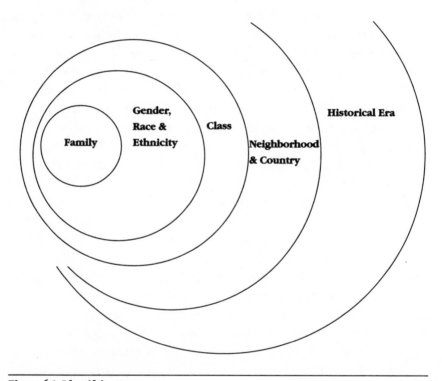

Figure 6.1. Identifying towers

Discursive Practices

Anyone who has spent some time in another country can testify to different constructions of "proper" behavior. My first experience happened in England during my college years. A friend and I were standing side by side, talking with less than subdued excitement, as we waited in line to get tickets for the London Underground. Feeling a tap on my shoulder, I turned, only to have a blue-haired lady tilt her head up so she could look at me through the bottom half of her bifocals while shrilly piping, "Here in England *we* queue properly." Not wanting to be an ugly American, I moved directly behind my friend and stopped talking as both of us faced squarely forward and proceeded to walk in lockstep toward the cashier.

All of us have similar stories of cultural difference—how in other countries heterosexual men freely embrace and kiss in public, how in some societies loud burping after a meal functions as a compliment to the chef. In other words, the discourse of cultural constructions affects us through the practices of those who surround us, practices reinforced by the spoken and written word.

It is for this reason that many people choose to homeschool their children, or to at least monitor television watching—for good reason. A study published in the respected journal *Pediatrics* reports that "watching sex on TV predicts and may hasten adolescent sexual initiation. . . . Alternatively, parents may be able to reduce the effects of sexual content by watching TV with their teenaged children and discussing their own beliefs about sex and the behaviors portrayed."[10] In other words, if parents draw attention away from the larger tower of contemporary sexual ethics back to the discourse written on their own family's tower, they can help shape behavior.

Nevertheless, many parents, having molded a child in a Christian tower, worry that the discourse of surrounding cultural constructions—the language written on other towers—will not just encourage the child to rebel and choose activities outside the family tower but will affect the child's *very definition* of right and wrong. After all, if a child knows her actions are "wrong" (which, in fact, may be part of her attraction to them), she is still being shaped by the discourse of her home life, acknowledging it as "true." However, leaving behind her parents' tower of knowledge, she may come to genuinely believe the language on surrounding towers that says there is nothing wrong with casual sex. Her knowledge is socially constructed.

And it's not just adolescents who stop looking at phrases from their Christian tower in order to focus on messages of the culture that surrounds them.

---

[10]R. L. Collins et al., "Watching Sex on Television Predicts Adolescent Initiation of Sexual Behavior," *Pediatrics* 114 (September 2004): 843.

While a mere thirty years ago divorce was considered something that evangelical Christians avoided, except under unusual circumstances, evangelicals today have been so molded by the discourse of surrounding towers that their divorce rate equals (some studies say exceeds!) that of American society as a whole.[11]

Religious Constructions

You may be wondering why I left out "religion" from my tower diagram above. There are several reasons. First, religion functions differently in different people's lives. For some, it is merely part of the discourse of their ethnicity—as in "Of course I'm Catholic; I'm Irish!" Second, sociologists have pointed out how class affects the expression of faith: the majority of Episcopalians are upper-middle to upper class while Pentecostals tend to be working class. In other words, the tower of religion is often embedded inside the tower of class. Third, even among white evangelicals "right" and "wrong" are often defined differently, depending on the cultural constructions of the country from which they come. My father tells of an incident in the 1960s when he was involved planning an international conference for the Christian Businessmen's Committee (CBMC). As U.S. delegates greeted German delegates in the airport, both were shocked by the other. The Germans couldn't believe how U.S. Christians had submitted to the prurient practices of secular society by allowing Christian women to wear bright red lipstick. Meanwhile, Americans were appalled that the Germans sullied "the temple of the Holy Spirit" by smoking cigars.

Of course, what divided these Christians was far less important to most of them than what united them: belief in a loving God who took human form, triumphing over the grave after dying on the cross. However, within this tower of Christian orthodoxy, Christians through the ages have constructed smaller towers and have often regarded the language of their tower as containing the only authentic way to know the truth of Christ. For example, until Vatican II in the 1960s, Roman Catholics taught that salvation through Christ could be achieved only through their church; in other words, Protestants were going to hell. Understandably, Protestants protested the exclusivity of this tower, pointing out the beliefs they held in

---

[11]For this and other examples of evangelical capitulation to surrounding cultural values, see Ronald J. Sider, *The Scandal of the Evangelical Conscience: Why Are Christians Living Just Like the Rest of the World?* (Grand Rapids: Baker, 2005).

common at the saving core of Christianity.

Catholics, of course, respond that Protestants have erected their own "infallible" tower: the Bible, the "Paper Pope of Protestantism," as some have described it. They also point out that, even if the Bible is as "infallible" as the pope, the Protestant emphasis on "the priesthood of all believers" leads to a multiplicity of biblical interpretations—towers within the tower of "Bible-believing" Christianity. And of course they are right. Protestantism contains within it numerous smaller towers, sometimes at odds with each other. Southern Baptists, American Baptists, Wisconsin Synod Lutherans, Evangelical Lutherans, Episcopalians, Methodists, Dutch Mennonites, the Dutch Reformed and so on often interpret the Bible differently at various points.

Figure 6.2 pictures how the tower of Christianity might look from the inside. Though all of the expressions of Christianity look differently depending what country and era they are surrounded by, Catholics might justifiably accuse Protestants of contributing to the "relativism" of postmodern culture. For without the guidance of a Holy Spirit-inspired pope who keeps Christians united in doctrine, any interpretation of Scripture might be constructed as long as enough people enter that particular tower of language to help maintain it. Indeed, while Mormons and Christian Scientists consider themselves Christians, many evangelicals would evict one or more of these faith traditions from the encompassing tower of Protestant Christianity.

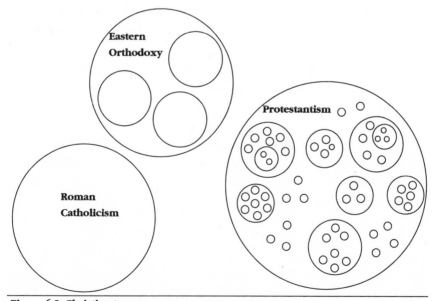

Figure 6.2. Christian towers

Fighting Relativism

Some Christians avoid accusations of relativism by asserting that their tower of language is the absolute truth and that all other expressions of Christianity are in error. For example, several years ago at the Christian college where I teach, I was accused of blasphemy by a student's mother after I said, in the classroom, that Jesus was tempted by lust according to the epistle to the Hebrews: "For we do not have a high priest who is unable to sympathize with our weaknesses, but we have one who has been tempted in every way, just as we are—yet was without sin" (Hebrews 4:15 NIV). The tower in which I grew up interpreted "tempted in every way" to mean "in *every* way," with lust among the "every." However, the accusing mother, who suggested that I should be fired for my blasphemy, evidently occupied a religious tower that did not allow any sexual references to Jesus on its walls. Ironically, Christians from other towers might point out that a denial of Christ's sexuality is a denial of his humanity—a denial proclaimed to be heresy early in church history.

A more tragic example can be seen in the persecution of Anabaptists in sixteenth- and seventeenth-century Europe. As we have seen (chapter five), these ancestors of Amish and Mennonite Christians criticized Lutheran Reformers for not taking the Reformation far enough. They thus incurred wrath from both Catholics and Protestants, who often burned Anabaptists at the stake.

What belief could generate so much animosity toward Anabaptists from other Christians? It was their stand on infant baptism. Because Anabaptists believed that individuals should not be baptized until they can make an intelligent assent to Christianity, other Christians executed them. And when some Anabaptists sang praises to Jesus on the way to their martyrdom, their tongues were forcibly stopped: sometimes their mouths were filled with gunpowder, other times wooden screws were used to hold down their tongues.

Ironically, of course, many evangelical Christians like myself grew up in a tower that established the Anabaptist view of baptism as the *only authentic* Christian belief—even though the Bible says nothing about an age of accountability for baptism. Thus, what the majority of Christians regarded as false teaching in one century is considered by many to be biblical truth several centuries later.[12]

---

[12]For a fascinating overview of how beliefs among evangelicals have changed over the centuries, see David Bebbington, *The Dominance of Evangelicalism: The Age of Spurgeon and Moody* (Downers Grove, Ill.: InterVarsity Press, 2005).

The Tower of Babel

When one tower of Christian discourse sets itself up as the absolute truth overriding all other Christian denominations, it becomes like the Tower of Babel. What strikes me about the story in Genesis is the arrogance of the builders, who believed that their construction could reach God:

> They said, "Come, let us build ourselves a city, and a tower with its top in the heavens, and let us make a name for ourselves; otherwise we shall be scattered abroad upon the face of the whole earth." The LORD came down to see the city and the tower, which mortals had built. And the LORD said, "Look, they are one people, and they have all one language; and this is only the beginning of what they will do; nothing that they propose to do will now be impossible for them. Come, let us go down, and confuse their language there, so that they will not understand one another's speech." (Genesis 11:4-7)

Though many people read this account as a primitive folktale explaining the myriad languages of the world, it gives much more honor to God if read not as divine worry over human power but as God's response to the presumption that humans can attain a God's-eye view of things. When Christians persecute Christians, whether through literal or figurative "firing," they presume that their construction of language is the true one: the tower that reaches into the heavens, the tower that encompasses the mind of God. But in the Babel story God undermines such an effort, causing a plurality of languages, as though to say no one language can capture absolute truth.

I am not the first to read the Babel story this way. In 2000, Christian philosopher James K. A. Smith stated, "The sin of Babel was its quest for unity—one interpretation, one reading, one people—which was an abandonment of creational diversity and plurality in favor of exclusion and violence." Five years before him, J. Richard Middleton and Brian J. Walsh began their discussion of Christianity and postmodernity by drawing a parallel between the Tower of Babel and modernism. Later in their book they acknowledged that Christians likewise "tend to construct perspectives, worldviews and metanarratives that erase difference and marginalize whatever does not fit." Significantly, years before Smith, Middleton and Walsh, Jacques Derrida wrote an essay called "Des Tours de Babel," arguing that in the Genesis 11 story God "opens the deconstruction of the tower, as of the universal language."[13] Moreover, while Derrida was still a

---

[13]James K. A. Smith, *The Fall of Interpretation: Philosophical Foundations for a Creational*

child, Christian theologian Reinhold Niebuhr published an essay titled "The Tower of Babel" to argue that

> true religion is a profound uneasiness about our highest social values. Its uneasiness springs from the knowledge that the God whom it worships transcends the limits of finite man, while this same man is constantly tempted to forget the finiteness of his cultures and civilisation and to pretend a finality for them which they do not have. Every civilisation and every culture is thus a Tower of Babel.[14]

Moving to Other Towers

Unlike those people who believe their particular tower rises above all others to encompass a universal language of truth, many Christians within their towers look beyond the language of their own Christian constructions to appreciate the reasons Pentecostals speak in tongues, Old Order Mennonites wear head coverings and Catholics go to confession. Often this appreciation will lead individuals to leave their particular tower of Christian discourse in order to enter another, some being attracted to the liturgy and ritual of the Episcopal Church, others to the guitars and clapping of charismatic worship.

Most Christians are comfortable with the move from one Protestant tower to another, many with a move from Protestantism to one of the earlier Christian traditions. But few would (or should) feel comfortable with the idea that all religious towers are alike and that it is a matter of personal preference whether one follows Christ or Krishna. This is not what postmodernism is about, nor is it what I am about. I believe in the absolute truth of God and have committed my life to following God Incarnate, Jesus Christ. This is not a faith I picked out of a smorgasbord of religions, preferring it to others as I do pecan pie to pumpkin. If anything, I believe that God picked me, placing me in a family that encouraged me to love the Lord my God with my whole heart, mind and soul. In other words, the tower I was born into developed my responsiveness to God—an idea consonant with the biblical in-

---

Hermeneutic (Downers Grove, Ill.: InterVarsity Press, 2000), p. 33; J. Richard Middleton and Brian J. Walsh, *Truth Is Stranger Than It Used to Be: Biblical Faith in a Postmodern Age* (Downers Grove, Ill.: InterVarsity Press, 1995), p. 170; Jacques Derrida, "Des Tours de Babel," trans. Joseph F. Graham, in *Poststructuralism as Exegesis,* ed. David Jobling and Stephen D. Moore (New York: Society of Biblical Literature, 1992), p. 7.

[14]Reinhold Niebuhr, *Beyond Tragedy: Essays on the Christian Interpretation of History* (New York: Scribner's, 1937), p. 28.

junction "Train children in the right way, / and when old, they will not stray" (Proverbs 22:6).

In this light, the idea that we are situated in towers of knowledge gives new meaning to the ages-old paradox of free will versus determinism. The multiple towers in which God has placed us shape our knowledge and practices even as we have a certain amount of freedom to roam among them. And admittedly, some people roam farther than others. Nevertheless, if we think in terms of transparent towers-within-towers of discourse, we can understand how the language written on the walls of surrounding cultural towers can seem vibrantly enticing to some children, drawing them away from the faith of their parents. This, of course, is consonant with orthodox Christian doctrine: God controls the direction of our life *and* we have the choice to freely follow Christ—or not. But notice: it is not a matter of religious picking-and-choosing, as though we could stand outside all towers in order to decide on "the best." The sanctification of personal choice is a modernist idea, based on the elevation of autonomous reason, which, as we have seen, eventually severed many intellectuals—and those they influenced—from God.

A Postmodern View of Reason

To understand the postmodern view of reason—strongly influenced by Foucault's *Madness and Civilization* (1961)—return again to your scissors and paste. Imagine setting up numerous construction-paper towers in an area as large as a football field. This field, surrounded by the high walls of a stadium, we will consider the tower of the twenty-first century. Now imagine its grass covered with a huge sheet of cardboard. This cardboard is the base on which you tape your transparent construction-paper tubes, standing them on end to make them look like towers rising up from the ground. As tubes, your towers have neither tops nor bottoms, so you can place smaller ones within larger tubes, as in figures 6.1 and 6.2 above. While you work on the concentric towers of Christianity, nearby one of your Jewish friends is taping down the embedded towers of Judaism, and beyond that your Muslim doctor has secured the embedded towers of Islam.

Consider the cardboard base, or ground, "reason." Now, if you think of the "Honey-I-Shrunk-the-Kids" within their language-inscribed towers, you recognize that people inside can see reason as the cardboard beneath their towers: a ground on which they are built. However, "reason" may look different from inside different towers, since it follows the contours of each particular tower's language. This illustrates the poststructuralist assumption that the various discourses surrounding us shape our awareness of the reason on which our thinking stands. Most people, of course, think their tower's form of reasoning to be correct, for it "grounds" the construction that makes sense out of life. For them, it seems only "common sense" to think the way they do. But "common sense" often differs from culture to culture.

Enlightenment thinkers, of course, naively assumed that when they exited religious towers they left behind narrow, confining perspectives to freely roam an open cardboard field of reason where truth was immediately accessible to the "freethinking" mind. The word *freethinker*, in fact, emerged at the beginning of "the Age of Reason" to designate "one who refuses to submit his reason to the control of authority in matters of religious belief; a designation claimed esp. by the deistic and other rejecters of Christianity at the beginning of the 18th c." *(OED)*. Freethinkers thought that reason enabled them to escape all encircling influences. And many modernists today, assuming they think freely and act autonomously, remain oblivious to ways that the surrounding discourse shapes their perceptions and behavior. In contrast, poststructuralists would point out that upon leaving one encircling construction of language, everyone, including themselves, merely enters into a larger surrounding tower.

This, however, does not imply that reason is eliminated from human consciousness. The cardboard ground is still there; it just takes different shapes under different towers.

The Prison Tower of Language

In *Discipline and Punish: The Birth of the Prison* (1975) Foucault uses a tower to explain how discourse has the power to shape knowledge and behavior. He discusses a plan developed by Jeremy Bentham, in the eighteenth century, for a prison that would inculcate "reasonable" behavior in its clientele. Called "Panopticon," the prison had cells built around a central tower from which a guard could watch each cell through windows.

According to Bentham, the prisoners, under constant surveillance from tower guards who expect certain behavior, would eventually conform to those expectations, whether they could see a guard watching them or not. They have internalized the behavioral constructions represented by the tower in order to police themselves. Foucault uses this as a metaphor for self-policing in any area of life:

It is not necessary to use force to constrain the convict to good behaviour, the madman to calm, the worker to work, the schoolboy to application, the patient to the observation of the regulations. . . . He who is subjected to a field of visibility, and who knows it, assumes responsibility for the constraints of power; he makes them play spontaneously upon himself; he inscribes in himself the power relation in which he simultaneously plays both roles; he becomes the principle of his own subjection.[15]

As in my construction-paper towers, it is the tower, representing discursive practices, that has power to regulate the knowledge of "correct" behavior. People think they are acting on their own when it is really their placement in particular towers that regulates their behavior.

Of course, in my transparent tower parable, individuals can wander among the various towers that encircle us—unlike the prisoners in Bentham's Panopticon. Nevertheless, poststructuralists assert that when we exit one tower, we enter either another adjacent to it or a larger tower that encircles them both. To bring this closer to home, they might say that people who "reject" Christianity, thinking they are leaving behind "religious constructions" for the freedom of rational thought, are merely entering into another construction: one built by modernism. Language, for the poststructuralist, is inescapable, leading one Marxist critic to describe our confinement to towers of discourse as "the prison house of language."[16]

Escaping the Prison House of Language

Ironically, it was people helped out by postmodernists' emphasis on the cultural construction of knowledge who led the most convincing assaults on its prison walls. In fact, it is due to these people that some consider postmodernism to be passé.

Poststructuralists drew attention to small towers on the periphery of the huge towers of twentieth-century Western countries. They did so in order to demonstrate that people in these towers perceive reality differently from those in the primary towers of culture. They are "other" to the dominant discourse. "Other" towers on the margins thus became important to postmodern discussions about "de-centering," giving respect to people who had formerly been disdained by modernists, from white portrait painters to black Pentecostal preachers.

---

[15]Foucault, *Discipline and Punish*, pp. 202-3.
[16]Fredric Jameson borrowed this phrase from Nietzsche for the title of his book *The Prison-House of Language* (Princeton, N.J.: Princeton University Press, 1972).

As margins became more central, thanks to poststructuralists like Derrida, minorities were given voice in a new way. And one of the things some voiced was a suspicion of poststructuralism.[17] They pointed out that if poststructuralism were taken to its logical extreme, such that every single human thought is a construction of culture, then people would be unable to identify injustice in their tower, let alone change it. After all, if discourse controls the very way individuals perceive reality, they are going to see the reality of their own culture as good—since their culture is what defines the good.

There is no question that people in one tower can see what is *bad* about other towers, as when Foucault endorsed the overthrow of the shah of Iran, visiting the country in 1978 to support the revolution. However, when Ayatollah Khomeini picked up the stones after the revolution and constructed a tower more imprisoning than anything built by the shah, Foucault and other Western-educated revolutionaries realized that their political assumptions could not be imposed on a Muslim culture from without. Change must happen from within. But how can change occur if culture controls the perceptions of its constituents? Such a poststructuralist scenario destroys any sense of agency—any sense that one can be an agent of cultural change from within a tower. The tower is a prison house of language.

People in formerly marginalized towers—black females, for example—were especially sensitive to this issue because they recognized how the dominant discourse of the tower in which their smaller towers were placed encouraged blacks and women to accept their status as less worthy of power and respect. Once poststructuralism gave them this insight, however, these minority scholars wanted to change the cultural tower in which they lived—the larger tower that controlled beliefs about minorities. In other words, they wanted *agency:* a concept of free will that allows people to alter the discourse of their own towers.

Agency Within the Towers: Postcolonialism

The issue of agency became especially pronounced in a field of study that grew out of poststructuralism: postcolonialism. Influenced by Edward Said,

---

[17]This became especially pronounced among black feminist critics. For a helpful overview of the white feminist appropriation of poststructuralism and the womanist response, see Elizabeth Abel, "Black Writing, White Reading: Race and the Politics of Feminist Interpretation," *Critical Inquiry* 19 (Spring 1993): 470-98.

who published *Orientalism* in 1978, postcolonialists discuss the effect of discourse on natives of European colonies. Such people were, and still are, shaped by the intersection of two towers: that of their native culture and that of the country that colonized them.

India is a prime example. In 1857 England established official rule of the subcontinent, setting up a civil service government and proclaiming Queen Victoria "Empress of India." Natives were taught to speak English and to follow English customs and mores. However, most natives still used their birth language when not interacting with their imperialist rulers. In poststructuralist terms, this meant that many natives were shaped by two radically different, often conflicting, discourses. To function, they might feel as if they were running back and forth between two touching towers, acting and thinking differently in each tower. So part of them felt British, part of them felt Indian. Imagine it like the image to the left in figure 6.3.

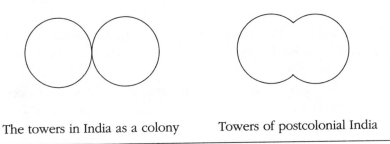

The towers in India as a colony   Towers of postcolonial India

Figure 6.3. Colonial and postcolonial towers

By the time India established self-rule, making it "post-colonial," multiple generations had lived a double-tower existence for so long that the two towers had merged, intersecting with each other, as on the right in figure 6.3. Unlike their ancestors, these postcolonial people do not feel like they are running back and forth between discourses. They are instead a hybrid of both. In fact, an Indian postcolonial scholar named Homi Bhabha characterizes their mental state as "hybridity." The descendants of colonized people are shaped by discourses both Indian and English. Problematically, however, the English part of their hybrid tower looks down on the native part of their hybrid tower as culturally inferior, and the English language perpetuates this inferiority. This can be demonstrated in connotations of the word *native*. Technically, the term is value neutral, as in "I am a native of California." However, when *native* is used by English speakers to refer to the once-colonized, non-white peoples of Africa and Asia, it elicits images of "primitive" behavior like head-hunting and wild dancers wearing animal pelts.

Because the discourse of Enlightenment progress fed European imperialism, postcolonialism, like postmodernism, is antimodernist. However, postcolonial studies also discusses how the hybrid subject might exercise agency to establish a sense of the self that neither submits to the English discourse of native inferiority nor hides out in the native part of the tower in naive denial of English influence.

Foucault himself seems to have changed his attitude about agency. Having once celebrated the "death of the self," he made an about-face, such that in 1980 he started talking about "the return of the self." Rather than focusing on the "domination" of discourse over knowledge, he started looking for "technologies of the self" that might allow individuals "to transform themselves," agreeing with Kant that "the ontological condition of ethics" is "free will." However, rather than returning to the secular humanism of modernism, Foucault was attracted to premodern models of free will: the restraint of Greek Stoics and the renunciation of medieval Christians. In a 1980 lecture at UC-Berkeley, he praised the "richness" of the Christian tradition, saying, "No truth about the self is without the sacrifice of the self."[18] This does not mean he became a Christian, at least as far as we know. But it does mean that his standing-room-only listeners were given a way to think about Christianity that differed from modernist sneers.

Beyond the Towers of Language: A Christian Response

Here's how people of faith might say that there is something beyond the prison house of language. Think again of the transparent towers that surround us. Rather than looking down to focus on the ground of reason in order to argue that our construction of religion is more "reasonable" than that of Hinduism or Islam—which is exactly what people in other towers are doing—we can look up to the light beyond all towers of language to believe in a God who transcends all human constructions. Here's how John the Baptist expressed it: "The one who comes from above is above all; the one who is from the earth belongs to the earth, *and speaks as one from the earth.* The

---

[18]Michel Foucault, "Technologies of the Self," in *Technologies of the Self: A Seminar with Michel Foucault,* ed. Luther H. Martin, Huck Gutman and Patrick H. Hutton (Amherst: University of Massachusetts Press, 1988), p. 18, and quoted in James Miller, *The Passion of Michel Foucault* (New York: Doubleday, 1993), pp. 318, 322, 333, 324.

one who comes from heaven is above all" (John 3:31 NIV, emphasis mine).

I think there is something quite profound about this view that God comes from heaven, a place "above." Of course, modernist skeptics use "heaven" as an example of the primitiveness of Judeo-Christian theology. After all, they say, science long ago established that the earth is round and the heavens not only surround us but are actually expanding as the edges of the universe move away from us at an incredible speed.

But perhaps the idea of God in heaven "above" the heavens was the Jews' Holy Spirit-inspired sense that God is above, or transcends, human understanding. As with the Tower of Babel, all attempts to reach God in language are deficient, since everyone "who is from the earth belongs to the earth, and speaks as one from the earth"—speaks according to the discourse of the towers in which he is embedded.

In his book *Miracles* C. S. Lewis discusses this issue: "Most certainly, beyond all worlds, unconditioned and unimaginable, transcending discursive thought, there yawns forever the ultimate Fact, the fountain of all other facthood, the burning and undimensioned depth of the Divine Life." However, Lewis makes clear, this does not mean that God is some amorphous, intangible entity. It is language that is too amorphous for God, who "is unspeakable not by being indefinite but by being too definite for the unavoidable vagueness of language."[19] Unfortunately, some Christians make language—the language inscribed on their particular tower—as definite as God, turning it into a Tower of Babel.

Christian Mysticism

For other Christians, the unreachable transcendence of the Absolute often generates hunger for mystical union with God that would elevate the soul above "the vagueness of language." Because Protestantism developed simultaneously with modernism, which emphasized reason and reading over mystery and sacrament, it has tended to be suspicious of mystical experiences. But mysticism has been part of orthodox Christianity for two thousand years. In his letter to the Romans, the apostle Paul alludes to God's mystical accommodation for the inadequacy of language: "The Spirit helps us in our weakness; for we do not know how to pray as we ought, but that very Spirit intercedes with sighs too deep for words" (Romans

---

[19]C. S. Lewis, *Miracles: A Preliminary Study* (New York: Macmillan, 1947), pp. 160-61, 193. The language of the Bible will be addressed in chapter eight.

8:26). Even more dramatically, Paul told the Corinthians about a man (pre-sumably himself) who "was caught up to the third heaven" where he "heard things that are not to be told" (2 Corinthians 12:2, 4).

Echoing Paul is Augustine, who is valued not only for articulating many of the doctrines considered orthodox in the Western church but also as "the Prince of Mystics." He writes in his *Confessions,* "I was swept away to you by your own beauty, and then I was torn away from you by my own weight and fell back groaning toward these lower things."[20] Seven centuries later, Bernard of Clairvaux (1090-1153) uses the same image of falling back after his mystical union with God: "Thee I often pass through in the heart, as I cannot in the body, for being earthly flesh and fleshly earth, soon I fall back."[21] Notice how all three engage the idea of God above—transcending—earthly existence.

Postmodern Mysticism: The Case of Lyotard

Significantly, several of the most famous poststructuralists have allowed for the possibility that there is something that transcends both reason and lan-guage. Take Jean-François Lyotard, for example. As we have seen (chapter two), Lyotard challenges the arrogance of modernist metanarratives, like those of Marxists and scientists who validate their truth claims through an appeal to universal reason. But, Lyotard argues, while such thinkers as-sume that their reason is unbiased, leading to self-evident truth, their thinking is actually shaped by language games. For Lyotard, then, when modernists impose their versions of truth on others, their behavior be-comes "terroristic"—a term that has special resonance for Americans after the destruction of New York's World Trade Center on September 11, 2001.[22] Those Twin Towers were destroyed by people who thought their own tower, or construction, of truth was pure; their terrorism was moti-vated by an assumption that everyone plays by a problematic "language game" except themselves.

In order to avoid terroristic attacks—both literal and metaphoric—Lyotard proclaims the need for "dissensus," rather than "consensus," about our truth

---

[20]*The Confessions of St. Augustine,* trans. Rex Warner (New York: New American Library, 1963), 7.17.153.

[21]Quoted in Rudolf Otto, *The Idea of the Holy: An Inquiry into the Non-rational Factor in the Idea of the Divine and Its Relation to the Rational,* trans. John W. Harvey (London: Oxford University Press, 1950), p. 35.

[22]Lyotard, *The Postmodern Condition,* pp. 10-13, 63-65.

claims: an agreement to disagree, as it were. However, he also endorses the idea that there may be something beyond language: "We can conceive the infinitely great, the infinitely powerful, but every presentation of an object destined to 'make visible' this absolute greatness or power appears to us painfully inadequate. Those are Ideas of which no presentation is possible. Therefore, they impart no knowledge about reality (experience)."[23] In other words, humans have a sense that there is a "greatness" that transcends our "experience" of "reality." It is so great, or "sublime," as Lyotard names it, that we cannot limit it to rational concepts.

Unlike modernists, then, Lyotard endorses our intuitions of transcendence, intuitions that allow for the existence of that which we cannot scientifically prove—like, perhaps, the "absolute greatness" of God. This may explain why, late in his life, Lyotard became interested in "the Prince of Mystics," Augustine. In *The Confession of Augustine,* Lyotard writes as though looking up through a glass-topped tower: "And yet, we from below, we scarcely read these signs that are still too high, still too dazzling. . . . We mumble our way through the traces left by the absolute that you are; we spell the letters."[24]

Opening a (La)can of Worms: The Case of Jacques Lacan

The distinction Lyotard makes between "reality" and "absolute greatness" was anticipated by Jacques Lacan (1901-1981), a French psychoanalyst and philosopher who influenced poststructuralism. Regarded today as a postmodern reinterpreter of Freud, Lacan distinguishes between "reality," as constructed by language, and the "real" that is beyond language. He calls language "the Law of the Father" to assert that both knowledge and behavior are shaped for us as soon as we enter into the symbolizing system (our towers) of words.

For an analogy, think of American children's belief in Santa Claus. Because parents tell them about Santa's roof-romping visits and society surrounds them with images of the rotund gift giver in stop-sign colors, children assume the "truth" of Santa's existence. Some even go through minitraumas when they discover that Santa is merely a cultural construction. His

---

[23]Ibid., p. 78.
[24]Jean-François Lyotard, *The Confession of Augustine,* trans. Richard Beardsworth (Stanford, Calif.: Stanford University Press, 2000), p. 40. See also *Augustine and Postmodernism: Confessions and Circumfession,* ed. John D. Caputo and Michael J. Scanlon (Bloomington: Indiana University Press, 2005), pp. 58-65, 82-88.

construction, in fact, operates like Foucault's Panopticon: from his North Pole guard tower, Santa surveys children's activities in order to reward them. He becomes an expression of "the Law of the Father"—language—that controls behavior.

Lacan, then, assumes all of language operates this way, molding perceptions not only of the proper and improper but also of the true and not true. Nevertheless, he asserts that a "real" exists beyond the "reality" written on our tower walls, generating an unquenchable "desire" for that which cannot be captured in language. Though we cannot reach the "real," hints of the "real" reach us, subtly invading our everyday reality in the form of dreams, slips of the tongue and odd bodily symptoms that have no physiological explanation.[25]

Though Lacan does not identify "the real" with any kind of mystical absolute, his hints of "the real" remind me of biblical and medieval stories of how God invaded the everyday reality of humans: Jacob's dream of the angels ascending and descending a ladder to heaven; an angel appearing in a dream to Mary's betrothed, Joseph; Saul struck blind on the Damascus Road; St. Francis bearing the mark of the stigmata, bloody wounds appearing on his hands and feet. Christians, then, might appropriate Lacan's constructs to say that even though language cannot capture the Real, the Real nevertheless makes itself felt, creating in us an unquenchable desire to know that which transcends reality.

Lacan had a strong influence on poststructuralist feminists, who argued for a knowledge that is "prediscursive": knowledge assimilated before discourse, "the Law of the Father," shapes the way we think. They relate prediscursive knowledge to the body, as in the wordless connection a mother has with her baby—communication based not on conventional language but on nursing, cuddling, rocking, cooing. Feminist scholar Kathryn Bond Stockton describes this prediscursive knowledge as "real-bodies mysticism": a "belief in something real that escapes and exceeds human sign systems."[26] But notice: as soon as one begins talking about prediscursive knowledge, one opens up the possibility that one can know in her heart—apart from language—that there is a God. As famously stated by the bril-

---

[25]Slavoj Zizek builds upon Lacan's religious implications in *The Fragile Absolute: Or, Why Is the Christian Legacy Worth Fighting For?* (New York: Verso, 2000).

[26]Kathryn Bond Stockton, *God Between Their Lips: Desire Between Women in Irigaray, Brontë, and Eliot* (Stanford, Calif.: Stanford University Press, 1994), pp. 13-14.

liant mathematician and apologist for Christianity Blaise Pascal (1623-1662), "The heart has its reasons, which reason does not know." But Pascal also acknowledged that "our linguistic instruments are too blunt ever to touch the truth."[27]

Significantly, several postmodern feminists influenced by Lacan—the most famous being Julia Kristeva and Luce Irigaray—started talking about God in their writings decades ago, as their emphasis on the body drew attention to what I would call the incarnational, rather than language-based, nature of truth. As Kristeva was to note in 1979, "Feminist ideology leaves the door open to the return of religion, whose discourse, tried and proved over thousands of years, provides the necessary ingredients for satisfying the anguish, the suffering, and the hope of mothers."[28]

An Impossible God: The Case of Jacques Derrida

The postmodern thinker most fully engaged with the "return of religion" is the famous godfather of deconstruction. This might come as something of a shock to anyone familiar with Derrida's oft-quoted aphorism "There is nothing outside of the text." This phrase, first published in *Of Grammatology* (1967), was Derrida's way of describing the multiple towers of language that surround us. For him, our view of reality is always conditioned by these verbal constructions, and, because every tower is either surrounded by or competing with other towers of discourse, there is no getting completely outside the towers of language to think independently of them. The best we can do is assess their "play" of language.[29]

By this Derrida does not mean we "play" freely with language on our tower walls. As we have seen, for him deconstruction is not something one

---

[27]Blaise Pascal, *Pensées and the Provincial Letters*, trans. W. F. Trotter (New York: Random House, 1941), p. 95; the second quotation is translated by and quoted in Peter Brooks, *Troubling Confessions: Speaking Guilt in Law and Literature* (Chicago: University of Chicago Press, 2000), p. 71.

[28]Julia Kristeva, "Women's Time," in *Critical Theory Since 1965*, ed. Hazard Adams and Leroy Searle (Tallahassee: Florida State University Press, 1986), p. 482. See also C. W. Maggie Kim, Susan M. St. Ville and Susan M. Simonaitis, eds., *Transfigurations: Theology and the French Feminists* (Minneapolis: Fortress, 1993).

[29]Jacques Derrida, *Of Grammatology*, trans. Gayatri Chakravorty Spivak (Baltimore: Johns Hopkins University Press, 1998), p. 158. James K. A. Smith similarly explains that "when Derrida claims that there's nothing outside of the text, he means that there is no reality that is not always already interpreted through the mediating lens of language." See his "Who's Afraid of Postmodernism? A Response to the Biola School," in *Christianity and the Postmodern Turn: Six Views*, ed. Myron Penner (Grand Rapids: Brazos, 2005), p. 225.

does; it is inherent in language itself. Therefore, rather than playing *with* language, Derrida wants to draw attention to the play *within* language—to its looseness, as in the "play" or "give" of a slack rope.[30] Because language is slack in its ability to fully contain absolute truth, Derrida hopes to move it aside, the way one might move a slack rope obstructing the view, so that those inside a tower might peer through the cracks to notice how people in other towers display truth differently. But notice, the only way to assess the play of language is to be inside the tower, acknowledging that the language of our tower defines our understanding of truth. As Derrida explains in *Of Grammatology,* "The movements of deconstruction do not destroy structures from the outside. They are not possible and effective, nor can they take accurate aim, except by inhabiting those structures. Inhabiting them *in a certain way,* because one always inhabits, and all the more so when one does not suspect it."[31]

To inhabit "in a certain way" is to constantly check for language's play, not only to draw attention to the constructed nature of our towers but also to create peepholes that enable us to see beyond to how other towers define reality and thus to open ourselves up to "the other." Significantly, Derrida uses the phrase "falling back"—reminiscent of the Christian mystics—to describe our efforts to see what is beyond the "closure" of our towers:

> Within the closure, by an oblique and always perilous movement, constantly risking falling back within what is being deconstructed, it is necessary to surround the critical concepts with a careful and thorough discourse . . . and, in the same process, designate the crevice through which the yet unnameable glimmer beyond the closure can be glimpsed.[32]

Then, toward the end of the 1980s, Derrida started looking up.[33] Rather than peering horizontally through the play of language on multiple towers-within-towers-within-towers, he took a vertical glance to consider what he called "*the* impossible": the existence of an unnameable glimmer of transcendence beyond language's ability to fully predict or define what it may be. It is "impossible" because the only way we can talk about the Above or

---

[30]See Niall Lucy, *A Derrida Dictionary* (Oxford: Blackwell, 2004), p. 95.

[31]Derrida, *Of Grammatology,* p. 24, his emphasis.

[32]Ibid., p. 14.

[33]Many would argue that theology was implicated in Derrida's work from the start. See Stephen D. Moore, *Poststructuralism and the New Testament: Derrida and Foucault at the Foot of the Cross* (Minneapolis: Fortress, 1994), pp. 21-25, 39-41.

Beyond is by naming it, which automatically limits it, pulling it back into our tower of language—like the "fall" back to earth of the Christian mystics.

Nevertheless, Derrida increasingly began to speak of the "possibility" of "the impossible," quoting famous Christian philosophers like Augustine, "the Prince of Mystics," and Kierkegaard, "the Knight of Faith" (1813-1855), as well as St. Paul. Derrida's phrase "the impossible" thus seems to echo Tertullian, the early church father (160?-230?) famous for saying *certum est, quia impossibile:* "It is certain, because it is impossible."[34]

As scholars pressed him on "the impossible," Derrida sometimes substituted the word *God* for it, while still calling himself an atheist. Then, at the 2002 meeting of the American Academy of Religion in Toronto, John Caputo, probably the most famous interpreter of Derrida,[35] asked the godfather of deconstruction to explain what he means when he says that he prays. In front of at least a thousand people (I know; I was there!), Caputo asked, "If you rightly pass for an atheist, to whom are you praying? How would your prayers be answered?"

Derrida's answer was long and complicated, but one of his statements reminded me of the moment I crawled out from under the dining-room table:

> When I pray, I am thinking about negative theology, about the unnamable, the possibility that I might be totally deceived by my belief. . . . I consider that this suspension of certainty, this suspension of knowledge, is part of an answer to the question, "Who do you expect to answer these prayers?" That suspension must take place in order for prayer to be authentic. If I knew or were simply expecting an answer, that would be the end of prayer. That would be an order—just as though I were ordering a pizza![36]

In other words, prayer for Derrida is acknowledgment of a possible Other so far beyond language that to give a name would be to enclose the Other

---

[34]Kevin Vanhoozer notes, "If there is a faith proper to postmodernity, it is this: a faith in these 'impossibilities'—impossible, that is, in terms of modern forms of thinking." See his "Pilgrim's Digress: Christian Thinking on and About the Post/Modern Way," in *Christianity and the Postmodern Turn: Six Views,* ed. Myron B. Penner (Grand Rapids: Brazos, 2005), p. 101 n. 25.

[35]See Caputo's essay "Confessions of a Postmodern Catholic: From Saint Thomas to Derrida," in *Faith and the Life of the Intellect,* ed. Curtis L. Hancock and Brendan Sweetman (Washington, D.C.: Catholic University of America Press, 2003), pp. 64-92. His most thorough work on religious elements in Derrida is *The Prayers and Tears of Jacques Derrida: Religion Without Religion* (Bloomington: Indiana University Press, 1997).

[36]A transcript of the interview with Derrida appears in *Derrida and Religion: Other Testaments,* ed. Yvonne Sherwood and Kevin Hart (New York: Routledge, 2005), pp. 27-49. I quote from pp. 30-31.

in his tower and thus limit that Other to human constructions, to a Tower of Babel. For Derrida, the prayers of many religious people reduce that Other to a cosmic delivery man who is at the beck and call of their individual tastes and preferences—with or without anchovies.

In contrast, the "negative theology" to which Derrida alludes is a component of Christian and Jewish mysticism, wherein God is described mainly in terms of what God is not, in acknowledgment that God far transcends all positive verbal descriptions.[37] One famous example of negative theology appears in a sixth-century text called *Mystical Theology*. In its prologue, the Christian author speaks as though placed inside a prison tower of language. Addressing the Trinity, he writes,

> Direct us towards mysticism's heights
> beyond unknowing beyond light beyond limit,
> there where the unmixed and unfettered and unchangeable
> mysteries of theology
> in the dazzling dark of the welcoming silence
> lie hidden, in the intensity of their darkness
> all brilliance outshining, our intellects overwhelming,
> with the intangible and invisible and illimitable:
> Such is my prayer.[38]

Derrida's interest in prayer and the "beyond" establishes a postmodern parallel with these premodern words.[39]

Responding to the God Above All Towers

If we conceptualize a God who transcends all towers of discourse, it implies that the same God can be seen from within the towers of all religions—as long as the people inside them choose to look up, seeking to know the one God who is above all language. This idea troubles most evangelicals and elicits ac-

---

[37]See Harold Coward and Toby Foshay, eds., *Derrida and Negative Theology* (Albany: State University of New York Press, 1992).

[38]Quoted in David C. Downing, *Into the Region of Awe: Mysticism in C. S. Lewis* (Downers Grove, Ill.: InterVarsity Press, 2005), p. 68. As one medieval scholar notes, Derrida engages "the tradition of apophatic spirituality that includes Meister Eckhart and Pseudo-Dionysius the Areopagite"—the latter being the author of the prayer I just quoted. See Bruce Holsinger, "Medieval Studies, Postcolonial Studies and the Genealogies of Critique," *Speculum* 77 (2002): 1224.

[39]Foucault's work has also been compared to negative theology. See James Bernauer, "The Prisons of Man: An Introduction to Michel Foucault's Negative Theology," *International Philosophical Quarterly* (December 1987): 365-80.

cusations of relativism. I therefore devote the entire next chapter to grappling with this disturbing problem. Until then, I want to share how I, committed to following Christ, deal with the postmodern concept of plural towers.

First of all, even though I can't *prove* that Christianity is true in a way that would satisfy a scientific materialist or logical empiricist, I can nevertheless testify that the tower of orthodox Christianity rings true to human experience—including my experience with language. What makes Christianity distinctive from other religions is the belief that since language cannot reach God, God reached down to us, taking the form of a servant who bore the sins of the world on his flesh. God chose to present the divine in human form, tangibly entering into our "reality," our "experience"—to use the words of Lyotard—even unto death. Jesus instantiates "real-bodies mysticism." Truth, for the Christian, is not a well-articulated proposition, it is a Person: "*I AM* the way, and the truth, and the life."

To embody the truth that shows us the way to life, God placed Jesus in a human position, situated among constructions of discourse: a male body placed in the Jewish tower, surrounded by Roman-ruled Palestine, of two thousand years ago. By taking on real-bodies flesh, God demonstrated that the body as well as its inherent situatedness—its inability to be located in more than one spot at a time—is part of the created order and therefore is "very good" (Genesis 1:31).

Positioned in the tower of orthodox Judaism, Jesus embodied what Richard Rorty calls the "strong poet": the "maker of new words, the shaper of new languages," that is, words and languages that enable individuals to think in new ways, to think outside the tower, as it were, while still identifying with it.[40] Christ's role as strong poet becomes most obvious through the parables; rather than simply delivering new propositions and rules to replace those of the Pharisees, Jesus creates poetic fictions (parables) that imaginatively describe how the truth is best *performed:* the prodigal son, the good Samaritan, the laborers in the vineyard, the ten maidens, the wise steward, the hidden talents. Furthermore, as a strong poet Jesus defied certain sentences on the tower in which he was situated by healing on the sabbath and touching the unclean. His miracles were parables made literal; one might call them *actualized* parables. Jesus, the Truth, made people free.

As followers of Christ, then, we are called to be living parables as well,

---

[40]Richard Rorty, *Contingency, Irony and Solidarity* (New York: Cambridge University Press, 1989), p. 20.

performing the truth in such a way that people will want to know the Strong Poet who transformed us into walking words of love. As Paul exhorted the Corinthians,

> Love never ends. But as for prophecies, they will come to an end; as for tongues, they will cease; as for knowledge, it will come to an end. For we know only in part, and we prophesy only in part; but when the complete comes, the partial will come to an end. . . . For now we see in a mirror, dimly, but then we will see face to face. Now I know only in part; then I will know fully, even as I have been fully known. (1 Corinthians 13:8-12)

In Paul's day, mirrors reflected "dimly" because they were usually made of polished metal. Hence, it would be unwarranted for someone in his culture to believe that she had an accurate picture of her own image. And Paul's context implies a similar lack of warrant for the Christian who assumes he has a clear and accurate vision of God.

Though mirrors are infinitely more accurate in our own day, Paul's metaphor of seeing "as in a mirror" should give us pause. For what we think we know about God is often a reflection of ourselves—selves shaped by the "tongues," "prophecies" and "knowledge" that are written on the walls of our "partial" towers. Unfortunately, some Christians seem to spend more time polishing their mirrors than looking up in holy awe to worship a God who exceeds their wildest imaginings.

Of course, Enlightenment modernists have long disparaged Christians for polishing their tower mirrors. However, their proposed solution was to tear down the towers of Christianity, saying they blocked one's view of rational, objective truth. In contrast, postmodernists teach that we are all embedded in towers of discourse—that it is impossible to conceptualize reality without them.

The Christian therefore has as much right to talk about knowing the truth as does the secular humanist. However, for the Christian, knowing the truth is not a matter of Enlightenment certainty over the "reasonableness" of specific propositions. It is a matter of trusting a Person, God Incarnate, who entered into our discourse-laden world. Confident in our convictions about this truth, we also humbly recognize that the word *confidence* means, quite literally, "with faith." Therefore, rather than idolizing the language engraved on our towers, Christians are called to have faith in a relationship, believing that God still reaches down into our experience by way of the Holy Spirit, the One who intercedes for us "with sighs too deep for words."

PART FOUR

From Relativism to the Relating of Faith

7   The Haunting of Relativism

Much of this book has been haunted by relativism, a ghost that got especially feisty among the construction-paper towers of the preceding chapter. Indeed, if all humans see reality through the discourse that surrounds them, as poststructuralists assert, how can Christians possibly "speak the truth in love"? If we agree with the postmodern deconstruction of objectivity, don't we become like Pilate, whose cynical question "What is truth?" paved the way for the death of God? This chapter will deal with the thorny issue of relativism, not only explaining its relation to postmodernism but also suggesting how Christians might nevertheless proclaim, "You will know the truth, and the truth will make you free" (John 8:32).

A Tricky Treatment of Relativism

My childhood home was especially fun at Halloween. Set back from the road on a gravel driveway, its seven gables were shrouded by overhanging trees, making the house look spooky even without the aid of construction-paper witches or skeletons. One memorable Halloween, my father decided to perform a role as he responded to the knock of trick-or-treaters. Hiding behind the front door, he emitted a creepy cackle as he opened it to costumed solicitors, most of whom screamed. Parents, however, kept coming back for repeat performances. My sister, brother and I were delighted that terrified children did not wait to get their Halloween candy, since it meant we would enjoy more leftovers. But we also felt baffled, never having seen this side of our no-nonsense father before.

Naturally, the various responses to the haunting laugh behind the door were relative to the context of the perceiver. Depending on the age and the relationship to my father of each participant, the same phenomenon was either frightening or funny—a real haunting or a great performance. This relativism, of course, did not undermine the fact that my father, and not a ghost, was behind the door.

Similarly, most postmodernists do not deny the existence of facts behind the doors of perception—facts that are better recognized and understood when one has more background knowledge, as do the parents of trick-or-treaters. However, postmodernists would attest that even facts can be affected by "positionality" and "discourse": one's position or placement in society and the language that society generates.

My first October in Pennsylvania, for example, I got in an argument about the "fact" of Halloween. I had just settled down in my favorite flannel nightgown to do some paper grading, when the doorbell rang at about 5:00 p.m. With embarrassment, I hid most of my body in its tattered flannel behind the door and stuck out my head to say "Yes?" A twelve-year-old girl, dressed as a witch, cheerily called out, "Trick or treat!"

As I opened the door wider, all I could think to say was "What do you mean?"

After a disconcerted pause, the girl explained, "Well, when I say 'trick or treat' you are supposed to give me candy."

Not wanting to appear like a flannel-clad dolt, I responded, "I know all that, but you're way too early. Trick-or-treat isn't till October 31, four days from now."

She paused, glancing into her yawning bag, before replying, "Nooooo, it's tonight."

As the witch glumly walked away, I honestly decided it was some kind of practical joke and returned to my grading. Ten minutes later the doorbell rang again, and this time my heart sank; perhaps it wasn't a joke! Sure enough, four ghoulishly costumed six-year-olds jubilantly greeted my raggedy gown with "Trick or treat!"

I intoned with rapidity, "I'm so sorry, but I'm from California, and in California we don't celebrate Halloween until October 31, and, you know, it's October 27 right now, and so I don't have anything for you because I wasn't going to do my shopping until tomorrow, and there's no grocery stores nearby, and, well, I am *so* sorry."

As the children continued to hold out their gaping bags, their smiles now turning to open-mouthed gasps of disbelief, one six-year-old finally said,

"It's OK lady: it's OK." Shoulders sagging under the weight of adult dysfunction, the ghouls turned to make the trek to a less quirky and more capable giver of goodies.

As soon as they were gone, I threw on a coat and drove to the nearest convenience store, where I explained to the clerk (nattily dressed as a pumpkin) how in California people don't give out candy until October 31. She just shook her head, as though to say, "You decadent Californians." As I later learned, my locale in Pennsylvania designates the Thursday before Halloween as trick-or-treat night, in order to safeguard children from adolescent excesses on October 31. An event the natty clerk and I both considered universal—at least for Americans—turned out be culturally defined.

This small incident, of course, does not imply the absence of universals or that "everything is relative." However, postmodern thinkers would assert that we make many assumptions—more than we realize—similar to those of my ghoulish and pumpkiny neighbors, who assumed a cultural construction to be universal practice.

Let me provide a more serious example. I distinctly remember the year that my parents no longer let me eat the popcorn balls and apples I brought home from trick-or-treating. They cited incidents in which children had either been poisoned by homemade treats or cut by razor blades hidden in fruit. At the time I sorrowed over the sullied holiday, but today most children take it for granted that perverts will try to get their jollies one way or another. The discourse of Halloween dramatically changed during my lifetime.

And I mean *discourse*. In 1985 sociologists Joel Best and Gerald Horiuchi published the results of extensive research about tainted Halloween candy. Studying twenty-six years of newspaper accounts, along with interviews of police and hospital workers, Best and Horiuchi came to the conclusion that "the number of kids critically injured by horrible Halloween misdeeds is" (are you ready?) "zero." They could find *no evidence* "that a kid has ever been killed or seriously injured by a contaminated treat received while trick-or-treating."[1] In other words, a fact that most Americans have believed true for decades turns out to be generated by discourse, a discourse so convincing that it has affected the behavior of Americans for several decades now.

---

[1]Quoted in Barry Fox, "Holiday Gets Its Spirit from Old Celtic Custom," *Patriot News* (Harrisburg, Penn.), October 25, 2002, p. 3. For the original study, see Joel Best and Gerald Horiuchi, "The Razor Blade in the Apple: The Social Construction of Urban Legends," *Social Problems* 32 (1985): 488-99.

"Who originated this discourse?" some may ask. Once again, that is a modernist question, for it assumes the power of autonomous individuals to initiate change. The postmodern poststructuralist, in contrast, says that discourse is generated by and through interaction within communities; it is socially constructed. Significantly, the authors of the Halloween candy study recognized the problem to be cultural, naming their report "The Razor Blade in the Apple: The Social Construction of Urban Legends." This is important to keep in mind as we consider postmodern relativism. For even the idea of relativism is socially constructed.

The Relativism of Relativism

Like the word *foundationalism* discussed in chapter four, the word *relativism* means different things in different contexts. For this reason, even a cultural conservative like Jacques Barzun objects to the way the word often gets dressed up like a Halloween bogeyman:

> In the realm of ethics, the most blatant absurdity of the day [2000] is wrapped up in the bogey word *Relativism*. Its current misapplication is a serious error, because it affects one's understanding of physical and social science and derails any reasoning about the morals of the day. Nine times out of ten, the outcry against Relativism is mechanical, not to say absentminded. Everybody is supposed to know what the term means; it has become a cliché that stands for the cause of every laxity; corrupt or scandalous conduct is supposed the product of a relativist outlook.[2]

Barzun implies that the word *relativism* has become a part of the discourse of the day, people viewing it like a razorblade in a popcorn ball. Philosopher Paul O'Grady also employs a Halloween term to assert that even individuals commonly called "relativists" speak against it:

> Relativism is nearly universally regarded as a bogeyman. Hardly any philosopher wants to be called a relativist; nearly everyone is against it—whatever it is. Even those who are regarded by their fellow philosophers as archetypal relativists vigorously deny that they are relativists and indeed launch strong attacks on what they see as relativism.[3]

There is good reason that so-called relativists—at least the intellectually

---

[2]Jacques Barzun, *From Dawn to Decadence: Five Hundred Years of Western Cultural Life, 1500 to the Present* (New York: HarperCollins, 2000), p. 761.
[3]Paul O'Grady, *Relativism* (Montreal: McGill-Queen's University Press, 2002), p. 3.

sophisticated ones—hate the term, for they know that relativism itself is relative to its contexts. Furthermore, as soon as someone says "Everything is relative," she makes an absolutist statement, implying that her own view of relativism is not relative. As theologian David K. Clark notes, such a position either "is self-referentially incoherent or commits the self-exempting fallacy."[4]

I am not arguing that relativism does not exist. What bothers me (as well as many others) is the indiscriminate use of the word *relativist* to attack someone who is sympathetic to alternate definitions of reality. If the redefinition of *truth* is relativistic, then Jesus was a relativist. Challenging traditional interpretations of the Fourth Commandment, for example, Jesus made the subversive statement "The sabbath was made for humankind, and not humankind for the sabbath" (Mark 2:27). In other words, honoring the sabbath and keeping it holy is *relative to* human need, as the biblical context implies: Jesus' statement follows an attack by Pharisees who saw Christ's disciples picking some "heads of grain" on the sabbath (Mark 2:23). Christ's redefinition reflects the relativism of truth: honoring the sabbath means different things in different contexts. Note the dictionary definition of relativism: "any theory holding that criteria of judgment are relative, varying with individuals and their environments."[5] Of course, other dictionaries might define it differently: the word *relativism* is relative.

How do we discriminate, then, between real threats to our faith and new ideas that some people have costumed up like Halloween bogeymen? Attempting an answer, this chapter will make three basic points:

1. Relativism is not a result of postmodernism.

2. There are many different kinds of relativism.

3. Postmodern thinkers reflect these various kinds of relativism, some of which harmonize with Christianity better than others.

Our Relativist Relatives: A History of Relativism

Scholarly arguments for relativism go back at least as far as classical antiquity.[6] But since postmodernism is largely a response to modernism, I will limit my look to the modern era, in order to make the point that people who

---

[4]David K. Clark, "Relativism, Fideism and the Promise of Postliberalism," in *The Nature of Confession: Evangelicals and Postliberals in Conversation,* ed. Timothy R. Phillips and Dennis L. Okholm (Downers Grove, Ill.: InterVarsity Press, 1996), p. 111.

[5]*The Random House College Dictionary,* s.v. "relativism."

[6]See Nicholas Rescher, *Pluralism: Against the Demand for Consensus* (Oxford: Clarendon,

consider relativism to be a result of postmodernism are historically naive.

It is no coincidence that in 1905 Einstein called his famous construct the "special theory of relativity" even though it is based on a constant: the speed of light. Rather than call it "the theory of constancy," he reflected the discourse of modernists, who were questioning the constancy of traditional ideas, especially ideas about God. Significantly, C. P. Snow has suggested that if Einstein had not developed the special theory of relativity in 1905, someone else soon would have; "it was an idea waiting to happen," as Bill Bryson puts it.[7] A poststructuralist would say that it was already a part of the discourse of modernism.

Indeed, when Darwin published *On the Origin of Species* in 1859, he gave modernists "empirical evidence" for ethical relativism. As Richard Weikart notes, "By basing morality on biological instincts, Darwin's evolutionary explanation for ethics provided a rational, scientific account for the development of nonrational human impulses."[8] Those who appropriated Darwin's theory liked the fact that it eliminated the need for a God who provided universal moral directives. For them, humans who outlasted other species must have evolved the most fortuitous ethics, illustrating the famous coinage of Herbert Spencer (1820-1903): "the survival of the fittest."

One of the intellectuals who gravitated toward evolutionary ethics was the German philosopher Friedrich Nietzsche (1844-1900). In the 1870s he started to question the way different cultures construct not only ethics but also truth itself. In one essay he echoes Pilate's famous question, "What, then, is truth?" in order to answer with "Truths are illusions about which one has forgotten that this is what they are." Societies, according to Nietzsche, smugly assume they know the truth about things because they have forgotten that their interpretations of reality are constructions of language: "metaphors, metonyms, and anthropomorphisms . . . which after long use seem firm, canonical, and obligatory to a people."[9] This sounds like poststructur-

---

1993), pp. 80-82. Joseph Margolis engages the theory of Protagoras (480?-421? B.C.) in *The Truth About Relativism* (Oxford: Blackwell, 1996).

[7]See Bill Bryson, *A Short History of Nearly Everything* (New York: Broadway, 2003), p. 123. When it comes to Einstein's *general* theory of relativity, established in 1917, I surrender analysis to the modernist concept of "genius." Einstein went where no one had gone before, beyond the speed of light.

[8]Richard Weikart, *From Darwin to Hitler: Evolutionary Ethics, Eugenics and Racism in Germany* (New York: Palgrave, 2004), p. 22.

[9]Friedrich Nietzsche, "On Truth and Lie in an Extra-moral Sense," in *The Portable Nietzsche*, ed. and trans. Walter Kaufmann (New York: Penguin, 1976), pp. 46-47.

alism, and indeed Nietzsche has influenced many postmodern thinkers. He, in fact, was one of the first nineteenth-century agnostic philosophers to question the truth claims of science—at a time, as we have seen, when scientific "truth" had displaced Christianity for many European intellectuals. He challenged the modernist assumption "There are only facts" with the statement "No, facts is precisely what there is not"; instead we have "only interpretations."[10]

If even anticipating postmodernism, Nietzsche still reflected modernist sensibilities, asserting that people must exercise "a will to power" in order to rise above their particular society's interpretation of truth. He calls the rare individual who can exercise such power an *Übermensch,* or "Superman."[11] Ironically, even as he rallies the Übermensch to separate from culture, Nietzsche demonstrates how much he himself is embedded in culture, for, as we have seen, one of the "truths" of modernism is the autonomy of genius. Nietzsche's celebration of Übermensch autonomy, therefore, was not autonomous.

Another German contributor to modernist relativism was Ernst Haeckel (1834-1919), who believed that the "truth" of evolution had supplanted Christian views of human nature. While Nietzsche assumed that morality is culturally constructed, Haeckel asserted that it is biologically determined: morality changes over time as species change. What he shared with Nietzsche, however, was the view that Christianity erroneously "exalts altruism to a command, while rejecting egoism."[12] In 1899, Haeckel's book discussing Darwinian ethics, *Riddle of the Universe,* became a bestseller.

These modernist theories influenced Adolf Hitler in the 1930s. Exercising a "will to power," Hitler absolutized his idea of "ethnic cleansing" with Haeckel's evolutionary view of moral relativism. Because Aryans were more evolved than Jews, Gypsies and other ethnic minorities, Hitler felt free to rise above the traditional Christian language that all people are equal in the sight of God. For him, morality was relative to one's place on the evolutionary chain.

---

[10]Friedrich Nietzsche, *The Will to Power,* ed. Walter Kaufmann, trans. Walter Kaufmann and R. J. Hollingdale (New York: Vintage, 1968), p. 267. German philosopher Martin Heidegger echoes Nietzsche when he writes, in 1927, "An interpretation is never a presuppositionless apprehending of something present to us." See *Being and Time,* trans. John Macquarrie and Edward Robinson (New York: Harper & Row, 1962), p. 192.

[11]Nietzsche, *Will to Power,* pp. 463-64.

[12]Quoted in Weikart, *From Darwin to Hitler,* p. 25.

The Postmodern Reaction: Multiculturalism, Skepticism and Succotash

Unlike those modernists who absolutized evolutionary relativism, postmodernists do not regard human significance as relative. Neil Leach, in fact, asserts that "far from promoting relativism, in some respects *poststructuralism could be seen as a defense against relativism.*"[13] Postmodernism subverts modernist assumptions about human progress, evolutionary or otherwise, instead asserting that all people have value—no matter their race, class, religion, gender, ethnicity or sexuality—and that their voices deserve to be heard. One manifestation of postmodernism is therefore "multiculturalism," which demands equal respect for peoples who formerly had been "marginalized" or "demonized" by the dominant culture—as Christians had been by Enlightenment humanists.

In the early days of postmodernism, in fact, there was an almost giddy exuberance over the possibilities for multicultural perspectives. Theorists were joyfully repudiating the strict rules of Enlightenment rationalism—rules that often resulted in skepticism. Though skepticism is as old as Greek philosophy, it is no coincidence that one of the most famous skeptics of all time, David Hume (1711-1777), wrote during the Age of Reason. As O'Grady notes, "Scepticism and relativism differ. Relativism accepts that alternative accounts of knowledge are legitimate. Scepticism holds that the existence of alternatives blocks the possibility of knowledge."[14]

When someone assumes that absolute truth can be reached through the objectivity of reason, and then discovers that many smart people disagree about the truth, that person can easily become skeptical about the possibility of ever attaining authentic knowledge. This often happens to Christians who have never been challenged to grapple with what they believe and why others believe differently. As soon as they leave a protective environment where everyone around them assumes Christian truth is self-evident, they become skeptical not only about Christianity but about all religious conviction.

Postmodern theorists, however, are not skeptics. They do not say there is no way of knowing truth. Instead they say there are multiple, competing truths. This, of course, is where they get their reputation for relativism, a rel-

---

[13]Neil Leach, introduction to "Poststructuralism," in *Rethinking Architecture: A Reader in Cultural Theory,* ed. Neil Leach (New York: Routledge, 1997), p. 248, emphasis mine.
[14]O'Grady, *Relativism,* p. 97.

ativism that often looks like succotash—a mishmash of different ways of thinking that not many have been willing to sort out. Perhaps due to their suspicions about the language games of philosophy, most postmodernists have not adequately responded to the many different kinds of relativism that professional philosophers discuss, failing to distinguish lima bean relativism from corn kernels of insight.[15]

Though I intensely dislike succotash, preferring to keep my vegetables separate, I understand the postmodern resistance to traditional philosophic distinctions. Different philosophers define relativism differently, a fact that underscores the limitations of language. One philosopher will call "epistemic relativism" what another calls "ontological relativism," while both reject the kind of relativism named by the other term. Or different philosophers will use the same name, like "conceptual relativism," to describe very different phenomena. Nevertheless, despite all the differences in style and argument, philosophers have convinced me that *either* a blanket dismissal *or* a blanket endorsement of relativism is too simplistic. We therefore need to consider the different forms of relativism manifest in postmodern thought.

Postmodern Relativisms: A Medley

Based on the work of several contemporary philosophers, I have identified six kinds of relativism manifest in postmodern thinkers.[16] However, because of the problem with philosophical terminology, I have followed the lead of Richard Rorty's "strong poet": one who invents vocabulary to encourage new ways of understanding. I use alliteration to name the six different kinds, from the most simplistic, *bird relativism,* to the most complex, *building relativism.* In between is *brain relativism,* which has three subsets within it: *bouncing relativism, boundary relativism* and *bombardment relativism.* To understand distinctions among them, you need to think of the towers described in chapter six, once again imagining "Honey-I-Shrunk-the-Kids" situated in different language-covered transparent tubes.

Bird relativism. The most simplistic kind of relativist is the one who says, "All religions are the same," or "All religions lead to God." I call this bird relativism because it implies the ability to rise above all towers of per-

---

[15]For the many different kinds of relativism, see Susan Haack, *Manifesto of a Passionate Moderate* (Chicago: University of Chicago Press, 1998), p. 149.
[16]I repeatedly cite these philosophers in the discussion to follow.

ception, like a bird, and see them from an unbiased, Godlike perspective. This kind of relativism echoes modernist autonomy. However, while the Enlightenment modernist assumed a birdlike position to say "all religions are false," the postmodernist bird merely flies upside down to suggest that "all religions are true."

Ironically, bird relativists often feel contempt for someone who believes his religion is the one and only tower reaching into the mind of God: a Tower of Babel. But in actuality bird relativists are not that much different. In fact, they may be worse, assuming that *they* have a God's-eye view without the benefit of a tower. In his book arguing for a pluralism of perspectives, Nicholas Rescher eschews this kind of relativism: "To refuse to discriminate—be it by accepting everything or by accepting nothing—is to avert controversy only by refusing to enter the forum of discussion. It betokens fecklessness and vacuity."[17]

Another species of bird relativism appears in the statement "All religions have elements of truth in them, and my religion combines the best of all religions." Though I think it is possible, in fact imperative, for people in Christian towers to recognize elements of truth in other religions (more on that later), the bird relativist assumes she can fly above various towers, recognizing with a God's-eye view what is true in each and swooping down to gather various strings of "truth" to make her own special nest. This position reeks of naive modernist autonomy, or if the bird is part of a flock, the nest merely becomes another tower by which a group identifies itself in an all-encompassing synthesis. As Rescher notes, "The synthesist seeks somehow to co-ordinate dissonant positions in grand all-embracing synthesis. But of course every standpoint (perspective, doctrinal stance), however 'synthetic' it may be is just exactly that—just one more particular standpoint."[18]

I suspect that bird relativism explains why Richard Rorty denounces the very notion of relativism, despite the fact that most philosophers call him a postmodern relativist. Rorty identifies the word *relativism* with this bird brand, which has spread like flu among people who like to think of themselves as "postmodern." In *The Consequences of Pragmatism,* Rorty writes, "'Relativism' is the view that every belief on a certain topic, or perhaps about any topic, is as good as any other. No one holds this view. . . . If there were

---

[17]Rescher, *Pluralism,* p. 89.
[18]Ibid., p. 94.

any relativists, they would of course be easy to refute. One would merely use some version of the self-referential argument used by Socrates against Protagoras."[19] By "no one," he means no intellectually sophisticated thinker. In contrast, the kind of relativism philosophers align with Rorty reflects his pragmatism, which leads us to the next category: brain relativism.

Brain relativism. Compared to bird relativism, brain relativism is, well, brainy. It asserts that people in radically different cultures use their brains (by which I mean their *minds*) differently. Something logically true in one tower might be false in another. Due to their relative rationalities, people in radically different towers cannot judge each other's thought processes. As a result, there is no legitimate way to say that all religions are true or all are false. This seems to be the position taken by many early postmodernists.

Though brain relativism is untenable to many philosophers (whose vocation calls them to assess the legitimacy of various arguments for truth), perhaps something as radical as brain relativism was needed to destabilize Enlightenment rationalism. As we have seen, most modernist humanists operated (and still do) by a "correspondence" theory of truth, which holds that our statements about truth correspond to reality. But then they made (and still make) statements saying that Christian doctrine is not true— because it is neither rational nor empirically verifiable. In other words, what was true for Christians was false for Enlightenment rationalists. Therefore they crushed Christianity in order to avoid brain relativism.[20]

Ironically, then, the correspondence theory of truth, which many Christians battle to protect, was aggressively used during the so-called Enlightenment to repudiate Christianity. Postmodern brain relativists, in contrast, established that secular humanist truth is no different from Christian truth: they are simply different ways to explain reality. This postmodern battering ram destroyed the wall of separation between reason and faith built up by Enlightenment modernists.

However, once secular humanism was reduced to a rubble, exposed as just one tower of truth among many, postmodernists were left with no way to argue for ethical universals. At least secular humanists could appeal to universal rational principles for moral behavior, even though they

---

[19]Richard Rorty, *Consequences of Pragmatism: Essays, 1972-1980* (Minneapolis: University of Minnesota Press, 1982), pp. 166-67.

[20]For a critique of the "correspondence theory of truth," see Nicholas Rescher, *The Coherence Theory of Truth* (Washington, D.C.: University Press of America, 1982).

eliminated a need for Christ in the process.

Bouncing relativism: Gilles Deleuze and Félix Guattari. Some brain relativists replaced "reason" with "desire." Assuming that identification with any one tower molds identity in oppressive ways, Gilles Deleuze and Félix Guattari argued that the self should follow the free flow of its desires, avoiding contact with any institutionalized language for too long. The best way to picture their view is to think of my cardboard football field as a huge pinball machine. The self, then, is the metal ball that bounces off the towers, picking up impetus from the language written on the walls at each point of contact but refusing to go inside.

Though this pinball metaphor sounds too mechanistic to be believable, Deleuze and Guattari actually call the postmodern self a "desiring machine," telling people to "keep moving, even in place, never stop moving."[21] These postmodernists seem to assume that constant movement prevents the self from being shaped by any one tower. In fact, to keep their own theory from becoming a tower, they bounce from terminology to terminology, sometimes calling the free-flowing self "nomadic," other times a "schizo-subject."[22] They use terms like these, usually associated with instability, to make the point that the idea of an authentic, unchanging self—one that acts according to unbiased cognitive processes—is an Enlightenment fiction that regulates behavior. For them, the cliché "Be yourself" really means "Enter a different tower from the one you're in now": it's merely the exchange of one socially defined identity for another.

Their point can be illustrated at high schools all across the nation. When adolescents "rebel," defying the way parents and/or teachers define "proper" behavior, they usually end up entering into the discourse of a different tower: that of the goths, punks, surfers, skaters, druggies, you name it. Attempting to "be themselves," they merely conform to a different idea of "the self." This is why Deleuze and Guattari advocated bouncing among the towers of discourse.

Though it subverted Enlightenment rationalism, the postmodern emphasis on desire created its own problems, resulting in a celebration of sexual desire in the arts that became problematically graphic. It seems to me that

---

[21]Gilles Deleuze and Félix Guattari, *A Thousand Plateaus: Capitalism and Schizophrenia* (Minneapolis: University of Minnesota Press, 1987), p. 159.

[22]Ibid. Also see Gilles Deleuze and Félix Guattari, *Anti-Oedipus: Capitalism and Schizophrenia* (Minneapolis: University of Minnesota Press, 1983).

the pursuit of desire works only if the majority of people stay committed to the reasoned morality of their towers, providing a stable social environment against which nomadic players can bounce. With their emphasis on "desire," antielitist postmodernists unwittingly deconstructed their own agenda by perpetuating a different form of elitism, wherein they could follow their own desires with impunity as long as the common person held fast to her principles.

Boundary relativism: Neopragmatism and Richard Rorty. In contradistinction to how Deleuze and Guattari nomadically followed their desires, bouncing among competing and/or contradictory tower "truths," postmodern neopragmatists have asserted the need for ethics. However, it was not the brain relativism of Deleuze and Guattari that bothered these postmodernists; it was the idea of bouncing.

Acknowledging that different towers "incommensurably" define truth differently, neopragmatists advocate identifying with one tower and sticking with it. Ethics, then, is based on your commitment to live according to the vocabulary of your tower, even while acknowledging that people in other towers define reality, and hence morality, differently. Rather than asking why or how your tower justifies its ethical stance in contradistinction to other towers, you just go along with what works—with what is pragmatic. And if your tower has been around for a long time, you have reason to conclude that its definition of "the good" works. It is pragmatic.

Consonant with brain relativism, postmodern neopragmatism asserts that truth isn't "out there" beyond the towers to be discovered; it is instead "in here," or *inherent* (my pun) to a tower's discourse. For this reason it is impossible to completely understand how people in radically different cultures think, for you can understand a tower of thought only if you live inside it.

The most famous exemplar of neopragmatist brain relativism is Richard Rorty. In his famous book *Contingency, Irony and Solidarity* (1989), Rorty repeatedly puts "truth" and "out there" in quotation marks to indicate that vocabularies, and hence "truths," for different communities are human constructions and hence "contingent" rather than universal. Rorty argues that "morality is a matter of . . . 'we-intentions,'" and hence "the core meaning of 'immoral action' is 'the sort of thing *we* don't do.'"[23] He would encourage us, then, not to worry about the way other brains think; instead we must work hard to

---

[23]Richard Rorty is quoting Wilfred Sellars in *Contingency, Irony and Solidarity* (Cambridge: Cambridge University Press, 1989), p. 59.

maintain the language of our tower, practicing what it preaches.

For understandable reasons, some Christians have responded positively to Rorty's brain relativism, using it to argue that followers of Christ need to stop worrying about the epistemologies of other religions and simply commit themselves to Christianity, asserting that it is "true for us." This kind of postmodern fideism, however, is not endorsed by Rorty, who regards Christianity as no longer useful or pragmatic. For him, Christian towers were made unnecessary by secular humanism, which practices what Christianity preaches without all the metaphysical mumbo-jumbo.

Basically, Rorty is a modernist wolf in postmodern clothing.[24] Though he argues for brain relativism, he asserts that certain enlightened individuals— he calls them "ironists"—can separate from their tower's vocabulary to recognize the "contingency" of its "truths." In this he resembles Nietzsche, a brain relativist who nevertheless posited the Übermensch whose "will to power" might defy the language that formulated his thinking. As John McGowan summarizes, "Rorty's final appeal is to the timeworn notion of the genius who transcends his age."[25]

I call Rorty a "boundary relativist" because, though he limits truth and knowledge to the boundaries of each tower wall, he posits ironists who can cross the boundaries and inspect them from the outside. He does so because he sees a need for tower boundaries to transform. Since no truths are universal, towers must adapt to changes in the world in order to stay useful to those inside. Furthermore, those exceptional few who can cross the boundaries of their towers are encouraged to do so in order to promote the "postmodernist bourgeois liberalism" of the larger tower that surrounds all the smaller towers of "North Atlantic Democracies." Rorty endorses the tower of bourgeois liberalism because it calls for liberty and justice for all—not as a universal truth but as part of a vocabulary that is still pragmatic. For him, bourgeois liberalism, unlike Christian towers within it, teaches tolerance for people in all towers, even when their brains think differently.[26]

Rorty makes no attempt to justify this position, because to do so he would have to appeal to something that transcends the tower of bourgeois liberal-

---

[24]Significantly, in *Consequences of Pragmatism* Rorty aligns pragmatism with "literary modernism" (p. 153).

[25]John McGowan, *Postmodernism and Its Critics* (Ithaca, N.Y.: Cornell University Press, 1991), p. 193. McGowan's discussion of Rorty's inconsistencies is the best I've read.

[26]Richard Rorty, "Postmodernist Bourgeois Liberalism," *Journal of Philosophy* 80 (October 1983): 583-89.

ism.[27] Instead he posits the need for "ungroundable desires," including the "hope that suffering will be diminished, that the humiliation of human beings by other human beings may cease," because "cruelty is the worst thing we do."[28] I would respond by asking Rorty, "Which tower's definition of cruelty are you following?" From most towers the circumcision of females seems the utmost in cruelty, but certain Third World towers regard it as important to the well-being of society.

Even within the tower of American bourgeois liberalism, cruelty is defined differently. Some will say that affirmative action is cruel to both white males and minorities, for it ignores the qualifications and goals of the one and eliminates incentive and pride of achievement for the other. Others, however, would say that it is cruel not to make accommodations for the racism and sexism that still permeate our culture.

Rorty seems to deconstruct his own argument. He establishes that there is no way to get outside of one's tower of perception, and yet his idea of "cruelty" transcends towers of perception. As Dorothy L. Sayers noted in 1941, "Even the most anti-religious of our thinkers" believe that "fully enlightened humanity" is not "cruel." And then she asks "But why? What makes us so sure about this?" She answers by asserting, "At the very basis of our thought and behaviour there lies a pair of assumptions which are wholly religious—which reason cannot prove and for which science can offer no evidence. We assume that both our conception of the good and our human reason are really valid."[29] According to Sayers's paradigm, Rorty is fundamentally religious. We might therefore ask him how he reconciles his "ungroundable desires" with an identifiable ground: his religious sense that cruelty is bad. If Rorty is going to religiously establish the paradox of a groundless ground, why not embrace the paradox of a God who became human in order to redeem all definitions of cruelty through love?

Bombardment relativism: Stanley Fish's neopragmatism. Fish is much more consistent in his brain relativism than Rorty, recognizing that bourgeois liberalism is simply one among many human constructions. Like Rorty, he argues that human agency operates according to the rules of the language game with which one identifies. For him, any individual "agent

---

[27]For this reason O'Grady aligns Rorty with "epistemological relativism" (*Relativism*, pp. 106-12).
[28]Rorty, *Contingency, Irony and Solidarity*, p. xv.
[29]Dorothy L. Sayers, "The Religions Behind the Nation," in *The Church Looks Ahead: Broadcast Talks* (London: Faber, 1941), p. 70.

cannot distance himself from these rules, because it is only within them that he can think about alternative courses of action or, indeed, *think at all.*[30]

On one level Fish is a friend of faith, arguing that Christians should not only maintain the upkeep of their towers but also emphatically proclaim that the doctrine on their walls is true. However, as a brain relativist, Fish asserts that people of all religions should do the same, shoring up their towers with all their might.[31] In *The Trouble with Principle* (1999) he writes,

> To put the matter baldly, a person of religious conviction should not want to enter the marketplace of ideas but to shut it down, at least insofar as it presumes to determine matters that he believes have been determined by God and faith. The religious person should not seek an accommodation with liberalism; he should seek to rout it from the field.[32]

I call this position bombardment relativism for obvious reasons. Though Fish asserts that all religions are incommensurable, with none having greater access to universal truth than any other, he advocates a Tower of Babel mentality for the people within each construction, encouraging them to regard all others as false.

The trouble with this position became obvious on September 11, 2001, when al-Qaida operatives sought to destroy actual, tangible, empirically verifiable U.S. towers on the field of Manhattan. In fact, after the bombardment of New York's Twin Towers, numerous people started blaming postmodern multiculturalism for the attacks.[33]

This is quite odd, since the Muslim terrorists surely did not read postmodern theory. If anything, Christians can understand al-Qaida's viewpoint, which might be summarized as follows: American consumerism has led to a decadent obsession with material objects, fueling a discourse that places creature comforts above the Creator. In contrast, Muslims are willing to sacrifice their very lives in service to their Creator.

How, then, can we say that the bombing of the World Trade Center was "wrong"? Wrong by whose standards? This is where postmodern brain rela-

---

[30]Stanley Fish, "Consequences," in *Against Theory: Literary Studies and the New Pragmatism*, ed. W. J. T. Mitchell (Chicago: University of Chicago Press, 1985), p. 113, emphasis mine.

[31]Rescher calls this "indifferentist relativism" (*Pluralism*, p. 80), while Joseph Runzo calls it "conceptual relativism" in *Reason, Relativism and God* (New York: St. Martin's, 1986), p. 62.

[32]Stanley Fish, *The Trouble with Principle* (Cambridge, Mass.: Harvard University Press, 1999), p. 250.

[33]See for example, Edward Rothstein, "Attacks on U.S. Challenge the Perspectives of Postmodern True Believers," *New York Times*, September 22, 2001, late edition, A17.

tivism falters. If we endorse the bombardment position of Fish, we cannot say that the actions of al-Qaida are universally immoral; we can say only that they are immoral *according to our tower's language* of morality.

And this is exactly what Fish did. Several weeks after 9/11, he published an essay in the *New York Times* titled "Condemnation Without Absolutes," asserting,

> The only thing postmodern thought argues against is the hope of justifying our response to the attacks in universal terms that would be persuasive to everyone, including our enemies. Invoking the abstract notions of justice and truth to support our cause wouldn't be effective anyway because our adversaries lay claim to the same language. (No one declares himself to be an apostle of injustice.) . . . Postmodern thought tells us that we have grounds enough for action and justified condemnation in the democratic ideals we embrace, without grasping for the empty rhetoric of universal absolutes to which all subscribe but which all define differently.[34]

On one level he is right: the universal absolutes of Enlightenment humanism—rational truth, freedom, justice—cannot be used to condemn al-Qaida. After all, the attackers were motivated by a sense of justice, based on their own reasoned and empirically verifiable truth about American decadence. Immediately after the attacks, in fact, an American Christian, Jerry Falwell, used the same form of reasoning. Both Falwell (until he recanted) and Osama bin Laden regarded the attack on the Twin Towers as a judgment from God.

On another level, of course, Fish's argument is appalling. Though we can condemn—and should condemn—what from our "democratic" tower looks like pure evil, the argument suggests that we must simultaneously allow people from nondemocratic towers to act in ways they consider "true" and "just."[35] How then shall we live? How then *can* we live?

The answer, I think, is not to bomb the bedrooms out of that foreign tower. To do so is merely to duplicate actions that we condemn, as though to say, "al-Qaida is right; we must destroy people who disagree with our definition of morality." Instead, we must convincingly argue for a transcendent

---

[34]Stanley Fish, "Condemnation Without Absolutes," *New York Times*, October 15, 2001; available at www.nytimes.com/2001/10/15/opinion/15FISH.htm.

[35]In *Just War Against Terror: Ethics and American Power in a Violent World*, Jean Bethke Elshtain gives the example of the French Revolution: "Those who guillotined thousands in the Place de la Concorde in Paris and called it 'justice' were pleased to speak of revolutionary terror as a form of justice" (Elshtain, "The Importance of Words," *Cresset* 66 [2002]: 40).

Creator who established all of creation as "good" because it reflects the Goodness that created it; a Creator who desires all humans to turn in love toward the Love that created them, re-turning that love toward fellow creatures; a Creator who therefore regards the killing of innocent people as inimical to the Good and the Love behind the created order; a Creator, in other words, who transcends all towers of discourse.

Without some kind of universal absolute, we cannot say that Hitler's extermination of six million Jews or Stalin's starvation of seven million Ukrainians is universally evil; we can say only that the actions are evil *to us*—those of us, at least, molded by different towers of discourse.

Building relativism. In his book *Relativism,* philosopher Paul O'Grady argues that some forms of relativism are more philosophically viable than others: "One can keep a classical conception of truth as absolute, while still having other forms of relativism and not falling into self-refutation."[36] I use the term "building relativism" to denote a postmodern relativism that allows for absolute truth.

I chose the term because *building* can operate both as a noun and a verb. As a noun *building* reminds us of the tower buildings that shape our thought; but as a verb *building* implies that certain towers can lead us toward—build toward—a truth that transcends language. The building relativist, then, believes that facts indeed exist apart from discourse, but because facts are viewed differently from within different language-covered tower walls, those facts differ from tower to tower.

Let me give an example. In 1787, someone in New Jersey sent a dinosaur bone to Caspar Wistar, a famous anatomist, in order to get the strange fossil identified. However, since dinosaurs were still unknown to scientists (the word itself would not be invented for another fifty-four years), Wistar could not really *see* the bone. He shunted it off to a closet as an anomaly, a fact without meaning. Similarly, two decades later, when Merriwether Lewis and George Rogers Clark traveled through an area of Montana so thick with dinosaur bones that they could have tripped over them, they did not *see* them as fossils. Though they stopped to inspect one specimen, as Bill Bryson notes, "they failed to make anything of it." Lewis and Clark did not perceive the bones as significant because they had no conceptual framework—no tower of discourse—to give them meaning. The bones indeed existed—that

---

[36]O'Grady, *Relativism,* p. 34.

is an empirical fact—but the bone-facts had no value until a vocabulary was developed with which they could be interpreted.[37]

Occasionally, one hears of Christians who actually deny the *fact* of dinosaur bones. Because the Bible never mentions dinosaurs, they assert that dinosaur bones cannot exist. Looking at bones through Bible verses inscribed on their tower walls, these Christians have established a different truth for the bones from the truth that other people accept.

But bonelike objects that we can see and touch do exist, even if some people perceive them as dinosaur bones and others as geological anomalies or even secularist hoaxes. Their absolute truth coexists with our building relativism. For the building relativist, the human mind and objects in the universe are not independent of each other. Instead they are interdependent: the facts of the world contribute to the building up—or out—of our towers, even as our towers mold the way we see the facts.

Building Out Our Towers

By building "out" I mean that certain towers become larger, to accommodate more facts, while still remaining identifiable buildings. For example, many scientists situated in Christian towers, while looking through their Bible-inscribed walls at Darwin's dangerous idea, have determined that the facts they see outside their towers endorse natural selection. They therefore suggest that Christianity can include evolution without giving up the biblical truth that God created the heavens and the earth. They thus "build out" their walls with "theistic evolution," saying God was the first cause of the evolutionary process and still participates in it.[38]

Residents in some Christian towers may eject such scientists, saying that the literal six-day creation on their walls is absolute truth and that no one is going to "monkey with" those walls. But notice, these tamper-resistant Christians are not much different from Stanley Fish's bombardment relativists: both refuse to acknowledge that there may be legitimate truths outside their walls.

If the human mind and facts of the universe are interdependent, then the fact of other towers must be part of that interdependence. If we indeed believe that facts are "out there," then a discussion of the different ways we

---

[37]Bryson, *Short History of Nearly Everything*, pp. 79-83.
[38]See part three, "Theistic Evolution," of *Debating Design: From Darwin to DNA*, ed. William A. Dembski and Michael Ruse (Cambridge: Cambridge University Press, 2004).

see those facts is not only possible but also desirable. To know the facts better without giving up on our tower's definition of truth, we want to understand how people in other towers see them.

While acknowledging that those in other towers see facts differently, the building relativist attempts to build bridges between buildings. Of course, people in towers of Babel do so as well, but they tend to insert tire rippers in their bridges so that the discussion of truth can go only one way: the way that leads inside their tower, which they consider the only tower that "corresponds" to truth.

In contrast, building relativists assume that two-way interactions between buildings can occur, that we can understand how people in other towers justify their truth claims *even as we disagree with them,* believing that our reasoning makes more sense of life as we experience it. This, of course, distinguishes building relativists from brain relativists, who assert that justifications for truth can be understood only within one's tower.

Most building relativists call themselves "perspectivalists" or "pluralists," avoiding the term *relativism* because of its association with bird relativism and the various forms of brain relativism. Rescher, for example, advocates a pluralism based on "perspectival rationalism (or contextualism)":

> Such a preferentialist position combines a pluralistic acknowledgement of distinct alternatives with a recognition that a sensible individual's choice among them is *not* rationally indifferent, but rather constrained by the probative indication of the *experience* that provides both the evidential basis and the evaluative criteria for effecting a rational choice.[39]

For Rescher, people see facts differently from within different towers, but they can justify their perspective in ways that make sense to people in other towers. Building relativism thus justifies evangelism, allowing Christians to talk to others about how and why they see reality the way they do.

Christian Pluralism

There are numerous Christian pluralists, the most famous being Alasdair MacIntyre and the initiators of "postliberal narrative theology": Hans Frei and George Lindbeck. Since a great deal has been published about these

---

[39]Rescher, *Pluralism,* p. 114. Note also Christian philosopher Merold Westphal: "In short, perspectivism is the relativism that insists that we are not God, that only God is absolute." See "Onto-theology, Metanarrative, Perspectivism, and the Gospel," in *Christianity and the Postmodern Turn: Six Views,* ed. Myron B. Penner (Grand Rapids: Baker, 2005), p. 152.

"postmodern conservative theologians" and their followers,[40] I would rather discuss James K. A. Smith, who has created a solid bridge between his knowledge of postmodernism and his background in Pentecostalism—a Christian theology that welcomes plural tongues.

In *The Fall of Interpretation: Philosophical Foundations for a Creational Hermeneutic,* Smith argues that interpretive pluralism is a reflection of God's plan for humanity. After quoting from Derrida's essay on the Tower of Babel, Smith affirms the idea that pluralism reflects the *goodness* of creation: "Yahweh, then, turns out to be a pluralist, one on the side of diversity and the multiplicity of others. And that is why creation is a pluralist idea and why a creational hermeneutic attempts to honor this diversity not as the original sin but rather as primordially good." In other words, having created humans with bodies rather than as mere spirits, God seems to have regarded as "very good" (Genesis 1:31) human situatedness, for situatedness is the result of embodiment—of incarnation. Furthermore, God's gift of tongues at Pentecost—an experience of the body—explicitly communicates the goodness in diversity to followers of Christ: "For at Pentecost Yahweh's pneuma affirms the multiplicity of creation and the post-Babelian era, in direct contrast to the quest for unity that initiated the construction of the tower (Acts 2:1-12)." Smith's point is affirmed by the Bible itself, which gives different perspectives—multiple tongues—on the same incidents, depending in the situatedness of each writer. Hence, while a modernist might point to discrepancies in the Gospels in order to discredit Christianity, Smith would celebrate the differences, saying, "The truth, in creation, is plural." Furthermore, since "the New Testament writings are themselves interpretations of a person and an event," we need to be open to differing interpretations of Scripture in our own day, trying to understand the situatedness of contemporary interpreters.[41]

---

[40] Alasdair MacIntyre, *Whose Justice? Which Rationality?* (Notre Dame: University of Notre Dame Press, 1988); Hans Frei, *The Eclipse of Biblical Narrative* (New Haven, Conn.: Yale University Press, 1974); George Lindbeck, *The Nature of Doctrine: Religion and Theology in a Postliberal Age* (Philadelphia: Westminster, 1984). Nancey Murphy regards them all as exemplars of "postmodern conservative theology" in *Anglo-American Postmodernity: Philosophical Perspectives on Science, Religion and Ethics* (Boulder, Colo.: Westview, 1997). For intelligent evangelical engagement with postliberal narrative theology, see *The Nature of Confession: Evangelicals and Postliberals in Conversation,* ed. Timothy R. Phillips and Dennis L. Okholm (Downers Grove, Ill.: InterVarsity Press, 1996), and Robert C. Greer, *Mapping Postmodernism: A Survey of Christian Options* (Downers Grove, Ill.: InterVarsity Press, 2003).

[41] James K. A. Smith, *The Fall of Interpretation: Philosophical Foundations for a Creational Hermeneutic* (Downers Grove, Ill.: InterVarsity Press, 2000), pp. 59-60, 53.

Smith's celebration of pluralism would have helped me out immensely when I encountered Christian pluralism for the first time—and nearly had a faith crisis.

My Battle with *The Last Battle* of C. S. Lewis

When I first read Lewis's Narnia Chronicles in college, I loved how the stories retold the message of salvation through the work of a Christlike lion named Aslan. The ending of the final chronicle disturbed me, however. In *The Last Battle,* Aslan's followers are journeying "further up and further in" toward a place beyond the towers of Narnia where they will be united with Aslan in glory. On the way, they meet Emeth, a Calormene soldier, who has spent his life worshiping Tash, the Calormene god. Emeth relates how, upon meeting Aslan, he immediately recognized him to be the true "Glorious One" and despaired: "I am no son of Thine but the servant of Tash." In other words, "My Calormene tower of religion blinded me to the truth." However, rather than consigning Emeth to hell for his wrong belief, Aslan assures him, "Child, all the service thou hast done to Tash, I account as service done to me."[42]

Unlike Emeth, I was not comforted by these words. It sounded to me as if Lewis was condoning universalism: the idea that whether you believe in Aslan or Tash, Christ or Krishna, as long as you're sincere you'll still get to heaven. This idea that all religions are the same went against everything I was taught about Christianity. After all, Christ said, "I am the way, and the truth, and the life. No one comes to the Father except through me" (John 14:6). In light of this verse, I wondered how Lewis could be so highly regarded by evangelicals. Shouldn't he get points off?

Not until postmodern theorists introduced me to the idea of "discourse" did I understand what Lewis was doing. I concluded that John 14:6 could be interpreted differently depending on the towers in which earnest followers of Jesus are situated. Many people in evangelical towers interpret "No one comes to the Father except through me" to mean that people cannot come to God unless they explicitly ask Christ into their heart (even though the verse does not say that). Lewis's tower, which was Anglo-Catholic, also had the words "No one comes to the Father except through me" written distinctly on the walls, and Lewis certainly believed that people come to God only through Christ's death and resurrection. However, he did not limit that

---

[42]C. S. Lewis, *The Last Battle* (New York: Collier, 1956), p. 164.

process to a certain act of intellectual assent the way most evangelicals do. As he clarifies in *Mere Christianity,* believers within a tower of Christian orthodoxy "know that no man can be saved except through Christ; we do not know that *only those who know Him* can be saved through Him."[43] In other words, *explicit* belief is not necessarily a precondition for salvation. For Lewis, who was drawn to Christian mysticism, God's ways far transcend both our language and our understanding.[44]

Once I stepped out on the bridge between Lewis's position and my own evangelical tradition, I saw that *The Last Battle* does not simplistically assert that "all religions lead to God," as a bird-brained relativist might do. In fact, when Emeth suggests that Aslan and Tash are one and the same thing, Aslan growls in disapproval, saying, "We are opposites." Aslan goes on to assert (though not in so many words) that he, unlike Tash, is *the* way, *the* truth and *the* life. However, Aslan also suggests that his ability to function as the way, the truth and the life does not depend on human knowledge; it transcends towers of discourse: "If any man swear by Tash and keep his oath for the oath's sake, it is by me that he has truly sworn, though he know it not, and it is I who reward him. And if any man do a cruelty in my name, then though he says the name Aslan, it is Tash whom he serves and by Tash his deed accepted." Lewis implies that following Aslan/Christ is not simply a matter of using the "right" name inscribed on certain tower walls; it is a matter of performing the way the Creator intended creatures to perform. This means not only keeping oaths and avoiding cruelty but also seeking the One who is above all: "Unless thy desire had been for me thou wouldst not have sought so long and so truly. For all find what they truly seek."[45] At the same time, Lewis endorses the tower of orthodox Christianity, establishing that Aslan/Christ is the true incarnation of God on Narnia/Earth. It's just that the saving work of God Incarnate does not depend on human language—or even knowledge—to fulfill God's purposes.

Significantly, Emeth never uses the name Aslan—the "right" language—when he describes this encounter. Instead he either refers to "the Glorious One"—One who is above all names—or says "the Lion," in reference to

---

[43]C. S. Lewis, *Mere Christianity* (New York: Macmillan, 1969), p. 65.

[44]See David Downing's groundbreaking study *Into the Region of Awe: Mysticism in C. S. Lewis* (Downers Grove, Ill.: InterVarsity Press, 2005).

[45]Lewis, *The Last Battle*, p. 165. Brian McLaren reads this Narnian incident the same way I do in his lovely book *A New Kind of Christian: A Tale of Two Friends on a Spiritual Journey* (San Francisco: Jossey-Bass, 2001), pp. 81-93.

Aslan's incarnated image: a form of "real-bodies mysticism." And Aslan speaks his own name with Emeth only in the statement quoted above, to make the point that the name itself is not the means to salvation. Thus, according to Lewis's interpretation of Scripture, most likely inspired by Matthew's sheep and goats passage (Matthew 25:31-46), the "Glorious One" will save people no matter how their tower is inscribed as long as they look up: seeking the Name that is above every tower's name. They will be saved by the blood of Aslan/Christ—whether they know his name or not.

At one time I would have angrily responded to this idea with "Why, then, be a Christian? If, as Aslan suggests, it's just a matter of truly seeking him, or, as Matthew 25 suggests, it's just a matter of treating others as though they were Christ, what difference does it make which religious tower I am in?"

Today I can answer with confidence, "It makes a big difference!" On this issue, postmodern pragmatism, despite its brain relativism, served my faith. Even though it's impossible to get entirely outside of language to attain a God's-eye view of things, neopragmatists argue that some discourses work better than others at promoting life, liberty and the prevention of cruelty. A necessary correlate of this would be that some religions work better at directing human sights toward a loving Creator who desires—and deserves—love and discipleship in response. Rorty, though an avowed atheist, identifies Christianity as one of "the great moral and intellectual advances of European history."[46] It was life affirming, despite all of the violence done in the name of Christ. In fact, violence usually occurs when people use Christ's words not as signs pointing up but as cement to reinforce their political and cultural assumptions, blocking their view of other towers.

I would argue, as I do more thoroughly in the last chapter of this book, that the tower inscribed with the ancient creeds of orthodox Christianity makes more sense of God's love and human need than any other tower I have surveyed. Admittedly, I make this claim from within a Protestant tower that affects the way I see, and speak about, all other towers; but poststructuralism has convinced me that this limitation is true of all humans. I therefore have as much right to speak about my belief in the existence of Christ as does the scientist about belief in the existence of quarks. Both of us are confined to language humans have constructed. The physicist employs words like *charm* and *flavor* to denote qualities of subatomic particles that

---

[46]Rorty, *Contingency, Irony and Solidarity*, p. 48.

far exceed the meaning of those words, and I employ diction like *atonement* and *sanctification* to speak of holy behavior that far exceeds the limits of my English tongue. I, like the scientist, believe in the truth of something I cannot see because I have built my knowledge on authorities preceding me as well as upon personal experience—as did Lewis.

The Relationality of Truth

Throughout the Chronicles of Narnia, Lewis implies that truth is far more than abstract rational information; truth is relational, involving persons, human and divine, communing and communicating in dynamic interaction. In *Prince Caspian,* several children, skeptical about Aslan's presence, see him only after they listen to Lucy's testimony about where the lion is leading and, trusting her, start to follow. Once they act on Lucy's witness, Aslan becomes apparent to them: the blind can see. For the Christian, truth is indeed "out there," but we understand it only by trusting and following. The truth coexists with our "positionality": it meets us where we are so that we might follow. In the Hebrew Scriptures, a disembodied God spoke from a burning bush in order to lead the twelve tribes of Israel through the wilderness of Sinai to the Promised Land. Later the embodied God set faith on fire by leading twelve disciples through the wilderness of sin to another Promised Land.

Like Aslan with Emeth, then, the truth meets human beings on their own ground. It reminds me of something I learned in a Young Life Bible study. As I was leading some high schoolers through the Gospels, one of the girls, having just licked the cream out of an Oreo, burst out, "What's the deal with all the different ways Jesus healed the blind? Couldn't he make up his mind?" Though she was being sassy, she had a point. Whereas Jesus heals two blind men in Nazareth by touching their eyes (Matthew 9:27-31), outside of Jericho he responds to Bartimaeus's plea for sight without any touch; he simply says, "Go; your faith has made you well" (Mark 10:46-52; Luke 18:35-43). On the same journey from Jericho to Jerusalem, Jesus heals two other men without saying anything, this time merely touching their eyes (Matthew 20:29-34).[47] In Jerusalem, Jesus puts mud, made with his saliva, on the defective eyes of a man who was born blind and then instructs him to "wash in the pool of Siloam" (John 9:1-11); only then is he healed. When Jesus encounters a blind man in Bethsaida, however, he leads him out of town and then spits directly

---

[47]Many scholars think that this healing was the same as the Bartimaeus healing, only remembered differently by different Gospel writers—thus demonstrating the pluralism of perception.

on his eyes before laying hands on him. But the healing doesn't totally take, and Jesus must lay his hands on the eyes a second time (Mark 8:22-26).

My Oreo-relishing high schooler wondered why, if Jesus was God, he wasn't more pragmatic, or at least more consistent, employing the same quick-fix technique each time. Today I would answer her that Jesus, the Truth, seems to acknowledge each person's "positionality"—not merely in terms of where her body is positioned but also in terms of her soul's position, its psychological and spiritual makeup. He knows that some people need only to be touched in order to accept divine healing; others, however, have to participate in their healing much more dramatically in order to be assured of their wholeness. One blind man needed to feel mud on his eyes, another that and then some. Truth, then, is relative to each; all come to the light differently. Nevertheless, it is the same Truth they come to: Jesus is the way, the truth and the light. The relativity is relational; it is based on the positionality of human perception and response rather than on the mere position of God. The same sun melts butter and hardens clay.

The most significant postmodern thinkers acknowledge that truth is relational as well: it is perceived through the beliefs, values and practices of the community—the human relations—within which a human is positioned. In contrast to Enlightenment humanists, postmodernists assert that human beings cannot discover truth on their own. Christian orthodoxy affirms this. If human beings could discover truth on their own, there would be no need for revelation, no need for the Holy Spirit, no need for the Bible, no need for Christian fellowship. Even Christ—God on earth—formed a community around himself, affirming the power of relationships to discern and transmit truth.

Proclaiming the Truth in Love

What, then, can we do when self-proclaimed postmodernists (usually the less informed ones) respond to the competing truth claims of different religions with the statement "There are no absolutes; all truth is relative"?

We can answer with the retort given by more sophisticated postmodernists: to say "There are no absolutes" is to make an absolutist statement. It's like saying, "There's only one truth: there is no truth." To be consistent, postmodernists must be open, like Jacques Derrida, to the possibility of "the Impossible": that there may be something—the "messianic"—that transcends human language. It is "impossible" because as soon as we attempt to communicate this Truth, we conform it to our towers.

Why even try, then?

Because language, like Truth, is relational.

Postmodern multiculturalism draws attention to the fact that all humans engage language in order to relate to others. The desire to communicate and the things being communicated—love, anger, hope, despair, joy, awe, beauty, justice and peace—are universal impulses, even if seen and expressed differently. Similarly, the majority of humans around the world attempt some kind of relationship with an absolute, albeit in radically different ways.

This near universal desire to know the Truth signals to me that there is a Truth desiring to be known, a Truth that created humans to desire the Truth. Augustine, addressing God in the first paragraph of his *Confessions,* put it this way: "You made us for yourself, and our heart is restless until it rests in you."[48]

In contrast, the modernist proclaimed, "You can rest in the fact that enlightened human reason, unlike religion, enables us to make statements that correspond with reality. Therefore you will know the truth, and the truth will set you free—free from dependence on religion." The postmodernist challenged the hubris of this correspondence theory of truth, giving Christians the opportunity to proclaim, "You shall know the Truth, which is not a disembodied concept grasped with autonomous reason. The Truth is a Person who has related to our position as embodied human beings in order to relate to us. And through this relationship, the Truth will set you free—but not in order to autonomously choose from rival explanations of reality. The Truth will set you free from sin, a freedom made possible only within relationship. Forgiveness, whether human or divine, can only occur relationally, one person confessing so the other—including the Transcendent Other—can forgive."

Believing, in all humility, that we have been forgiven, Christians are called to do unto others as we would have them do unto us. This includes attempting to understand how and why people in other towers relate to the truth differently from the way we do. Remembering that Jesus provided light for the blind in radically different ways, we need to be open to what many Christians would call "the impossible": the idea that people who do not see

---

[48]Augustine, *Confessions,* trans. Henry Chadwick (Oxford: Oxford University Press, 1991), p. 3.

Jesus might eventually come to the light because of Jesus, the Truth who can relate to us whether we see him as Truth or not.

Absolute Love, after all, loves absolutely—despite our building relativism.

Identifying Truth

THE BEST AND WORST
OF POSTMODERNISM

T hroughout this book I have been identifying ways
that postmodernism serves Christian faith, and I would like to end the book
by asserting how Christian faith can serve postmodernists. Before I do so, I
need to discuss some negative aspects of postmodernism, suggesting how
they have sullied Christianity. Only by confronting our own complicity with
the worst of postmodernism, I will argue, can Christians establish an identity
worthy of our name, employing the best of postmodernism to (1) rethink
how we read the Bible and (2) lovingly relate the truth of Christ.

The Worst of Postmodernism: When the Surface Is the Substance

One of the celebrated postmodernists of the 1980s was Jean Baudrillard, a
professor of sociology at the University of Paris Nanterre. A former Marxist
(like many postmodern theorists), Baudrillard argued that Marxism could no
longer critique capitalism, because capitalism had changed. While Marxism
responded to the capitalism of the Industrial Revolution, postmodernism responds to what Daniel Bell called, in 1973, a "post-industrial society."[1]

Thus, rather than being fueled by its modes of industrial production, the
Western economy is now fueled, according to Baudrillard, by the sign. Con-
sumers buy signs rather than products; they purchase objects that bring
them status rather than products that fulfill needs. This is evident not only

---

[1] Daniel Bell, *The Coming of Post-industrial Society* (New York: Basic Books, 1973).

in the expensive cars cruising through poor urban neighborhoods but also in the Hummers parked outside upscale suburban homes. Postmodern society, then, is what Guy Debord calls the "society of the spectacle," where identity is based on surface appearances.[2]

This is different from Jesus' reference to "whitewashed tombs." He, of course, was speaking of religious people who "on the outside look righteous to others" but "are full of hypocrisy and lawlessness" on the inside (Matthew 23:27-28). For Baudrillard there is no distinction between outside and inside: the surface *is* the substance; people *are* what they own or perform. America has therefore become the culture of the "simulacrum": a sign that does not point to anything except its own power as a sign.

For instance, a Hummer, once signaling military utility, is now a sign for its own power as a status symbol. Or, better yet, consider this caption from my local newspaper: "Actress Kate Mulgrew, seen lately in *Star Trek: Voyager* as the first female captain to star in a Trekkie series, will be the guest of the White House tomorrow at an issues briefing touting women's achievements in science."[3] A fictional *sign* of women's achievement in science is treated like the real thing.

In the postmodern "society of the spectacle," even people's faces have become signs, not of themselves but of someone else. Richard Fleming, a Beverly Hills plastic surgeon, publishes every year a list of the most popular requests he gets from his patients. In 2004 he reported that women tended to want Angelina Jolie's lips, Nicole Kidman's nose or Catherine Zeta-Jones's eyes, while men asked for Jude Law's lips, Keanu Reeves's nose or Johnny Depp's jaw. In postmodern society, then, rather than seeking the bread of life, people dish out a lot of dough in order to become simulacra.[4]

Postmodern simulacra are abetted by the Internet, which got its start, significantly enough, in the 1960s. Like many other theorists, Stuart Sim regards the Internet as "the exemplary postmodern object, and arguably even the architecture of postmodern culture."[5] This is because signs from cyberspace appear on our computer screens without any indication of their place of origin or of the substance behind them. I'll never forget the time I overhead a six-foot-tall, two-hundred-pound adolescent male in California telling a

---

[2]Guy Debord, *The Society of the Spectacle* (Detroit: Black and Red, 1976).
[3]*Patriot News* (Harrisburg, Penn.), March 9, 1995.
[4]Walter Scott, "Personality Parade," *Parade Magazine*, April 25, 2004, p. 2.
[5]Stuart Sim, ed., *The Routledge Companion to Postmodernism* (New York: Routledge, 2001), p. 284.

friend about his time in a chat room that day: "Today I was a 110-pound single mom from Texas." The Internet allowed him to fabricate an identity that had no substance: it was a simulacrum. And I don't even want to know what the guy as "single Texan female" was writing to another person— although that other person, unknown to him, was probably a simulacrum as well, an identity fabricated by words on a screen. Postmodernism, says Baudrillard, has thus replaced reality with "hyperreality."[6]

Baudrillard so relished the idea of hyperreality that he eventually became a simulacrum of himself, publishing such outrageous ideas and inaccuracies that scholars stopped taking him seriously. But in the early 1980s he was a defining voice of postmodernism, aligning it with the information technology and consumerism of Western culture. It is no wonder that Marxists launched such vicious attacks against postmodernism!

Unfortunately, like culture at large, many Christians have bought (into) the power of the sign, purchasing objects they do not need and lifestyles they cannot afford. This may explain why, in 2002, only 6 percent of "born again" Christians tithed; much of their money, evidently, was spent on status signs. In *The Scandal of the Evangelical Conscience,* Ronald J. Sider lists statistic after statistic, gathered by reputable polling agencies, demonstrating that evangelical behavior in the twenty-first century is not that much different from secular culture. He quotes theologian Michael Horton to say that "evangelical Christians are as likely to embrace lifestyles every bit as hedonistic, materialistic, self-centered, and sexually immoral as the world in general."[7] In other words, evangelicals have embraced postmodern hyperreality with a vengeance.

I would rather have us embrace some of the postmodern perceptions presented in earlier chapters of this book. After all, one of those perceptions is validated by Sider's book: the discourse of culture molds behavior and identity—even for born-again Christians.

A Postmodern View of Identity

Identity is a concept which creates problems for many postmodern theorists. For them, the word *identity* is too closely tied to the modernist notion of an "authentic self" which refuses to follow the conventions of culture.

---

[6]Jean Baudrillard, "The Orders of Simulacra," in her *Simulations,* trans. Paul Foss, Paul Patton and Philip Beitchman (New York: Semiotext(e), 1983).

[7]Ronald J. Sider, *The Scandal of the Evangelical Conscience: Why Are Christians Living Just Like the Rest of the World?* (Grand Rapids: Baker, 2005), p. 17.

Conformism was regarded as the unforgivable sin by many modernist existentialists, who were willing to risk alienation in order to protect their autonomous identity.

For the postmodernist, in contrast, people are not identical to their own sense of self, for every human is inevitably molded by culture. To a certain extent, Christian orthodoxy agrees with this, recognizing how the society in which we are embedded shapes both perception and behavior. Even St. Paul admits that he is not identical to himself: "I do not understand my own actions. For I do not do what I want, but I do the very thing I hate." He attributes this disjunction, of course, to sin: "Now if I do what I do not want, it is no longer I that do it, but sin that dwells within me" (Romans 7:15, 20). I am struck by the distinction Paul makes between the "I" and the self that performs "sin." But what elicits this performance? Obviously not the "I" (note how Romans 7:15-25 reiterates this).

Where, then, does sin come from? I was taught to answer, "From the human heart," and I still believe this. But the Bible repeatedly implies that the heart is influenced by external forces. If we look back to the story of sin's origin in Genesis, we see that it comes from outside the self. Consonant with the poststructuralist sense that language shapes human behavior, a serpent's words, not its actions, direct the performances of Eve and Adam. Subject to a power outside the "I," Adam and Eve perform new selves, their story anticipating Paul's statement "So I find it to be a law that when I want to do what is good, evil lies close at hand" (Romans 7:21).

Postmodernism also views the self as subjected to forces, embedded in language, which become internalized. Therefore, rather than the word *identity*, many employ the word *subjectivity* to refer to the self, because the self is both subject to and the subject of language. As in Paul's reiterations in Romans 7, the "I" of a sentence, though grammatically its "subject," is not entirely in control of its subjectivity. Perhaps this explains Paul's emphasis, throughout his letters, on the need for Christians to actively participate in a society of believers, a church community or fellowship group whose language might shape a new subjectivity, one that displaces our subjection to sin.

Christians, then, are called not to be autonomous, existentialist believers but to edify each other (1 Corinthians 14:26). The word *edify*, of course, is related to the word *edifice*. When we edify others, we "build them up." So also we are "constructed" by the society in which we are positioned. St. Peter was especially attuned to the construction metaphor, perhaps because Jesus designated him as the "rock" on which the church would be built (Matthew 16:18). In his first letter, Peter writes, "Like living stones, let yourselves be built into a spiritual house, to be a holy priesthood. . . . For it stands in scripture: 'See, I am laying in Zion a stone, / a cornerstone chosen and precious; / and whoever believes in him will not be put to shame'" (1 Peter 2:5-6).

Christians like myself believe this cornerstone is Christ, whose subjection to death on the cross made possible the construction of a new subjectivity for those who subject themselves to him in trusting relationship. Jesus himself refused an existentialist identity, even though he had every right to assume that his "authenticity" as the Son of God—"identical" to God, in fact—elevated him above the rest of humanity. He was perhaps the only man to walk the earth who deserved Nietzsche's name for a person demonstrating culture-defying authenticity: *Übermensch*. Coining the aphorism "God is dead," Nietzsche asserted that the Übermensch becomes his own god. Jesus, however, refused the status of Übermensch, for he "did not regard equality with God / as something to be exploited, / but emptied himself, / taking the form of a slave, / being born in human likeness" (Philippians 2:6-7). And he surrounded himself with a group who could define him to us, "constructing" his ministry through their Gospels in order to attest that he was (and is!) God's own Son, resurrected from the dead.

How do we know this? We take it on faith, believing it has been revealed to us through Scriptures inspired by the Holy Spirit. And, as I have been arguing throughout this book, the best of postmodernism allows us to share this faith with impunity.

The Best of Postmodernism: The Religious Turn

Sometimes called "the religious turn," postmodernism has made a radical difference among academicians. In the 1970s Paul Feyerabend, a philosopher of science influenced by Thomas S. Kuhn, outraged modernists when he asserted that religious explanations for the origins of life must be taken as seriously as scientific ones. As Stuart Sim notes, Feyerabend, though not a Christian, went so far as to argue that since "there is simply no common ground between the Creationist and Darwinian views of the origins of humankind they should be taught in schools on an equal basis."[8] Two decades later,

---

[8]Sim, *Routledge Companion to Postmodernism*, p. 244. Paul Feyerabend's two most famous works are *Science in a Free Society* (1978) and *A Farewell to Reason* (1987).

famed evolutionary biologist Stephen Jay Gould created a firestorm of controversy when he not only demonstrated how modernist science had unfairly
dismissed religion but also argued that religious explanations for reality must
be valued.[9]

Attitudes have also changed in the humanities. As most professors can
attest, secular conferences that once avoided religious issues, if not reviled
them, now include respectful discussions of how faith informs their academic discipline, from philosophy to political science. I realized something amazing had happened when I read about a presentation at Yale
University by two of our country's most famous African American scholars,
Cornel West and bell hooks. After someone sang Tommy Dorsey's "Precious Lord," hooks, an advocate of postmodernism, began by saying,
"Both Cornel and I come to you as individuals who believe in God. That
belief informs our message." Encouraged by postmodern theory to establish their "positionality," they felt free to witness to their faith. More re-
cently, a local chapter of the secular organization that made poststructuralism famous, the Modern Language Association, announced a 2005
conference called "God Is Undead: Post-secular Notions in Contemporary
Literature and Theory."[10]

Reviews of scholarly books repeatedly acknowledge the change postmodernism has made. In 2003, for example, scholars received announce-
ments for publications that reflect "the 'return to religion' now evident in European philosophy." A reviewer stated, "One of the most important recent
trends in 19th-century studies has been the rescue of religion from the academic discard bin." Blackwell, a respected British publisher, summarized it
well: "The reintroduction of religion into the market is a defining characteristic of postmodernity."[11]

---

[9]Stephen Jay Gould, *Rocks of Ages: Science and Religion in the Fullness of Life* (New York: Bal-
lantine, 1999).

[10]bell hooks and Cornel West, *Breaking Bread: Insurgent Black Intellectual Life* (Boston: South
End, 1991), p. 8. The Northeast Modern Language Association Conference, focusing on ways
that "religion has found a way back into the academy," was held in Cambridge, Massachusetts, March 31-April 2, 2005.

[11]Taken from a catalog blurb for Michel Henry, *I Am the Truth: Toward a Philosophy of Christianity,* trans. Susan Emanuel (Stanford, Calif.: Stanford University Press, 2003); the *Choice*
review (May 2003) of Cynthia Scheinberg, *Women's Poetry and Religion in Victorian England:
Jewish Identity and Christian Culture* (Cambridge: Cambridge University Press, 2002); and the
catalog description for Graham Ward, *True Religion* (Oxford: Blackwell, 2002).

A Postmodern View of Religion

To understand a postmodern view of religion, imagine a room, with windows in all four walls, where a group of fifteen people sit in a circle facing each other. Each is strapped into a wheelchair that has a ring of metal placed around the occupant's forehead, holding the head in place. Depending on which direction a person's wheelchair faces, the occupant will perceive reality differently. He can see the people across the circle quite easily, while those at his sides are knowable only through sound. This is how all of us see reality; the placement of our body in time and space—our positionality—limits our perceptions like a band around our forehead. We see religion, then, as that which transcends this room of human existence: it is the spiritual reality that exists beyond the windows of our life environment.

Secular humanists, of course, deny the existence of anything beyond and concentrate only on things in the room: the reasoning abilities of the people as they respond to each other and things verifiable to their senses. Many modernists refuse to even glance out the windows and put all their energy into denying that anything is out there to be seen. Postmodernists, however, wheel their chairs around the circle, listening to how different groups, positioned at different spots, describe what they see out the windows.

And they attest that people facing one set of windows see something different outside from the view of those facing the opposite direction. People sitting in one part of the circle see Allah, those in another see Jehovah, those looking out other windows perceive a universal Oversoul. Furthermore, postmodernists note that when people talk about the truth of their perceptions, someone facing one direction will say, "I believe in absolute truth, and only my window reveals it." Another will retort, "You are wrong; absolute truth appears only out my window." And a third will shout, "No! To see absolute truth you must look out my window!" Religious truth seems relative to the place where the absolutist is situated.

Even the word *absolute* is situated, meaning different things to different people. In philosophy, absolute means "independent" or "free-standing," such that "absolute truth" is independent of individual thinkers and their various windows on reality. This is what I have meant in earlier chapters when I talk about "absolute truth" beyond all towers of perception. Some evangelical intellectuals, however, assert that we should not call God "the Absolute," and they have good reason. The word has been compromised by modernists, who replaced God with numerous alternate definitions of the Absolute:

as universal spirit, as will, as the life force behind evolution, as consciousness, as experience, as the space-time matrix of all reality, and so on. While for Kant the Absolute was unknowable, Christian orthodoxy asserts that God became known through Christ. Hence, rather than "independent" or "freestanding," God desires to be in relationship with humanity. This is why some say God should not be described as absolute. As we can see, even among Christians there are plural ways of seeing "the Absolute."

It is important to realize, then, that postmodernists do not *prescribe* something called "religious pluralism." Postmodernists merely *describe* what they see: the world is filled with people who have conflicting vocabularies for absolute truth. How should Christians respond? If we proclaim, "All of you are wrong; only *we* see absolute truth!" what distinguishes our behavior from the similar proclamations of seriously committed Buddhists, Muslims and Jews? All we are doing is reinforcing postmodern descriptions of religious behavior.

I believe that Christians *do* have the clearest window on truth, but attempting to knock bottles of Windex out of the hands of competing religions is not the best response. Instead, Christians should be embodying—incarnating—how Christianity differs from other religions, in such a way that people long to look out our window at what inspires our actions. Think of the word *convert*: the Latin root word, *vertere,* means to turn. People "convert" when they turn in a new direction. We want to turn people toward our window, believing that once they see Jesus, whose incarnation inspires our own fallen imitations, there's no turning back.

The Problem with the Religious Turn

Good developments can have negative consequences. When the cane toad was introduced to the Australian ecosystem, for example, it effectively did its job, eating up the crop-destroying pests it was meant to eradicate. Joy over the return of threatened crops, however, soon turned to despair. Because cane toads had no natural predators in Australia, they burgeoned, reproducing so excessively that they became worse pests than the ones they destroyed.

Similarly, when poststructuralism was introduced to Western culture, it effectively nibbled away at faith-destroying modernism. The return of religious crops, however, created a new problem: an excessive multiplicity of faith vocabularies, with an indiscriminate emphasis on tolerance for all. Tolerance, of course, is a good thing. But postmodernists who argue most vo-ciferously for tolerance are often intolerant of anyone who disagrees with their definition of tolerance. They just want to keep turning, rather than commit themselves to one view of truth.

The problem with the religious turn of postmodernity, then, is not getting people to turn toward a Christian window but getting them to spend serious time looking through it so that we can explain to them the significance of what they see. The sophisticated information systems that are the identifying mark of postmodernity—film, radio, television and especially the Internet—expose people to more competing claims for "truth" than ever before. This allows seekers to sample superficial feel-good elements from many different religions. Rather than seeking understanding beyond their own life experiences, some of these individuals—often called "New Age"—do not consider what frames our windows of faith. It's more like they're looking through the windows that protect salad bars from snotty sneezes as they pick and choose elements that satisfy their personal palates. How do we get people to turn from the bread at the end of the salad bar in order to seek the Bread of Life?

I would begin to answer this important question by once again quoting the words of Jesus: "Do to others as you would have them do to you" (Matthew 7:12). If we want people to take our community's window on Christ seriously, we need to take the existence of other windows seriously, seeking to understand why people believe the way they do. This includes taking critiques of Christianity seriously. Rather than getting defensive, we need to rethink our language and how it identifies us. One descriptor I'd like us to reconsider is the identifying term employed by many evangelicals: *Bible-believing*. Perhaps it would be more helpful—and accurate—to characterize ourselves as *Christ-following*.

Identifying Biblical Truth

Christian identity is molded by what we identify as biblical truth. Problematically, there are multiple biblical truths that sometimes seem to conflict with each other. When a rich young ruler asks, "What must I do to inherit eternal life?" Jesus replies that the way to salvation is threefold; first he tells the ruler to follow the commandments, next to "sell all that you own and distribute the money to the poor," and finally to "come, follow me" (Luke 18:18, 22). In contrast, Jesus explains eternal life quite differently to Nicodemus: "For God so loved the world that he gave his only Son, so that every-one who believes in him may not perish but may have eternal life" (John 3:16).

There are several ways to respond to this discrepancy. I name them *one-window readings, window-glass readings* and *multipaned readings.*

One-window readings. Some Christians argue that only one of the ac-counts above gives a window on the absolute truth of eternal life. Some will foreground John's story, saying that salvation is entirely based on belief in Christ's resurrection. Others will cite Luke's story, noting that Christ says nothing about "right belief" but instead calls the rich young man to "right action." These "social action" Christians, however, are often repudiated by those looking through John's window, and vice versa. Both windows are framed by numerous verses in the Bible that support their view of truth, and people positioned at each window often quote their framing Bible verses to invalidate the view through the other window. One-window readers treat the Bible itself like a salad bar, picking and choosing verses that confirm their vision.

Window-glass readings. Those who advocate glass readings would say that the Gospels attributed to Luke and John are viewing Christ's ministry through differently framed glass, glass that reflects, like windows at night, the authors' different positionalities. Indeed, even conservative Bible schol-ars will tell you that the focus of John's book is quite different from that of the other Gospels, that John emphasizes belief much more than the others do. Liberal critics will point out that only John's Gospel includes the story of Lazarus's resurrection, a dramatic oversight for the other writers, since the incident, if it really happened, must have been the talk of the town. These critics will suggest that John made up the story to bolster the believability of Christ's forthcoming resurrection. For them, John's Gospel-glass mirrors his own interests.

Glass scholars therefore inspect the Gospel windows in order to ascertain which has the most solid frame around the truth—which is most "authentic." Often, however, the inspection is made from the perspective of a very dif-ferent window, so that the scholar validates whichever Gospel accords with *her* view of truth. The worst examples occur among demythologizers, who, having decided in advance that supernatural elements in Scripture are im-plausible, pronounce as "inauthentic" parts of Scripture that describe super-natural events. These readers so focus on each Gospel glass that they fail to gaze *through* the glass with faith-filled trust in the sight all share in common: Christ's death and resurrection for humanity.

Multipaned readings. Christians should acknowledge that while there are numerous windows on absolute truth, we believe we look through the most solidly framed and clearest one. However, at the same time, we also recognize that our one window has numerous panes of glass, divided by wooden or metal lattices, as seen in old country houses. Thus, depending on which pane a Christian is situated before, she, like the Gospel writers, will view Christ's teaching differently. In fact, as with any multipaned window, she can probably see two views at once, while remaining very aware of the latticework dividing them.

This certainly was the case for the apostle Paul. In his letter to the Romans, he looks at "eternal life" through the same pane of glass as Luke, saying that God "will repay according to each one's deeds: to those who by patiently doing good seek for glory and honor and immortality, he will give eternal life" (Romans 2:6-7). However, Paul changes perspective a bit later, presenting a more John-like view: "If you confess with your lips that Jesus is Lord and believe in your heart that God raised him from the dead, you will be saved" (Romans 10:9). Paul's plural perspectives show us that eternal life is not an either-or proposition but a commitment to both-and living.

In the language of postmodernism, we might say that the binary opposition between belief and action contains its own deconstruction, for both right belief and right action are marked with a trace of that which they repudiate. On the one hand, being Christ to others necessitates belief in his teachings; on the other hand, belief, if it has no works, is dead (James 2:17).

Paneful Readings of Scripture

For Christians used to one-pane readings of the Bible, the discovery of other panes can be, well, painful. I know the feeling. Though I read my Bible diligently throughout my adolescence, I simply did not *see* the verses outside my framed perspective on truth. I overlooked the fact that in Philippi, Paul and Silas tell their jailer, "Believe on the Lord Jesus, and you will be saved, you *and your household*" (Acts 16:31, emphasis mine). When I finally noticed this verse, I was shocked, having been taught that one person's decision to follow Christ does not cover a multitude of sinners. I found even more disturbing Paul's emphatic statement to the Galatians: "Listen! I, Paul, am telling you that if you let yourselves be circumcised, Christ will be of no benefit to you" (Galatians 5:2). Why, then, did my "Bible-believing" parents allow my brother to be circumcised?

Many readers will retort that I am quoting these verses out of context, that they must be considered in light of surrounding verses and of the historical situation that Paul is addressing. And they would be exactly right. Truth is *situated* in contexts. Nevertheless, I have discovered that sometimes people who discount verses that don't accord with their worldview—saying they must be read in context—often treat other verses as autonomous, decontextualized nuggets of truth and use them as stones to throw at other people's windows.

For example, some who regard as absolute truth Paul's prescription that "the husband is the head of his wife" (1 Corinthians 11:3) disregard Paul's very next sentence: "Any woman who prays or prophesies with her head unveiled disgraces her head" (1 Corinthians 11:5). In fact, I have heard Christians dismiss Anabaptists who honor this verse—Mennonite and Amish women who wear prayer veils—as "works oriented."

Augustine, the great definer and defender of Christian doctrine, had little patience with one-pane interpretations of the Bible. Discussing Genesis in his *Confessions,* he emphatically states,

> See how stupid it is, among so large a mass of entirely correct interpretations which can be elicited from those words, rashly to assert that a particular one has the best claim to be Moses' view, and by destructive disputes to offend against charity itself, which is the principle of everything he said in the texts we are attempting to expound.[12]

Augustine's emphasis on charity implies that we need to be humble in our use of the Bible as an arbiter of universal truth, for many times the truths we find are those we have been trained to see. After all, the Bible is not self-interpreting; it does not indicate which are its most important passages. Human beings are the interpreters, and all interpret according to the pane of glass before which they are positioned. The truth of Scripture is therefore as pluralistic as the multipaned window before which Christian communities throughout the ages and around the globe have positioned themselves.[13]

---

[12] *Confessions of St. Augustine* 12.25.35, quoted in James K. A. Smith, *The Fall of Interpretation: Philosophical Foundations for a Creational Hermeneutic* (Downers Grove, Ill.: InterVarsity Press, 2000), pp. 177-78.

[13] As discussed in chapter seven, Jamie Smith provides an apologetic for interpretive pluralism. In fact, he identifies the Fall with what I call "one-window" interpretation: "The central effect

This, however, does not mean that interpretation is arbitrary. From the very beginning of the church, views through the Hebrew Scriptures, as with the New Testament much later, have had a focus: standing on the other side of the biblical window is Jesus, who, like a prism refracting the glory of God, casts light on all panes of biblical glass—if even at different angles. According to Luke 24:27, even Jesus interpreted "Moses and all the prophets" in terms of himself. Jesus is the site/sight that gives purpose to the plural panes of Christian interpretation.

Arming Plural Truths: The Biblical Canon

As Augustine illustrates, interpretive pluralism is not a result of postmodernism. Postmodernism merely gives us a new vocabulary with which we can talk about it. While many modernists saw scriptural discrepancies as evidence that the Bible was not "true," postmodernists would attribute discrepancies to the pluralistic situatedness of interpretation. I, in fact, see the different perspectives presented by the four Gospel accounts as validation of biblical truth. Writing out of their situatedness, Matthew, Mark, Luke and John saw the facts differently. Each reported differently, for example, the number and identities of the women who discovered Christ's empty tomb. If, as some suggest, the entire New Testament was written centuries after Christ in order to substantiate and legitimate a fiction about his resurrection, one would think that the conspirators would work harder to get their stories straight. Instead, the plural perspectives of the Evangelists reflect the embodiment of truth.

Christian pluralism is also reflected in how the New Testament was put together. Numerous documents were floating around during the first centuries of the church, all of which were considered authoritative to at least one congregation committed to following Christ. Church leaders therefore set up councils to discuss the truths that the majority held in common and to select the documents that best presented those truths. These councils rejected some documents that earnest followers of Christ held as sacred, while accepting others as necessary to the faith. The selection process, of course, was not capricious. The zealous circulation of certain documents among early Christians, as Norman Perrin and Dennis Duling note, "could almost

---

of the Fall with regards to interpretation is domination—the domination of texts and the domination of others by the oppressive imposition of one interpretation." See *Fall of Interpretation*, p. 187 n. 24.

be described as a prerequisite to final inclusion in the New Testament, for books not found generally useful, and hence not copied and circulated, would not have found their way into the canon."[14] Thus after a great deal of prayer—as well as argument—a council in 397 finally determined which books should be considered sacred Scripture. Our Bible canon, then, is a product of the situatedness of both Christian and Jewish traditions. Indeed, there is no historical or biblical evidence that God wrote on a wall revealing which books to include and which to leave out.

Dorothy L. Sayers was especially attuned to the ancient traditions of the church, which she studied intently. She disagreed with those who placed the authority of the Bible above church tradition. When in 1942 an American asked her to "write a book about the Scriptural sanction for the doctrine of the Trinity," she refused, explaining that the doctrine of the Trinity, a word never mentioned in the Bible, "was hammered out at the Council of Nicaea" in the fourth century. She writes,

> But since you demand Scriptural warrant for everything, where is your Scriptural authority for the Scriptures themselves? On what texts do you rely for the make-up of the Canon as we have it? Where, for example, does the Lord say that there are to be those four Gospels and no more? or that the *Revelation of Peter* and *The Shepherd of Hermas* are not authoritative—though the first was read in churches as early as the second century, and the second was included in the *Codex Sinaiticus* as late as the fourth century? The doctrine of the Trinity was worked out and formulated in the Church—the same Church that is the authority for the Canon itself.[15]

Sayers recognized that truth is an expression of belief formulated by an interpretive community. In fact, she is quick to point out that the word *dogma,* used to describe the traditional doctrines of Christian belief, originally meant "opinion."[16] The word *opinion,* of course, sends up all kinds of red flags, making us think of "seekers" picking and choosing tasteful opinions from the salad bar of faith. But that is a modernist interpretation of "opinion," tied to the idea that autonomous individuals can reach truth on their own. In contrast, the premodern Christian view, like the postmodern

---

[14]Norman Perrin and Dennis Duling, *The New Testament: An Introduction* (New York: Harcourt Brace Jovanovich, 1982), p. 450.

[15]*The Letters of Dorothy L. Sayers, 1937-1943: From Novelist to Playwright,* ed. Barbara Reynolds (Cambridge: Carole Green, 1997), p. 367.

[16]As Lesslie Newbigin notes, "'Dogma' derives from *dokein,* 'to seem.'" See *The Gospel in a Pluralist Society* (Grand Rapids: Eerdmans, 1989), p. 5.

view, is that opinion, or dogma, arises out of an interpretive community whose members believe with all their hearts, souls and minds that their shared opinion is truth. Christians also believe, however, that God guided this process of dogma formation and that the Holy Spirit continues to guide us in the understanding of its truth, speaking to us through the biblical canon established by Christians in the fourth century.

Taking Aim with the Canon

The word *canon* comes from an ancient Greek word meaning "measuring rod" or "ruler." Whether made of wood or plastic, a ruler is based on a human formulation that communities agree to follow as an absolute standard of measurement. While U.S. rulers measure by inches and feet, European countries conform their rulers to a metric system. However, even though millimeters and inches are human constructions, we choose to obey them, for if people were to take them lightly, airplanes, houses and clothes would all fall down. Rulers are absolutely necessary, and hence become necessary absolutes.

The same, then, can be said of the biblical canon, which is the "rod" or "ruler" by which we take measure of God's revelation in history. Having been established by humans as the absolute guide for following Christ, the canon should not be altered by addition or subtraction. As New Testament theologian Luke Timothy Johnson argues,

> An unlimited canon is no measure, any more than a foot ruler can gain inches and still be a foot ruler. Because it is closed, the canon can perform the function of mediating a specific identity through successive ages of the church. Because the church today reads the same writings as were read by Polycarp and Augustine and Aquinas and Luther and Barth, it remains identifiably the same community, and on that basis can debate with those earlier readers their interpretations and realizations.[17]

It is the same ruler, but we measure different things with it. Just as Americans in the 1920s never dreamed that we would someday be measuring the inches of our cell phones and iPods, they also never dreamed that many Christians would someday be measuring the biblical place of women preachers and gay marriage.

---

[17]Luke Timothy Johnson, *Scripture and Discernment: Decision Making and the Church* (Nashville: Abingdon, 1996), p. 36.

Unfortunately, the history of Christianity is filled with examples of people who turn their ruler into an idol, making it so inflexible that it can't measure new things. Christians in the fourteenth century persecuted John Wyclif for translating parts of the Bible into English, and church leaders burned William Tyndale's 1525 English translation. The abusers of Wyclif and Tyndale believed that the ruler could function properly only in Latin, that Latin was the truly sacred language.

It took almost a century before Christians in England would recognize that language is a human construction, like inches and meters, but when authorized by an interpretive community, it operates as an absolute guide to truth. As a result, the 1611 Bible, authorized by King James, became a new expression of the old standard of measurement, enabling English readers to see the truth in a new light. Just as a tape measure, different from an unbending wooden ruler, can measure different surfaces without losing its absolute standard, the Bible, translated into new languages, can speak in new ways to communities of people who acknowledge its authority.

Therefore, as Johnson argues, the incredible diversity and apparent contradictions within Scripture are its strength. Its pluralistic pronouncements and parables can speak to the pluralistic experiences of Christians, a pluralism generated by our positionality, whether in thirteenth-century Assisi or twenty-first-century Aspen, whether in a Mennonite or a Methodist fellowship, whether in times of joy or times of sorrow. To refuse the pluralism of Scripture is to make an idol of only one voice within it, as though to say that the space between the three- and four-inch mark on a ruler is the only segment a carpenter can legitimately employ for accurate measurements.

What is to prevent, then, people from reading into Scripture anything they want?

One form of prevention is to stop thinking like modernists who celebrate the radical autonomy of thought. From the very beginning of Christianity, to follow Jesus was to participate in community, whether a group of twelve disciples—seeking God like the twelve tribes of Israel—or a contemporary megachurch of twelve thousand believers. As Johnson notes, the books of the Bible "were written to be read before many hearers at worship, and so they are read in the church today. They are also read for purposes of public discussion and discernment. The Scripture as Scripture is appropriated by a community. Therefore, the act of interpretation (the hermeneutical process) must also involve the community."[18]

The canon, then, is absolute, even though it measures different things at different times as communities are positioned differently. The ones who made it absolute, a community of Christians in 397, determined its measurement by an absolute established and expressed in the community-endorsed creeds of the early church, like the Nicene Creed of 325 and the baptismal creeds that preceded it. We believe, of course, that both times these fathers of our faith were guided, not only by the Holy Spirit, but also by three centuries of believers who had faith that a carpenter in the first century was himself the measure of all truth.

Relating Faith

How, then, do I relate my faith to others, especially postmodern others, who often preach tolerance of all communities rather than commitment to any single one? Of course, the most perceptive ones recognize that we are all committed to some kind of discourse, whether we realize it or not. But they would still consider proselytizing a form of "violence" or "terror." Though these words seem excessively negative, an experience I had in grad school, while teaching a writing course, helps me understand.

Still struggling to figure out how to be a good teacher, I felt harried by one of my students, who wore me out with his attacks on Christians. He turned most of his papers, and many of his comments during class discussion, into diatribes against Christianity. His language was so bitter, his metaphors so violent, that I finally asked him for an explanation. He informed me that during high school he had "accepted Christ" at a Young Life camp. But when he told his Jewish parents about his conversion, they were so horrified that they hired a "deprogrammer" to kidnap him in order to convince him about the idiocy of Christianity. Whether their motivation was from modernist disdain or in protection of Judaism I do not know. What I do know is that their son was psychologically battered, so proselytized by anti-Christian assumptions that he could not stop witnessing to the "truth" of what he had learned: that Christianity was vile. However, his reiterations that he knew the absolute truth while all Christians were in error made even non-Christians in my classroom feel terrorized by his insistent rhetoric.

---

[18]Ibid., p. 32.

It made me wonder if my insistence that only Christians have the truth and all others are in error might similarly alienate people. I realized that when I put propositions above people, no matter how true I believed the propositions to be, I was violating the *imago Dei,* the image of God, in them. After all, shouldn't sharing my faith be an expression of love for them? Instead, I often acted as though I loved Christian propositions more than people.

To share the love of Christ, I needed to model the love of Christ—which meant meeting people on their own ground, relating to them in their positionality. Only then did I have a right to share my own positionality, explaining how Christ *relates to me:* how he makes a difference in the way I see reality, why he makes life worth living, why I believe the way I do.

The faith we are called to relate is a relating faith.

Poststructuralist Relating

Of course, most poststructuralists would relate my belief in Christ to the fact that I grew up surrounded by Christian discourse. I was born not only to evangelical parents but also in a country where most people believe in God in some form or other.[19] They would say I am a Christian because both theistic and christological language molded, and continue to control, my perceptions. As we have seen, however, some of the most influential poststructuralists started doubting such a deterministic scenario, primarily because it eliminates agency, the possibility of turning.

Most poststructuralists, like most Christians, would affirm that change usually results from exposure to competing discourses, as when children raised in Christian homes abandon their faith for a different window on reality. But many poststructuralists came to believe that ethics makes little sense without the concept of free will or the idea of a universal moral center to which all humans, despite the particularity of their discourse, might be held accountable. Of course, postmodernists feel uncomfortable referring to universals, because much cruelty has been enacted in the name of them. However, their very abhorrence of "cruelty" (as in Rorty) or their belief in "justice" (as in Derrida) demonstrates a universal that most share

---

[19]A survey by the National Study of Youth and Religion, conducted from 2001 to 2005, determined that 71 percent of American teenagers (ages thirteen to seventeen) believed in God and that 82 percent were affiliated with some kind of religious congregation. See Richard N. Ostling, "Religion 'Does Matter' to Teens, Study Finds," *Patriot-News* (Harrisburg, Penn.), February 24, 2005, p. A8.

(even as they deny the possibility of universals). Their universal posits the value of all humans and hence a respect for the pluralistic discourses that mold human thought. Several postmodernists have expressed their universal as an "openness to the other." Derrida, in fact, defended himself against accusations of nihilism with this desire: "I totally refuse the label of nihilism which has been ascribed to me and my American colleagues. Deconstruction is not an enclosure in nothingness, but an openness toward the other."[20]

Unfortunately, some Christians seem so closed to other perspectives and to the people who hold them, refusing to even consider alternate explanations for reality, that many postmodernists stopped listening to *any* Christians (thus deconstructing their own reputed "openness to the other"). How, then, can we draw them back to take a long look out our multipaned window? Perhaps by suggesting that their own vocabulary is written on our frame: "openness to the other" is fundamental to Christian orthodoxy.

The Othering of God

When I witness about the positionality of my faith to postmodern scholars, I inform them that key to Christian dogma is the doctrine of the Trinity. In 325 the Council of Nicaea determined, despite dissent from some earnest Christians, that Jesus was "begotten, not made," "of one Being with the Father." The "Nicene Creed" was formalized in 381 by the Council of Constantinople, which added that the Holy Spirit is to be "worshiped and glorified together with the Father and the Son."[21] Christianity thus became unique among religions for its view that *otherness* is inherent to God's nature.

While some religions have plural gods, and others have one supreme god, Christians believe that God is one and plural simultaneously. In fact, Christian orthodoxy, as established by ancient Christian councils, deems it heretical to assert that God is merely one substance with three manifestations or forms. Tradition, formulated into dogma in the fourth century, established that God, though one, is nevertheless three distinct persons. God's very nature is relational.

---

[20]Quoted in "Dialogue with Jacques Derrida," in *Dialogues with Contemporary Continental Thinkers: The Phenomenological Heritage,* ed. Richard Kearney (Manchester, U.K.: Manchester University Press, 1984), p. 124.

[21]Stanley J. Grenz, *Rediscovering the Triune God: The Trinity in Contemporary Theology* (Minneapolis: Fortress, 2004), pp. 7-8.

This explains John's reiterated statement "God is love" (1 John 4:8, 16). Though we are taught that God loves us, dying on the cross for us, dogma also teaches that God has been forever the same. Therefore, God is Love even before the creation of human beings. And because love, by its very definition, extends itself to an other, God's essence should be seen as other oriented, the persons of the Godhead unceasingly extending themselves to each other, each person continuously completed through relation to the others. Eastern Orthodox Christianity emphasizes this relating even more than do the Western panes of orthodoxy. According to theologian Catherine Mowry LaCugna, trinitarianism in the West was based on the idea of one "substance" in three persons, thus presenting God as primarily "something in and of itself." In contrast, the trinitarian theology of the East emphasizes that "communion underlies being": the three persons make up the Godhead. Hence "personhood," based on the model of a trinitarian God, implies "someone toward another."[22]

Dogma about the inherent relationality of the Trinity helps explain God's desire to create: otherness—whether in the form of stars, starlings or starfish—is inherently good because God—three in One—is good. The highest good was the creation of the *imago Dei,* "the image of God" manifest in human flesh: "So God created humankind in his image, / in the image of God he created them; / male and female he created them" (Genesis 1:27). Hence when the second person of the Trinity became flesh, he made visual the "openness to the other" that is inherent to God's nature. First and foremost, he became other to himself, taking on the physicality, and hence positionality, of human perception. Paul describes the process of Christ's "othering" in order to exhort the Philippians to put others first:

> Do nothing from selfish ambition or conceit, but in humility regard others as
> better than yourselves. Let each of you look not to your own interests, but to
> the interests of others. Let the same mind be in you that was in Christ Jesus,
>> who, though he was in the form of God,
>>> did not regard equality with God

---

[22]Catherine Mowry LaCugna, "God in Communion with Us: The Trinity," in *Freeing Theology: The Essentials of Theology in Feminist Perspective,* ed. C. M. LaCugna (San Francisco: Harper-Collins, 1993), p. 86. LaCugna's work is part of what Stanley Grenz calls a "twentieth-century renaissance of trinitarian theology" that got its start in the work of Karl Barth and Karl Rahner. The "triumph of relationality" that marks her trinitarian theology was "abetted by" the earlier work of Jürgen Moltmann, Wolfhart Pannenberg and Robert W. Jenson (Grenz, *Rediscovering the Triune God,* pp. 4, 118).

> as something to be exploited,
> but emptied himself,
>> taking the form of a slave,
>> being born in human likeness.
> And being found in human form,
>> he humbled himself
>> and became obedient to the point of death—
>> even death on a cross. (Philippians 2:3-8)

Even before the crucifixion, Jesus did not align himself with the powerful. Instead he related to the most radically "other" of first-century Palestine: tax collectors, women and sinners. In fact, the only time Jesus *explicitly* stated that he was the Messiah (he implied it many times) was to someone who embodied "otherness" in multiple ways: the "woman at the well" (John 4:7-26). Her ethnicity was so despised by Jews that many crossed the Jordan to avoid even touching the ground of Samaria; she was a gender not allowed numerous rights given to Jewish males; and she was probably reviled even by Samaritan members of her own sex for living with a man not her husband.

The example of Jesus, formalized by Christian doctrine, thus fulfills what is "written on the hearts" of postmodern theorists: that ethics must be based on "openness to the other." And, I would argue, it is also true.

The Truth of Christianity

Sayers reminds us that one definition of *true* is that of a carpenter who, employing some kind of ruler, establishes "that a line is 'out of true'"—as when a window frame is off kilter. She makes this point in order to discuss the work of creators, both human artists and God the Creator, saying that "truth" is tested by how long creations last: "If the structure is truly knit, it will stand any strain, and prove its truth by its toughness. Pious worshipers, whether of mortal or immortal artists, do their deities little honor by treating their incarnations as something too sacred for rough handling; they only succeed in betraying a fear lest the structure should prove flimsy or false."[23]

Ironically, people who denounce postmodernism imply that Christian dogma cannot withstand rough handling, betraying perhaps a subconscious fear that the structure of Christianity might prove flimsy or false. Postmodernism, however, has exposed the flaws not of Christianity but of modernism, arguing that the modernist line of thought—which disdained Christianity—

---

[23]Dorothy L. Sayers, *The Mind of the Maker* (San Francisco: Harper & Row, 1979), p. 92.

is "out of true." Modernism therefore lasted only three hundred years, while Christian orthodoxy has stayed true for over two thousand years.

And Christianity will outlast postmodernism. For even though postmodernism situates its ethic on "openness to the other," it has failed to conceptualize a transcendent Other that gives the concept meaning. For without a "prediscursive" or "extradiscursive" universal, postmodernism cannot explain why language about openness to the other should be taken any more seriously than pronouncements from the Qur'an, which, according to one Muslim scholar, "denounces, rejects and asks Muslims to oppose the Other or aspects of Otherness."[24] Christians, in contrast, can proclaim that the ethics of otherness have their origin, and hence their meaning, in a universal Other beyond language, an Other whose very nature endorses love of the other, an Other who became same with us in order to demonstrate universal love:

> Beloved, let us love one another, because love is from God; everyone who loves is born of God and knows God. Whoever does not love does not know God, for God is love. God's love was revealed among us in this way: God sent his only Son into the world so that we might live though him. In this is love, not that we loved God but that he loved us and sent his Son to be the atoning sacrifice for our sins. Beloved, since God loved us so much, we also ought to love one another. No one has ever seen God; if we love one another, God lives in us, and his love is perfected in us. (1 John 4:7-12)

Loving the other does not mean abandoning our beliefs. In fact, we have strength to love the other only because of our belief that a loving God wants all humans to return to their Creator, having made it possible through the death and resurrection of Jesus. Christian orthodoxy, of course, also establishes that our Creator will exercise justice when it comes to those who reject the good news. However, that is God's role and not our own. Jesus put it quite bluntly: "Do not judge, and you will not be judged; do not condemn, and you will not be condemned. Forgive, and you will be forgiven" (Luke 6:37).

We therefore proclaim our faith out of love for both the universal Other and the other that is the *imago Dei,* testifying that forgiveness, peace and hope can be found in Christ. At the same time, we humbly acknowledge that our perception is situated and our language is limited. This very acknowledgment opens us to the other among us, reflecting our trust that the transcendent Other intercedes for us with truth too deep for words.

---

[24]Farid Esack, *Qur'an, Liberalism and Pluralism: An Islamic Perspective of Interreligious Solidarity Against Oppression* (Oxford: Oneword, 1997), p. 116.

Appendix

INFLUENTIAL POSTMODERN PUBLICATIONS OF THE 1960s

Michel Foucault	*Madness and Civilization*	1961
Thomas S. Kuhn	*The Structure of Scientific Revolutions*	1962
Michel Foucault	*The Birth of the Clinic*	1963
Jacques Lacan	*Écrits*	1966
Michel Foucault	*The Order of Things*	
Jacques Derrida	"Structure, Sign and Play in the Discourse of the Human Sciences"	
Jacques Derrida	*Of Grammatology*	1967
	Speech and Phenomena	
	Writing and Difference	
Roland Barthes	"The Death of the Author"	1968
Gilles Deleuze	*Difference and Repetition*	
Michel Foucault	"What Is an Author?"	
Michel Foucault	*The Archaeology of Knowledge*	1969
Julia Kristeva	*Semiotike*	

Bibliography

WORKS THAT AID (MY) UNDERSTANDING OF POSTMODERNISM

Allen, Graham. *Intertextuality*. New York: Routledge, 2000.

Belsey, Catherine. *Poststructuralism: A Very Short Introduction*. Oxford: Oxford University Press, 2002.

Benhabib, Seyla. *Situating the Self: Gender, Community and Postmodernism in Contemporary Ethics*. New York: Routledge, 1992.

Bertens, Hans. *The Idea of the Postmodern: A History*. New York: Routledge, 1995.

Best, Steven, and Douglas Kellner. *Postmodern Theory: Critical Interrogations*. New York: Guilford, 1991.

Butler, Christopher. *Postmodernism: A Very Short Introduction*. Oxford: Oxford University Press, 2002.

Butler, Judith. *Bodies That Matter: On the Discursive Limits of "Sex."* New York: Routledge, 1993.

Butterfield, Bradley. "Ethical Value and Negative Aesthetics: Reconsidering the Baudrillard-Ballard Connection." *PMLA* 114 (1999): 64-77.

Caputo, John. *The Prayers and Tears of Jacques Derrida: Religion Without Religion*. Bloomington: Indiana University Press, 1997.

Caputo, John D., ed. *Deconstruction in a Nutshell*. New York: Fordham University Press, 1997.

Derrida, Jacques. *Of Grammatology*. Translated by Gayatri Chakravorty Spivak. Corrected edition. Baltimore: Johns Hopkins University Press, 1998.

———. "Structure, Sign and Play in the Discourse of the Human Sciences." In *Writing and Difference*. Translated with introduction and notes by Alan Bass. Chicago: University of Chicago Press, 1978.

Erickson, Millard J. *Truth or Consequences: The Promise and Perils of Postmodernism*. Downers Grove, Ill.: InterVarsity Press, 2001.

Foucault, Michel. *The Archaeology of Knowledge and the Discourse on Lan-*

guage. Translated by A. M. Sheridan Smith. New York: Pantheon, 1972.

———. *Discipline and Punish: The Birth of the Prison.* Translated by Alan Sheridan. New York: Vintage, 1979.

Greer, Robert C. *Mapping Postmodernism: A Survey of Christian Options.* Downers Grove, Ill.: InterVarsity Press, 2003.

Grenz, Stanley J. *A Primer on Postmodernism.* Grand Rapids: Eerdmans, 1996.

Hart, Kevin. *Postmodernism: A Beginner's Guide.* Oxford: Oneworld, 2004.

Heartney, Eleanor. *Postmodernism.* Cambridge: Cambridge University Press, 2001.

Hutcheon, Linda. *The Politics of Postmodernism.* New York: Routledge, 1989.

Jameson, Fredric. "Postmodernism, or the Cultural Logic of Late Capitalism." *New Left Review* 146 (August 1984): 53-93.

Jencks, Charles. *What Is Post-modernism?* New York: St. Martin's, 1986.

Kaplan, E. Ann. *Postmodernism and Its Discontents: Theories, Practices.* New York: Verso, 1988.

Kim, C. W. Maggie, Susan M. St. Ville, and Susan M. Simonaitis, eds. *Transfigurations: Theology and the French Feminists.* Minneapolis: Fortress, 1993.

Leitch, Vincent B. *Postmodernism: Local Effects, Global Flows.* Albany: State University of New York Press, 1996.

Linn, Ray. *A Teacher's Introduction to Postmodernism.* Urbana, Ill.: National Council of Teachers of English, 1996.

Lyotard, Jean-François. *The Postmodern Condition: A Report on Knowledge.* Translated by Geoff Bennington and Brian Massumi. Minneapolis: University of Minnesota Press, 1984.

———. *The Postmodern Explained: Correspondence, 1982-1985.* Translated by Don Barry et al. Minneapolis: University of Minnesota Press, 1993.

McGowan, John. *Postmodernism and Its Critics.* Ithaca, N.Y.: Cornell University Press, 1991.

Mitchell, W. J. T., ed. *Against Theory: Literary Studies and the New Pragmatism.* Chicago: University of Chicago Press, 1985.

Murphy, Nancey. *Anglo-American Postmodernity: Philosophical Perspectives on Science, Religion and Ethics.* Boulder, Colo.: Westview, 1997.

Murphy, Nancey, and James Wm. McClendon Jr. "Distinguishing Modern and Postmodern Theologies." *Modern Theology* 5 (April 1989): 1919-214.

Percesepe, Gary. "The Incredible Lightness of Being Postmodern." *Christian Scholar's Review* 20 (December 1990): 118-35.

Phillips, Timothy R., and Dennis L. Okholm. *Christian Apologetics in the Postmodern World*. Downers Grove, Ill.: InterVarsity Press, 1995.

Rorty, Richard. *Contingency, Irony and Solidarity*. Cambridge: Cambridge University Press, 1989.

Rose, Margaret. *The Post-modern and the Post-industrial: A Critical Analysis*. Cambridge: Cambridge University Press, 1991.

Sarap, Madan. *An Introductory Guide to Post-structuralism and Postmodernism*. 2nd edition. Hertfordshire, U.K.: Simon & Schuster International, 1993.

Sim, Stuart, ed. *The Routledge Companion to Postmodernism*. New York: Routledge, 2001.

Index